THE MASTER KEY SYSTEM

OTHER TITLES IN THE

LIBRARY OF
HIDDEN KNOWLEDGE

The New Science of Getting Rich

Natural Abundance

Coming in 2012

The Game of Life and How to Play It

As We Think, So We Are

THE MASTER KEY SYSTEM

Charles F. Haanel

Edited by Ruth L. Miller

LIBRARY OF
HIDDEN KNOWLEDGE

ATRIA BOOKS
New York London Toronto Sydney New Delhi

Hillsboro, Oregon

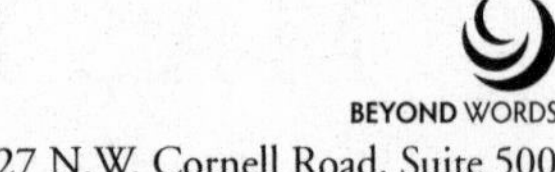

A Division of Simon & Schuster, Inc.
1230 Avenue of the Americas
New York, N.Y. 10020

20827 N.W. Cornell Road, Suite 500
Hillsboro, Oregon 97124–9808
503-531-8700 / 503-531-8773 fax
www.beyondword.com

Originally published in 1916 by Psychology Publishing, St. Louis, and the Master Key Institute, New York.

Managing editor: Lindsay S. Brown
Editors: Kayla Ballrot, Gretchen Stelter
Proofreaders: Marvin Moore, Jennifer Weaver-Neist
Design and composition: Nancy Singer Olaguera, ISPN Publishing Services

First Atria Books/Beyond Words hardcover edition February 2008

Manufactured in the United States of America

20 19 18 17 16 15 14 13 12 11

Library of Congress Control Number: 2007920776

ISBN: 978–1–58270–190–5
ISBN: 978–1–4165–8766–8 (eBook)
ISBN: 978–0–7435–7197–5 (audio)

The corporate mission of Beyond Words Publishing, Inc.: *Inspire to Integrity*

CONTENTS

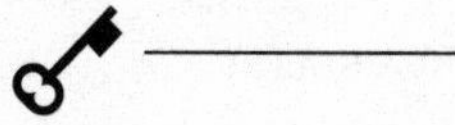

ORIGINAL TEXT

LESSONS

NOTE FROM THE EDITOR

THERE IS much wisdom to be gleaned from *The Master Key System*, but for many of us today, Haanel's language is cumbersome. He was writing for people of another era, who spoke and wrote a different kind of English than we generally use, and who responded to different kinds of examples.

Following is an alternative version of *The Master Key System*, "translated" into modern form and explaining some of Haanel's ideas in more familiar terms. You may find it useful to go back and forth between old and new, or simply to use this edited version and ignore the original text. Either way, you'll find *The Master Key System* to be a powerful guide on your path to success!

—*Ruth L. Miller*

UPDATED VERSION

FOREWORD

No matter how much we try, we can't stand still. Our human nature compels all of us to move and change throughout our lives.

At the same time, nobody who thinks about life wants to experience it as a vegetable. We want to improve and continue to develop mentally, throughout our lives—which can only happen if we improve the quality of our thoughts, along with the ideals, actions, and conditions that are the results of those thoughts.

So, throughout history, humanity has passionately sought "the Truth." People have explored every avenue to it and, in the process, have produced an entire field of literature. These works range from the trivial to the sublime, from divination and spells through all the philosophies to the final, lofty Truth known as "the Master Key."

The Master Key is the way to tap the great Cosmic Intelligence and attract from it all that the reader hopes and dreams, and in this book, the Master Key is given to the world.

Creative Thought

Every thing and institution we see around us, because it was created by human beings, existed first as a thought in some human mind. Thought, therefore, is constructive; it's creative.

Human thought is the Spiritual Power of the cosmos operating through humanity, so studying the creative processes of thought and how to apply them is one of the most important things we can do. It's how we can help improve the quality of human life on earth. The Master Key helps the reader use that power, both constructively and creatively.

Every condition and thing we desire to experience, we must first create in thought; the Master Key explains and guides the process for doing so.

A Note on Using This Book

This teaching was originally published as a correspondence course with twenty-four lessons, delivered one each week for twenty-four weeks. Today's reader, receiving the whole twenty-four parts at once, is therefore warned not to attempt to read this book like a novel. Instead, treat it as a course of study, taking in the meaning of each part—reading and rereading one part each week before moving on to the next lesson. Otherwise the later parts are likely to be misunderstood, and the reader's time and money will be wasted.

Used this way, the Master Key will help the reader experience a greater, more satisfactory personality, a new power to achieve any worthwhile personal purpose, and a new ability to enjoy life's beauty and wonder.

—F. H. Burgess
(Interpreted by Ruth L. Miller)

INTRODUCTION

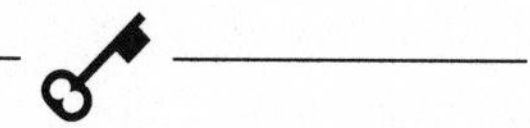

SOME PEOPLE seem to attract success, power, wealth, and achievement with little conscious effort. Others struggle to achieve anything. Still others fail completely to achieve their ambitions, desires, and ideals. Why is this so? Why should some people realize their ambitions easily, while others do so with difficulty and still others not at all?

The reason for the difference can't be in their physical form; if it were, only physically perfect people would be successful. The difference must, therefore, be in the mind. Mind must be the part of us that overcomes our environment and any obstacles in our path.

When the creative power of thought is fully understood, its effects are clearly marvelous. Students who learn that the power to accomplish comes from within recognize that they seem to be weak only because they've depended on help from outside. They rely on their own thought without hesitation, instantly standing tall, taking on a confident attitude, and working miracles.

The Master Key System

The Master Key is, therefore, based on a newly understood set of laws working in and with the mind. It brings to light the possibilities that lie dormant in each of us and tells how they may be brought into powerful action to increase anyone's energy, discernment, vitality, and intellectual capacity. The student who comes to understand these mental laws will possess an ability to obtain results not yet dreamed of, along with rewards that words can hardly express.

The Master Key teaches the use of Mind Power—true Mind Power—not any substitute or perversion. It has nothing to do with hypnotism, magic, or any of the more or less fascinating deceptions by which people are often led to think that something can be had for nothing.

The Master Key explains the correct use of both the receptive and active elements of the mind and teaches the reader how to recognize opportunities. It strengthens the will and reasoning powers, and teaches the development and best uses of imagination, desire, emotion, and intuition. Those who use it experience increased initiative and persistence, wiser choices, a deeper understanding and sympathy for others, and a thorough enjoyment of a meaningful life.

The Master Key enables the student to control the body and to experience health. It improves and strengthens the memory. It develops the kind of insight that is so rare: the kind that is the distinguishing characteristic of every successful leader; the kind that enables people to see the possibilities as well as the difficulties in every situation; the kind that enables people to discern opportunity close at hand. Thousands fail to see the opportunities within their grasp because they are busy focusing on situations that couldn't possibly provide any substantial return—but the Master Key changes that.

The Master Key develops internal power, which means that others instinctively recognize you as someone with force of character—they want to do what you want them to do. It means that you attract people and things to you; you are what some people call "lucky" and things come your way. You have come into an understanding of the fundamental laws of Nature and have put yourself in harmony with them; you are in tune with the Infinite; you understand the Law of Attraction, the natural laws of growth, and the psychological laws on which all advantages in the social and business world are based.

Experiencing abundance depends on recognizing the Law of Abundance and accepting the fact that Mind is not only *a* creative force, it's the *only* creator of all there is.[1] Because mental power is creative power, it gives you the ability to create for yourself. Certainly nothing can be created before we *know* it can be created! Only then can we act appropriately. And it's *not* taking something away from someone else; Nature never does things that way. Nature makes two blades of grass grow where one grew before, and Mind Power enables us to do the same thing.

The Master Key develops insight and wisdom, increased independence, and the ability and disposition to be helpful. It destroys distrust, depression, fear, and every form of lack, limitation, and weakness, including pain and disease. It awakens buried talents and supplies initiative, energy, and vitality—and it awakens an appreciation of the beautiful in art, literature, and science.

The Master Key has changed the lives of thousands of men and women by replacing uncertain and hazy methods and ideas with definite principles—the foundation upon which any effective system must rest. Elbert Gary, the first chairman of the United States Steel Corporation, said, "The services of advisors, instruc-

1 Mind with a capital "M" is one of the many names of the Creative Source of the universe. When the book of Genesis says, "Let us make man in our image," it's not saying "make a likeness of" but rather "make part of, or within, our form."

tors, efficiency experts in successful management are indispensable to most business enterprises of magnitude, but I deem the recognition and adoption of right principles vastly more important."

The Master Key teaches these right principles and suggests methods for their practical application. It teaches that the only value of any principle is in its application, and in so doing, it differs from most other courses of study. Many people read books, take home study courses, and attend lectures all their lives without ever making any progress in demonstrating the value of the principles involved. The Master Key provides methods to demonstrate and put into actual practice these principles in our daily lives.

A New Paradigm

A change is occurring in humanity's thinking. This change, silently transpiring in our midst, is more important than any shift the world has undergone since the European Renaissance of 600 years ago. The whole world is on the eve of a new consciousness, a new power, and a new realization of the resources within the self.

Science has recently made such vast discoveries, has revealed such an infinity of resources, has unveiled such enormous possibilities and such unsuspected forces that more and more scientists hesitate to declare certain theories to be firmly established, or to deny other theories as absurd or impossible.

The last centuries saw the most magnificent material progress in history, and the present century is set to produce the greatest progress in mental and spiritual power. The blinders of tradition are being removed from humanity, and as the last limiting vestiges of materialism are released, human thought is being liberated to reveal Truth, fully formed, before an astonished multitude. As a result, a new civilization is being born: old assumptions, with their associated customs, creeds, and cruelty, are passing, and a new paradigm, based on vision, faith, and service, is taking their place.

Consistent Laws

Each discovery of a new type of law has marked an epoch in human progress. The application of each discovery has reduced uncertainty in people's lives and replaced it with law, reason, and conviction in that area. For example, there's always been a fixed amount of natural resources in the world from which we derive electricity—quite nearly the same amount of resources, in fact, that have been around us for ages. Until someone recognized the law by which these could be implemented, we received no benefit. Now that the law is understood and the right tools are in use to apply it, practically the whole world has access to electricity. What's more, now we understand how best to use newer technologies to harness this voltaic power that's been there all along. Hydroelectric dams, wind farms, and solar cells are now replacing less efficient power sources, such as coal mines and nuclear facilities, as each technology makes way for the discovery of a cleaner, more efficient one. Indeed, historians of the future will say that we live in the Age of Electricity.

All laws were discovered by inductive reasoning; that is, by comparing a number of events until the common factor in all of them is seen. Applying this method has given humanity much of our prosperity and knowledge. It has lengthened life, mitigated pain, spanned rivers, and brightened the night with this splendor of day. It has extended the range of vision, accelerated motion, annihilated distance, facilitated communication, and enabled people to descend into the sea and travel beyond the atmosphere.

In the process, physicists have analyzed matter into molecules, molecules into atoms, and atoms into energy, and now they're suggesting that intelligence underlies this pattern of energy.

At the beginning of the twentieth century, Sir Ambrose Fleming, in an address before the British Royal Society, said, "In its ultimate essence, energy may be incomprehensible by us except as an exhibition of the direct operation of that which we call Mind or Will." Today, particle physicist Amit Goswami calls the universe "Self-Aware."

Let's consider the most powerful forces in the universe. In the mineral world everything is solid and fixed, held together by invisible bonds. The animal and vegetable kingdom is always changing, being created and re-created, through invisible information loops and processes. In the atmosphere we find heat, light, and other forms of energy. And in the vacuum of outer space, we find the powerful "quantum field." Each realm becomes finer and less material as we pass from the visible to the invisible, from the coarse to the fine, from low potentiality to high potentiality.

When we reach the invisible, we find energy in its purest and most powerful state. Since the most powerful forces of Nature are the invisible forces, we find that the most powerful forces of humanity are the invisible forces, our spiritual forces. And because thinking is the only activity of the spirit, and thought (including emotion) is the only product of thinking, the only way in which the spiritual forces can manifest is through the process of thinking. Addition and subtraction are therefore spiritual activities; reasoning is a spiritual process; ideas are spiritual conceptions; questions are spiritual searchlights; and logic, argument, and all the other methods of philosophy make up what could be called "spiritual machinery."

The laws governing this mental and spiritual world are as fixed and certain as are the laws of the material world. So spiritual law, like every other law, is universally applicable to all; it is constantly working and continuously bringing to each of us exactly what we have created. This is what was meant by, "Whatsoever a man soweth that shall he also reap."[2] Just as in the world of matter and energy, complying with a given law will always produce the desired result.

Today, because the scientific method is so widely used, an increasing number of people, when they observe or desire a result, seek the particular condition for achieving it. No wonder, then, that people have begun to apply this system of study to their thinking! Once it became clear that a specific desired result came after a particular pattern of thought, all that remained was to classify these patterns and discover the law.

The Law of Abundance, therefore, is just like electricity: only those who recognize the law and place themselves in harmony with it, applying the right tools and methods, can share in its benefits. And whoever fails to fully investigate and take advantage of the wonderful progress being made in this last great science will soon be as far behind as anyone who refuses to acknowledge and accept the benefits of electricity.

The Power of Thought

You will see—you must see—that we are at the dawn of a new day, where the possibilities are so wonderful, fascinating, and limitless they are almost bewildering. In the world of warfare two centuries ago, any man with a Gatling gun could have annihilated a whole army equipped with the weapons then in use.[3] In the world of medicine half a century ago, one man with a vaccine wiped out the worldwide scourge called polio. We're in the same kind of situation. Anyone with a knowledge of the possibilities

---

2 Galatians 6:9.

3 This is graphically illustrated in the film, *The Last Samurai* and is explained in great detail in regard to the real effects this kind of advantage had on human history in Jared Diamond's Pulitzer Prize–winning book, *Guns, Germs, and Steel.*

contained in the Master Key has an inconceivable advantage over any set of circumstances.

Would you like to experience more power? Develop your power consciousness. More health? Develop your health consciousness. More happiness? Fill your consciousness with happiness.

Every thought brings into action certain parts of the body—the brain, the nervous system, the muscles. Thought produces an actual physical change in the construction of the tissue. Therefore it's only necessary to have a certain number of thoughts on a given subject to bring about a complete change in the body's physical organization.

This is how failure is changed to success.

Mind creates negative conditions just as readily as favorable conditions, and when we consciously or unconsciously visualize any kind of lack, limitation, or discord, we create these conditions—as many people are doing all the time.

When thoughts of courage, power, inspiration, and harmony are substituted for thoughts of failure, despair, lack, limitation, and discord, the physical tissue is changed and the individual sees life in a new light. Old things have actually passed away; all things have become new. He or she is born again of the spirit. Life has a new meaning. The self is reconstructed and is filled with joy, confidence, hope, and energy.

People who've had this experience see opportunities for success that they missed before. They recognize possibilities that were once meaningless. Thoughts of success are radiated outward, and people show up to help them onward and upward; they attract to themselves new and successful associates, and this in turn changes their environment. Therefore, by this simple exercise of thought, we change, not only ourselves, but our environment, circumstances, and conditions.

Live the spirit of these things until they become yours by right. It will then become impossible to keep them from you.

The things of the world respond to a power within us which we can rule them by. You need not acquire this power; you already have it. But you need to understand it to use it; you need to control it; you need to fill yourself with it so that you can go forward and carry the world before you.

Day by day as you go on, you gain momentum, your inspiration deepens, your plans crystallize, and you gain understanding, you will come to realize that this world is no dead pile of stones and timber; it is a living thing! It's made up of all living things. The world is a thing of life and beauty.

Clearly, work with this kind of material requires understanding, but those who come to this understanding are inspired by a new light, a new force. They gain confidence and greater power each day. They realize their hopes, and their dreams come true. Life has a deeper, fuller, clearer meaning than before.

And now, lesson one.

LESSON ONE

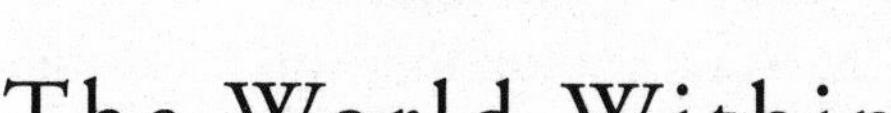

The World Within

There is a world within—a world of thought and feeling and power, of light and life and beauty—and, although invisible, its forces are mighty. The world within is governed by our mind. When we discover this world we will find the solution for every problem, the cause for every effect. And, since the world within is subject to our control, all laws of power and possession are also within our control.

Some would say that we can't express powers we don't possess; however, power is already within our grasp. The only way we can gain possession of power is to become conscious of it, and we can never become conscious of it until we learn that all power is from within.

We must "be" before we can "do," we can "do" only to the extent to which we "are," and what we "are" depends upon what we "think." Therefore, the first step is simply to think.

Outer Circumstances Reflect Inner Consciousness

The world without reflects the circumstances and the conditions of the consciousness within.

Since the world without is a reflection of the world within, what appears around us shows us what we have been thinking within. In the world within we can find infinite wisdom, infinite power, and infinite supply of all that is necessary. It's simply waiting for development and expression. If we recognize these potentials in the world within, they will take form in the world without. If we find wisdom in the world within, we'll have the understanding to discern the marvelous possibilities that are latent in this world within, and we shall be given the power to make these possibilities manifest in the world without. As we become conscious of the wisdom in the world within, we mentally take possession of it, and by taking mental possession, we come into actual possession of the power to bring into visible manifestation the essentials for our most complete and harmonious development.

Mental efficiency is contingent upon harmony; discord means confusion; therefore, he who would acquire this power must be in harmony with Natural Law. Harmony in the world within will be reflected in the world without as agreeable conditions, pleasant surroundings, and having the best of everything. It's the foundation of health and a necessary essential to all greatness, all power, all attainment, all achievement, and all success. Harmony in the world within means the ability to control our thoughts and to determine for ourselves how any experience will affect us. Harmony in the world within results in optimism and affluence; affluence within results in affluence without.

All possessions begin in consciousness. Life is an unfolding, not a process of adding on; what comes to us in the world without is the unfolding of what we already possess in the world within. All gain is, therefore, the result of a cumulative consciousness. And all loss is the result of a scattering consciousness.

The world within is the practical world in which the men and women of power generate courage, hope, enthusiasm, confidence, trust, and faith; in so doing, they are given the fine intelligence to see a vision—and the practical skill to make their vision real.

Conscious and Unconscious Mind

We relate to the world without by the objective, conscious mind, dealing with outward objects. The brain is the organ of this mind, and the nervous system puts us in conscious communication with every part of the body. This system of nerves responds to every sensation of light, heat, odor, sound, and taste.

When this mind thinks correctly, when it understands the truth, when the thoughts sent through the cerebrospinal nervous system of the body are constructive, these sensations are pleasant, harmonious. The result is that we build strength, vitality, and other constructive forces into our body.

But it is through this same conscious mind that all distress, sickness, lack, limitation, and forms of discord and disharmony appear in our lives. It is, therefore, through incorrect thinking in the objective mind that we experience destructive forces.

Perceiving and operating through the five physical senses, the conscious mind deals with the impressions and objects of the outward life. It has the faculty of discrimination, carrying with it the responsibility of choice. It has the power of reasoning—whether inductive, deductive, analytical, or syllogistic—and this power may be developed to a high degree. It's also where the will is located.

We relate to the world within by the unconscious, or subjective, mind.[4] This mind is located in the combination of nerves and hormones, and the glands, tissues, and vessels that connect them to control the regular functions that make physical life possible. It presides over all subjective sensations, such as joy, fear, love, emotion, respiration, perspiration, imagination, and other unconscious phenomena. Through it, we're connected with Universal Mind and brought into relation with the infinite constructive forces of the universe.

The conscious mind not only impresses other minds through logic and will, but it can also direct the unconscious mind. In this way the conscious mind becomes the responsible ruler and guardian of the unconscious mind. This function can completely reverse conditions in your life. It's often true that conditions of fear, worry, poverty, disease, disharmony, and evil dominate us by false suggestions accepted by the unguarded unconscious mind. The trained conscious mind can entirely prevent all this by vigilant protective action. It may properly be called "the watchman at the gate" of the great unconscious domain.

An unknown writer expressed the chief distinction between the two phases of the mind this way: "Conscious mind is reasoning will. Unconscious mind is instinctive desire, the result of past reasoning will."

The great secret of life is the coordination of these two centers of our being and the understanding of their functions. With this knowledge we can bring the objective and subjective minds into conscious cooperation and thus coordinate the finite and the infinite. Our future is entirely within our own control—not at the mercy of any capricious or uncertain external power.

---

4 Molecular biologist Candace Pert, author of *Molecules of Emotion*, says "your body is your unconscious mind" and points to the near-instantaneous reaction of the cells to a thought, memory, or perception as an indicator of this relationship.

One Consciousness

All religions and increasing numbers of scientists agree that there is but one principle, or consciousness, pervading the entire universe, occupying all space, and essentially the same at every point of its presence. Consciousness is all power, all wisdom, and always present, and when it thinks, its thoughts become objective things. All thoughts and things are within it. It is all in all.

As this consciousness is omnipresent, it must be present within every individual, so each of us must be a manifestation of that Omnipotent, Omniscient, and Omnipresent Consciousness. As there is only one consciousness in the universe, it necessarily follows that your consciousness is part of that Universal Consciousness, or in other words, all mind is Mind. There's no dodging this conclusion. The consciousness that focuses in your brain and body is the same consciousness focusing in the brain and body of every other being in the universe. Each of us is an individualization of Universal Mind.[5]

So, as all attributes are contained in Universal Mind, which is omnipotent, omniscient, and omnipresent, these attributes must be present as potential at all times in every individual. They are one.

Universal Mind simply exists. It is static, potential energy and can act or manifest only through individual beings. Mind is static energy; thinking is dynamic energy—two phases of the same thing. Thought may therefore be said to be the vibratory force formed by converting static Mind into dynamic energy.

Human consciousness consists only in our ability to think and feel. Thinking is our unique ability to act on the Universal and bring it into manifestation. Mind is creative, and our conditions, environment, and all our experiences in life are the result

---

5 Throughout this text, words such as Intelligence, Consciousness, and Truth will be capitalized when they directly refer to this invisible, creative source of power that is often called God.

of our habitual or predominant mental attitude. This means that our every thought is a cause and every condition an effect, so it's absolutely essential that you control your thoughts to bring forth only desirable conditions.

Life and Growth

The idea that "much gathers more" is true on every plane of existence; "loss leads to greater loss" is equally true. This is because all growth comes from within. This principle is evident throughout Nature: every plant, every animal, every human is a living testimony to this great law.

The world within is the Universal Fountain of Supply, and the world without is an outlet to the stream. The error of the ages has been looking for strength or power from without because our ability to receive depends upon our recognition of this Universal Fountain—this Infinite Energy—of which each of us is an outlet and each is made us one with every other person on the planet.

Recognition is a mental process and, as stated earlier, mental process, or thinking, is our ability to act on Universal Mind. To recognize the Universal Fountain within is therefore to interact with Universal Mind. And, as Universal Mind is the Intelligence that pervades all space and animates all living things, this mental interaction is the process of causation. (Remember, though, that this causation process is not an objective faculty but an unconscious process, occurring not in the individual mind but in Universal Mind, of which the individual is the active part, and its results may be seen in an infinite variety of conditions and experiences.)

In order to express life there must be Mind; nothing can exist without Mind. Universal Mind is the life principle of every atom, molecule, and cell that exists. Everything is continually striving to manifest more life, and, as Universal Mind is Omnipresent Intelligence, all are intelligent, and all manifestations of Mind are seeking to carry out the purpose for which they were created.

So, as Mind is everywhere, in all things, and forming all things, even the vacuum of space, we can say we live in a fathomless sea of plastic Mind Substance.[6] Everything that exists is some manifestation of this one basic Substance from which and by which all things have been created and are continually being re-created. Substance is ever alive and active. It is sensitive to the highest degree, taking form according to mental processes. Thought and feeling form the mold, or matrix, from which the Universal Substance manifests.

Power

This Master Key brings you into a realization of power that will be yours when you understand the relationship between the world without and the world within.

Clearly, the secret of all power, all achievement, and all possession rests in our thinking and the attitude of mind that is generated by our thought. This means that all power is from within and is absolutely under your control; power comes through exact knowledge and by applying exact principles. It should be plain that when you acquire a thorough understanding of this law and are able to control your thought processes, you can apply it to any condition. At that point, you will have come into conscious cooperation with the Omnipotent Law that is the fundamental basis of all things.

---

6 In terms of today's science, we would call this "the quantum field" which is made up of constantly interacting subatomic "wavicles," sometimes showing up as waves and sometimes as particles, which may best be described as tendencies toward binding ("bosons") or separating ("fermions"), and which form the basis for all things and all energy, everywhere.

Most people live in the world without; few have found the world within—yet *the world within makes the world without.* The world within is creative, and everything you find in your world without, you have created in the world within. The world within is the cause, the world without the effect, and to change the effect you must change the cause.

You will see at once that this is a radically new and different idea—most people try to change effects by working with effects. They fail to see that this is simply trading one form of distress for another. To remove discord, we must remove the cause, and this cause can be found only in the world within.

Applying the Principle

Remember that the value of any principle is in its application, and a practical understanding of this law will substitute abundance for poverty, wisdom for ignorance, harmony for discord, and freedom for tyranny. Certainly there can be no greater blessing in this world than these!

Now, apply the principle:

1. Select a room where you can be alone and undisturbed.
2. Sit erect, comfortably, but do not lounge.
3. Let your thoughts roam where they will, but be perfectly still for fifteen to thirty minutes.
4. Continue this for three or four days or for a week until you secure full control of your physical being.

Many will find this extremely difficult while others will manage with ease, but it is absolutely essential to secure complete control of the body before you are ready to progress.

In lesson two you will receive instructions for the next step; in the meantime, you must master this one.

Summary

- The world without is a reflection of the world within.
- The source of all power is the world within, the Universal Fountain of Supply, the Infinite Energy of which each individual is an outlet.
- Universal Mind is present in every atom, molecule, and cell that exists.
- We are related to the Universal Mind by the unconscious, or subjective, mind and to the objective world by the objective, or conscious, mind.
- Our ability to think is our ability to act upon the Universal Mind and bring Substance into form.
- The result of this interaction is cause and effect; every thought is a cause and every condition an effect.

LESSON TWO

Thought Is Energy

THOUGHT IS energy. Active thought is active energy; concentrated thought is concentrated energy. Thought that is concentrated on a definite purpose becomes power.

Our ability to receive and manifest power depends on our ability to recognize the Infinite Energy always dwelling within us, constantly creating and re-creating both body and Mind, and ready at any moment to manifest through us in whatever way we desire. Manifestation in outer life will be in exact proportion to our inner recognition of this truth.

All processes, even those of thought, rest on solid foundations. Difficulties are largely due to confused ideas and ignorance of our true interests. The powers, uses, and possibilities of the mind are incomparably more wonderful than the most extravagant accomplishment or dreams of material progress. Clear thinking and moral insight are, therefore, invaluable.

The Unconscious, Working Mind

The operations of the mind are produced by two parallel modes of activity, one conscious and the other unconscious.

In the early 1900s, the philosopher Donald Davidson said: "He who thinks to illuminate the whole range of mental action by the light of his own consciousness is not unlike the one who should go about to illuminate the universe with a rushlight." The dim light of a torch made of rushes is as inadequate for lighting the vastness of space as are the meager capacities of our logical thinking mind for understanding the depth and breadth of our full consciousness.

Analyzing our thought processes shows that the unconscious is the domain of our most important mental phenomena. The unconscious mind, also called our soul, works and provides for our benefit like a benevolent stranger, pouring only the sweet, mature fruits of its labors into our lap. The many processes of the unconscious occur with a certainty and regularity that would be unachievable if the possibility of error existed. It provides the essentials for all cognitive activity, while we haven't the slightest notion how it does so.

The value of the unconscious is enormous: it inspires us; it warns us; it furnishes us with names, facts, and scenes from the storehouse of memory. It directs our thoughts and tastes, and it accomplishes tasks so intricate that no conscious mind, even if it had the power, has the focus to undertake.

We can walk at will; we can raise an arm whenever we choose to do so; we can give our attention through eye or ear to any subject we want. On the other hand, we cannot willfully stop our heartbeat or the circulation of the blood, the growth of our stature, the formation of nerve and muscle tissue, the building of the bones, or the many other important vital processes.[7]

---

7 The ability to do these things intentionally has been demonstrated by highly trained yogis and fakirs in India and Tibet—but only under very limited circumstances and for relatively short periods of time.

The unconscious is also the source of understanding and wisdom beyond the norm. It must have been through the unconscious that Shakespeare perceived, without effort, great truths normally hidden from the conscious mind, that Phidias fashioned his famous bronze statues, that Raphael painted Madonnas, and that Beethoven composed symphonies.

In any skill, ease and perfection depend entirely upon the degree to which we no longer depend on our conscious awareness. Playing the piano, skating, using a keyboard, performing any of the crafts and skilled trades—all depend on the unconscious mind for their perfect execution. The marvel of playing the piano or typing while at the same time conducting a conversation shows the capacity of our unconscious powers. We're all aware of how dependent we are upon the unconscious, and the greater, the nobler, the more brilliant our thoughts are, the more obvious it becomes that the origin lies beyond our understanding. We find ourselves endowed with tact, instinct, and a sense of the beautiful in art, music, and so on, whose origin or dwelling place we are wholly unconscious.[8]

When we compare these two minds, the one decreed by the will of the moment and the other proceeding in consistent, rhythmic course, we see that the all-important life functions appear to have been intentionally withdrawn from the domain of our ever-changing outward will, and placed under the direction of a permanent and dependable power within us.

The unconscious mind draws logical and accurate inferences from premises furnished from outside sources. Where the premise is true, the unconscious mind reaches a faultless conclusion, but where the premise or suggestion is in error, the whole structure falls. Illness, distress, and disharmony prevail.

---

8 The ancient Greeks and Romans called these capacities of the unconscious "the Muses" and developed elaborate rituals to influence them and encourage their activity.

This happens because the unconscious mind doesn't attempt to prove or disprove what it receives. It accepts any suggestions as true and at once proceeds to act thereon in the whole domain of its tremendous field of work. It perceives directly by intuition rather than reasoning. Hence its processes are rapid. It doesn't wait for the slow methods of conscious reasoning. In fact, it can't use them.

The unconscious mind relies on the conscious mind to act as "the watchman at the gate" by guarding it from mistaken impressions. The conscious mind can suggest either truth or error. If the latter, it places the whole being in peril.

So, ideally, the conscious mind would be on duty during every waking hour. When the "watchman" is "off guard," or when its calm judgment is suspended for whatever reason, the unconscious mind is left open to suggestion from all sources. Films, television, and music are all potential sources of suggestion—with advertising designed to have a strong influence. Conditions are most dangerous during the excitement of panic, the height of anger, the impulses of an irresponsible crowd, or other times of unrestrained passion. The unconscious mind is then open to the suggestion of fear, hatred, selfishness, greed, self-depreciation, and other undesirable thought patterns from its surroundings.

The result is usually unwholesome in the extreme, with effects that may cause the mind and body distress for a long time. Hence it is of great importance to guard the unconscious mind from false impressions.

The unconscious mind is the seat of our instincts, principles, and aspirations. It's the source of our artistic and altruistic ideals. And because the unconscious mind can't argue or reason, these innate principles, or established instincts and ideals, can only be overthrown by an elaborate and gradual process of undermining them. We focus on a new suggestion, frequently repeated, which the mind must accept. This eventually leads to forming new and healthy habits of thought and life, for the unconscious mind is the seat of habit. That which we do over and over becomes mechanical; it's no longer an act of judgment but a pattern of deep, worn grooves in the unconscious mind. This is favorable for us if the habit is wholesome and right.

But if the unconscious has accepted harmful suggestions, the remedy is to recognize the omnipotence of the unconscious mind. In doing so, we suggest that freedom is present here and now. The unconscious being creative and one with Universal Mind will at once begin to create the freedom suggested.

To sum up: The normal functions of the unconscious on the physical side are to maintain regular and vital processes, preserve life and restore health, and care for offspring, which includes an instinctive desire to preserve all life and improve conditions generally.

On the mental side, the unconscious is the storehouse of memory: it maintains wonderful thought messengers unhampered by time or space; it's the fountain of practical initiative, will, and the constructive forces of life; it's the seat of habit.

On the spiritual side, it's the source of ideals, aspirations, and imagination, and it's the channel through which we recognize and interact with Universal Mind. Insofar as we recognize this Creative Source, we come into an understanding of power.[9]

The unconscious mind sleeps and rests no more than your heart or your blood does, which, of course, is never. It's been found that by plainly stating to the unconscious mind specific things to be accomplished, forces are set in motion both in the body and in our cir-

---

9 Carl Jung called it the "unconscious mind," separating it into the "subconscious," which has to do with maintaining our bodies and implementing habits of mind and body, and the "superconscious," which has to do with intuitive awareness and our ideals, aspirations, and principles. He suggested that both are united with all other minds in what he called the "collective consciousness."

cumstances that will lead to the desired result. Here, then, is a source of power that places us in touch with omnipotence. Here is a deep principle well worth careful study.

The operation of this law is interesting. Those who put it into operation find that when they go out to meet the person with whom they had anticipated a difficult interview, something has been there before them and dissolved the supposed differences; everything is changed and all is harmonious. They find that when some difficult business problem presents itself, they can afford to delay because something will suggest the proper solution; everything is properly arranged. In fact, those who have learned to trust the unconscious find that they have infinite resources at their command.

Someone may ask, "How can the unconscious change conditions?" The reply is, because the unconscious is a part of Universal Mind, and a part must be the same in kind and quality as the whole; the only difference is one of degree. The Whole, as we know, is creative—it is the only creator there is. So we find that the mind is creative, and as thought is the only activity that the mind possesses, thought must—by necessity—be creative also.

But we shall find that there is a vast difference between simply thinking and directing our thought consciously, systematically, and constructively. When we do the latter, we place our mind in harmony with Universal Mind, we come into tune with the Infinite, and we set in operation the mightiest force in existence: the creative power of Universal Mind.

This, as everything else, is governed by Natural Law, and this law is called the Law of Attraction, stated as: *Mind is creative and automatically resonates with its object to bring it into manifestation.*

Applying the Principle

In the last lesson, you performed an exercise for the purpose of securing control of the physical body. If you have mastered this you are ready to advance. This time you will practice controlling your thoughts.

1. Always use the same room, the same chair, and the same position, if possible. In some cases it may not be convenient to do so; simply make the best use of such conditions as may be available.
2. Now be perfectly still as before, but this time observe and then inhibit all thoughts. This will give you control over any thoughts of care, worry, and fear, and will enable you to entertain only the kind of thoughts you desire.[10]
3. Continue this exercise until you gain complete mastery.

At first, you may not be able to do this for more than a few moments at a time, but the exercise is valuable because it will be a practical demonstration of the great number of thoughts that are constantly trying to gain access to your mental world.

In the next lesson, you will receive instructions for an exercise that may be a little more interesting, but it is necessary that you master this one before proceeding to the next exercise.

Cause and effect is as absolute and undeviating in the hidden realm of thought as in the world of visible and material things. Mind is the master weaver, both of the interior garment of character and the outer garment of circumstance.

—JAMES ALLEN

---

10 The goal here is not so much to "empty the mind" as to cancel each thought as it emerges, choosing the silence, or emptiness, of "no thought." It's possibly what Jesus meant when he said, "Take no thought."

Summary

- The two modes of mental activity are the conscious and unconscious.
- The degree to which we experience ease and perfection depends solely on the degree to which we stop depending upon our conscious mind.
- The unconscious mind is essential to our well-being: it guides us and warns us, it controls the vital processes of life, and it is the seat of memory.
- The conscious mind has the capacity to discriminate and to reason; it is the seat of the will and it can impress the unconscious.
- "Conscious mind is reasoning will. Unconscious mind is instinctive desire, the result of past reasoning will."
- To impress the unconscious, we mentally state what is desired and intended, repeating it frequently, until it becomes our mental attitude.
- If the desire is in harmony with the forward movement of Universal Consciousness, natural forces are set in motion both within ourselves and in our environment to bring about the result.
- The Law of Attraction says that thought is a creative energy that resonates with its object to bring it into manifestation.
- In operation, conditions in our environment reflect the predominant mental attitude we maintain.

LESSON THREE

Radiating Attraction

YOU HAVE found that the individual mind may interact with Universal Mind and that the result of this interaction is cause and effect. Thought, therefore, is the cause, and your life experiences are the effect.

So you can see the importance of eliminating any tendency you may have to complain about your life conditions—as they have been, or as they are—because only *you* can change them and make them what you would like them to be.

To do so, you simply focus on the mental resources, always at your command, from which all real and lasting power comes.

Continue with this practice until you realize the fact that there can be no failure in the accomplishment of any goal in life that is harmonious with the Universal—as long as you understand your power and persist in your intent.

It must be so because the forces generated by our thinking are always ready to support our purposeful will. They're always crystallizing thought and desire into actions, events, and conditions.

Although in the early stages of any practice, each action is the result of conscious thought, repeated actions become habitual and automatic. So as we continue with this practice, the thought that controls each action and function passes into the realm of the unconscious. And it's essential that such thoughts and actions do become automatic, or unconscious, so the conscious mind can attend to other matters. Then these new actions will, in their turn, become habitual, then automatic, then unconscious, so that the conscious mind may again be freed from this detail and go on to still other activities.

When you realize this, you'll have found a source of power to manage any possible situation in life.

The Anatomy of Thought and Feeling

The interaction of the conscious and unconscious mind requires a similar interaction between the corresponding systems of nerves. Judge Thomas Troward[11] indicated the very beautiful method in which this interaction is effected. He said:

> The cerebrospinal system is the organ of the conscious mind and the sympathetic [nervous system] is the organ of the unconscious. The cerebrospinal is the channel through which we receive conscious perception from the physical senses and exercise control over the movements of the body. This system of nerves has its center in the brain.

---

11 Thomas Troward was a British judge in India at the turn of the nineteenth and twentieth centuries. He retired to the British Isles and presented a highly coherent theory of applied metaphysics, most clearly laid out in a book called *The Edinburgh Lectures.* His work profoundly influenced both Ernest Holmes and Emmet Fox, well-known religion philosophers.

> The sympathetic nervous system has its center in a bundle of nerve cells at the back of the stomach known as the *solar plexus.* It channels the unconscious mental activity that supports the vital functions of the body. The two systems are connected through the vagus nerve, which passes out of the cerebral region through the throat, sending out branches to the heart and lungs, and finally passing through the diaphragm, where it loses its outer coating and becomes identified with the nerves of the sympathetic system, making the body a "single entity" physically.

Every thought or idea received by the senses is subjected to reasoning in the cerebral cortex of the brain, which is the organ of the conscious mind. When the conscious, objective mind has been satisfied that the thought is true, it's sent to the nerve center at the solar plexus, or the "brain" of the subjective mind, to be made into our flesh and brought forth into the world as reality. At this point, it's no longer susceptible to any form of reasoning or argument. The unconscious mind cannot argue; it only acts. It accepts the conclusions of the objective mind as final.

This center at the solar plexus has been called the "sun" of the body (*solar* meaning "of the sun") because it's the distribution center for the energy that the body is constantly generating. This energy is very real energy, being distributed by very real nerves to all parts of the body, and this "sun" is a very real sun, throwing off energy in an "atmosphere" that envelops the body.[12]

---

12 In Oriental martial arts, this point is often called the "chi" or "ki" point. In Tibetan yoga it is called the tse bum or vase—a place where the internal energy, chi or, in Sanskrit, prana is stored and dispersed through the body by means of the intricate system of energy channels, or nadis, used by acupuncturists.

If the radiation from this center is strong enough in someone for the rest of us to feel it, we call that person "charismatic" and we say they have "personal magnetism." Such people may wield an immense power for good. The presence alone of such men or women will often bring comfort to troubled minds around them.

When the solar plexus is operating and is radiating life, energy, and vitality to every part of our bodies, the sensations are pleasant, the body is filled with health, and everyone we meet experiences a pleasant sensation.

If there's any interruption of this radiation, the sensations are displeasing because the flow of life and energy to some part of the body is stopped. This is the cause of every human ill—physical, mental, or environmental. The physical is affected because the "sun" of the body is no longer generating sufficient energy to revitalize some part of the body; the mental because the conscious mind depends on the unconscious mind for the vitality necessary to support its thought and is no longer receiving it; and the environmental because the connection between the unconscious mind and Universal Mind is being interrupted.

The solar plexus is the point at which the part meets with the whole, where the finite becomes Infinite, where the uncreated becomes created, the Universal becomes individualized, and the Invisible becomes visible. It's the point where life appears, and there's no limit to the amount of life an individual may generate from this solar center. This center of energy is omnipotent because, being the point of contact with infinite life and intelligence, it can accomplish whatever it is directed to accomplish.

This is the power of the conscious mind: the unconscious can and will carry out such plans and ideas as may be impressed on it by the conscious mind. And because conscious thought controls this sun center from which the life and energy of the entire body flows, the quality, the character, and the nature of the thoughts in our conscious mind determine the quality, character, and nature of energy the solar plexus radiates. It follows then that conscious thought also determines the nature of the experiences that result from that center's interaction with the Universal.

Letting Our Light Shine

With all this in mind, it becomes clear that the more energy we can radiate, the sooner we'll be able to transmute undesirable conditions into sources of pleasure and profit; all we have to do is "let our light shine."

Then the question is how to let this light shine, how to generate this energy. Here are some guidelines:

- Pleasant thought expands the solar plexus; unpleasant thought contracts it.
- Nonresistant thought expands it; resistant thought contracts it.
- Thoughts of courage, power, confidence, and hope all produce a corresponding state.

But the archenemy of the solar plexusis is fear, which must be eliminated before there's any possibility of letting any light shine. This enemy must be expelled forever for it's the cloud that hides the sun, causing a perpetual gloom. This is the personal devil that makes people avoid the past, the present, and the future; themselves, their friends, and their enemies; everything and everybody.[13]

When you find that you are really one with Infinite Power and you can consciously realize this power by a practical demonstration

13 A number of interpreters of the Bible, including Emmet Fox, Charles Fillmore and Ernest Holmes, suggest that this is what is meant when Jesus says "Get thee behind me, Satan" in response to Peter's expressions of fear regarding Jesus' final trip to Jerusalem (Matthew 16:23).

of your ability to overcome any adverse condition with the power of your thought, you have nothing to fear. Fear will have been destroyed and you will have come into possession of your birthright. When fear is completely destroyed, your light shines, the clouds disperse, and you find the source of power, energy, and life.

Our attitude toward life determines the experiences we encounter. If we expect nothing, we'll get nothing; if we demand much, we shall receive even more. The world is harsh only as we fail to assert ourselves. The world's criticism is bitter only to those who can't compel room for their ideas—and fear of this criticism causes many ideas to fail to see the light of day.

But people who know they have a radiating solar plexus won't fear criticism or anything else; they'll be too busy radiating courage, confidence, and power. They'll anticipate success by this mental attitude. They'll pound barriers to pieces and leap over the chasm of doubt and hesitation that fear has placed in their path. Knowledge of our ability to consciously radiate health, strength, and harmony will bring us into a realization that there is nothing to fear because we are in touch with Infinite Strength.

Applying the Principle

Knowledge can be gained only by applying information. We learn by doing, just as the athlete becomes powerful through practice.

As the following statement is supremely important, it will be presented in several ways so you can't fail to get the full significance of it. If you are religiously inclined, you can let your light shine. If your mind has a bias toward physical science, you can awaken the solar plexus; or, if you prefer the strictly scientific interpretation, you can impress your unconscious mind.

You've already learned that the unconscious is intelligent and that it is creative and responsive to the will of the conscious mind. What, then, is the most natural way to make the desired impression?

Concentrate on the object of your desire.

While you're concentrating, you're imprinting your thought upon the unconscious. This isn't the only way, but it's simple and effective, and the most direct way, so it's the way to achieve the best results. In fact, this method is producing such extraordinary results that many people think miracles are being accomplished. It's the method by which every great inventor, every great financier, every great statesman has been able to convert the subtle and invisible energy, or force, of desire, faith, and confidence into concrete facts in the objective world.

Why does it work? The unconscious mind is part of Universal Mind. Universal Mind is the creative principle of the universe; a part must be the same in kind and quality as the whole. This means that this creative power is absolutely unlimited; it's not bound by any precedent and consequently has no prior existing pattern by which to apply its constructive principle. Since the unconscious mind is responsive to our conscious reasoning and will, the unlimited creative power of Universal Mind is within control of the conscious mind of the individual.

When applying this principle in the following exercises, remember that you don't need to figure out how the unconscious will produce the results you desire. The finite cannot inform the Infinite. You need simply to say *what* you desire not *how* you are to obtain it.

You are the channel by which the undifferentiated is being differentiated, and this differentiation is being accomplished by appropriation of the substance of the universe. It only requires your recognition to set causes in motion that will bring about results in accordance with your desire. This is accomplished because the Universal can act only through the individual, and the individual can act only through the Universal; they are one.

For your exercise in this lesson, you will go one step further:

1. Sit in the same room, the same chair, and the same position.
2. Be perfectly still and inhibit all thought as far as possible, as you did before.
3. Now, relax, let go, let the muscles take their normal condition; this will remove all pressure from the nerves and eliminate that tension which so frequently produces physical exhaustion. Physical relaxation is a voluntary exercise of the will, and the exercise will be found to be of great value, as it enables the blood to circulate freely to and from the brain and body.[14]

Tension leads to mental unrest and abnormal mental activity of the mind; it produces worry, care, fear, and anxiety. Relaxation is, therefore, an absolute necessity in allowing mental faculties to exercise the greatest freedom. Make this exercise as thorough and complete as possible; mentally determine that you will relax every muscle and nerve until you feel quiet, restful, and at peace with yourself and the world.[15] The solar plexus will then be ready to function, and you will be surprised at the result.

Summary

- The cerebrospinal system of the brain is the organ of the conscious mind.

---

14 There are many guides to relaxing the body, but the essential process is to start at the toes and intentionally tighten and relax the muscles. Focus next on the muscles of the feet and do the same, then the calves, the thighs, and so on all the way up to the face—the forehead, jaw, and eye muscles. Sometimes it helps to use a CD or tape recording to guide the process. *The Relaxation Response,* by Dr. Herbert Benson, contains an excellent process.

15 In *The Relaxation Response,* Herbert Benson describes research results in which patients who slowed down their breathing began to relax their muscles; in patients whose muscles were relaxed, many other systems showed improved function.

- The sympathetic system of nerves is the organ of the unconscious mind, in which the solar plexus is the center.
- The solar plexus is the central point of distribution for energy that the body is constantly generating and radiating outward into the environment.
- This energy can be controlled and directed by conscious thought.
- We awaken the solar plexus by mentally concentrating on the conditions that we desire to see manifested in our lives.
- This distribution of energy may be interrupted by resistant, critical, or discordant thoughts but especially by fear, the archenemy.
- Every ill with which the human race is afflicted is the result of such interruption.
- Fear may be completely eliminated by an understanding and recognition of the true source of all power.
- Universal Mind is the creative principle of the universe, with infinite power and intelligence. As our unconscious mind is a part of Mind and is controlled by our conscious mind, we have access to infinite power through our conscious thought.

LESSON FOUR

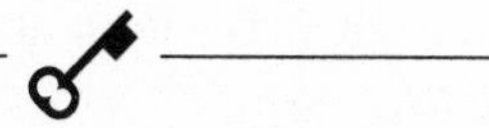

Energy Is Power

This Lesson will show you why what you think, do, or feel becomes what you are.

Thought is energy, and energy is power, but because all the religions, sciences, and philosophies of the world have been based on the *manifestation* of this energy instead of the energy itself, the world has been limited to effects, while the causes have been ignored or misunderstood.

The world until now has focused on these effects to the extent that the effects have names we are all familiar with, as opposed to anyone caring enough about what caused these things to be in the world in the first place. That's why we have God and the Devil in religion, positive and negative in science, and good and bad in philosophy. We have labeled the effects and forgotten, or never found, the causes.

The Master Key reverses that process. This system is interested only in cause, and letters received from students tell a marvelous story, indicating conclusively that they're finding the causes and are securing for themselves health, harmony, abundance, and whatever else may be necessary for their welfare and happiness.

Life is expressive, and our job is to express ourselves harmoniously and constructively. Sorrow, misery, unhappiness, disease, and poverty are not necessities, and with this system we're constantly eliminating them.

But this process of eliminating requires rising above and beyond limitation of any kind. People who have strengthened and purified their thought need not concern themselves about microbes, and those who understand the Law of Abundance will go at once to the source of supply.

This is how fate, fortune, and destiny will be controlled as readily as a captain controls his ship or an engineer his train.

Discovering the "I"

Your personality is made up of countless individual characteristics, peculiarities, habits, and traits. These are the result of your former method of thinking, but they have nothing to do with the real "I." When you say "I think," the "I" tells the mind what it shall think; when you say "I go," the "I" tells the physical body where it shall go; the real nature of this "I" is spiritual, and it's the source of the real power which comes to men and women when they realize their true nature.

So the "I" of you is not the physical body; that is simply an instrument the "I" uses to carry out its purposes. The "I" cannot be the mind, for the mind is simply another instrument that the "I" uses to think, reason, and plan.

The "I" is something else; something that controls and directs both the body and the mind; something that determines what the body and the mind shall do and how they shall act. When you realize the true nature of this "I," you will enjoy a sense of power greater than you've ever known.

One of the strongest affirming statements you can make is, *"I can be whatever I will to be."* It strengthens the will and helps you realize your power to accomplish. Every time you repeat it, you realize who and what this "I" is. Try to come into a thorough understanding of the true nature of the "I." If you do, you will become invincible—provided that your objects and purposes are constructive and in harmony with the creative principle of the universe. To make the best use of this affirmation, use it continuously, night and morning and as often during the day as you think of it. Continue to do so until it becomes a part of you; form a habit.

Unless you do this fully, you're better off not starting at all because modern psychology tells us that when we start something and don't complete it, or make a resolution and don't keep it, we're forming a habit of failure—absolute, ignominious failure.

So, if you don't intend to do a thing, don't start. If you do start, see it through even if the heavens fall. If you make up your mind to do something, do it. Let nothing and no one interfere. The "I" in you has determined, the thing is settled; the die is cast, there is no longer any argument.

If you carry out this idea, begin with small things that you know you can control then gradually increase the effort. Never, under any circumstances, allow your "I" to be overruled, and you'll find that you can eventually control yourself. And, while many men and women have found to their sorrow that it's easier to control a kingdom than to control themselves, when you have learned to control yourself, you will find the world within that controls the world without. You will become irresistible; people and things will respond to your every wish without any apparent effort on your part. This is not so strange or impossible as it may appear if you simply remember that the world within is controlled by the "I," and this "I" is a part of, or one with, the Infinite "I"—Universal Mind or Consciousness, usually called God.

This last is not just a statement or theory made for the purpose of confirming or establishing an idea; it's a fact, accepted by the highest religious thought as well as the best scientific thought.

Writer and philosopher Herbert Spender said: "Amid all the mysteries by which we are surrounded, nothing is more certain than that we are ever in the presence of an Infinite and Eternal Energy from which all things proceed." Theologian Lyman Abbott, in an address delivered before the alumni of Bangor Theological Seminary, said: "We are coming to think of God as dwelling in man rather than as operating on men from without."

Science goes a little way in its search and stops. Science finds the ever-present eternal energy, but religion finds the power behind this energy and locates it within humanity.

Through all the ages, humanity has believed in an invisible power, through which and by which all things have been created and are continually being re-created. We may personalize this power and call it God, or we may think of it as the Essence, Intelligence, or Spirit that permeates all things, but the effect is the same.

As far as the individual is concerned, the objective, the physical, the visible is the personal—that which can be perceived by the senses. The personal is conscious because it has a personal identity, or individuality.

The subjective is the spiritual, the invisible, and the impersonal. The impersonal, being the same in kind and quality as all other beings, is not conscious of itself and has therefore been termed the unconscious mind.

The personal—the conscious mind—has the power of will and choice, and can therefore select which methods to use to solve difficulties.

The impersonal, or spiritual, being a part of, or one with, the source and origin of all power, can necessarily exercise no such choice but has infinite resources at its command. It can and does bring about results by methods concerning the individual conscious mind, which being finite in nature, can have no possible conception.

Constructive Thought and Action

The greatest and most marvelous power that this "I" has been given is the power to think, but few people know how to think constructively or correctly. As a result, they achieve variable results. Most people childishly allow their thoughts to dwell on selfish purposes. When a mind becomes mature, it understands that *the germ of defeat is in every selfish thought.*

The trained mind knows that every transaction must benefit every person who is in any way connected with the transaction, and any attempt to profit by the weakness, ignorance, or necessity of another will inevitably operate to his or her disadvantage. This is because the individual is a part of the Universal. A part cannot antagonize any other part, but, on the contrary, the welfare of each part depends on honoring the interest of every member of the whole.

Those who recognize this principle have a great advantage in life. They don't wear themselves out. They can eliminate vagrant thoughts easily. They can readily concentrate to the highest possible degree on any subject. They waste neither time nor money on things that can be of no possible benefit to them.

Here is the secret of power, of mastery. To overcome does not mean to go without things. Self-denial is not success. *We cannot give unless we get; we cannot be helpful unless we are strong.* The Infinite is not bankrupt, and we who are the representatives of Infinite Power should not be bankrupt either. If we wish to be of service to others we must have power, but to get it we must give it; we must be of service.

The more we give, the more we shall get; we must become a channel whereby the Universal can express activity. The Universal is constantly seeking to express itself, to be of service, and it seeks the channel whereby it can find the greatest activity, where it can do the most good, where it can be of greatest service to mankind.[16]

The Universal cannot express through you as long as you are busy with your preconceived plans, your own purposes. Quiet the senses and seek inspiration. Focus your awareness within and dwell in the consciousness of your unity with Universal Omnipotence. Still water runs deep. Contemplate the many opportunities to which you have spiritual access by the omnipresence of power. Visualize the events, circumstances, and conditions that these spiritual connections may assist in manifesting.

Realize the fact that the essence and soul of all things is spiritual—that the spiritual is truly real because it is the life of all there is. When the spirit is gone, the life is gone; it is dead; it has ceased to exist.

These mental activities pertain to the world within, to the world of cause, and the conditions and circumstances that come about are the effect. This is how you become a creator. This is important work, and the higher, loftier, grander, and more noble the ideals you conceive, the more significant the work will become.

Applying the Principle

Thought is motion and is carried by the Law of Vibration very much the way that light or electricity is. Thought is a product of

---

16 This understanding is the inspiration for what we call "The Prayer of St. Francis," which starts (according to some translations) with "Make me a channel of your peace."

the spiritual "I," so it is divine, spiritual, and creative in nature. Thought takes form and expression by the Law of Growth and is given vitality by the emotions through the Law of Love.

So in order to express power, abundance, or any other constructive purpose, the emotions must be called upon to give feeling to the thought and then to give it form. How may this be accomplished? How may we develop the faith, the courage, the feeling that will result in accomplishment?

We do so by practice. Mental strength is secured in exactly the same way that physical strength is secured: by repeated exercise. We think something, perhaps with difficulty the first time; we think the same thing again, and it becomes easier this time; we think it again and again; it then becomes a mental habit. We continue to think the same thing, and finally it becomes automatic. We can no longer help thinking this thing because we are now positive of what we think; there is no doubt about it. We are sure; we know.

In the last lesson, you relaxed to let go physically. Now, you are going to let go mentally.

If you practiced the exercise given in the last lesson for fifteen or twenty minutes a day, you can no doubt relax physically. Anyone who isn't able to consciously, quickly, and completely do this is not yet a master of the self. Those who can't relax their bodies easily and effortlessly have not yet obtained freedom; they are still slaves to conditions. But let's assume that you have mastered the exercise and are ready to take the next step, which is mental freedom.

1. Take your usual position.
2. Remove all tension by completely relaxing.
3. Now, mentally let go of all adverse thoughts and emotions, such as hatred, anger, worry, jealousy, envy, sorrow, trouble,

> or disappointment of any kind. You may say that you can't "let go" of these things, but you can; you can do so by mentally determining to do so—by voluntary intention and persistence.[17]

Some people have difficulty doing this because they allow themselves to be controlled by their emotions instead of by their will. But those who are guided by the reasoned will achieve their goals. You may not succeed the first time you try, but practice makes perfect in this as in everything else. You must succeed in dismissing, eliminating, and completely destroying all negative and destructive thoughts because they are the seed that is constantly germinating into every kind of discordant conditions you may have been experiencing.

Balance is essential. Overwork, over-play, or too much activity of any kind produces mental apathy and stagnation, which, in turn, makes it impossible to do the more important, inner work of realizing conscious power. So seek the Silence frequently. Power comes through repose; it's in the Silence that we can be still, and when we are still, we can think. Thought is the secret of all attainment.

---

17 Some teachers suggest using visualization to do this: visualize such thoughts and emotions being carried away or washed away; imagine a cleansing light flowing through the body and mind; use a mental "laser" to burn away thoughts and images that do not serve our highest good—whatever images help the reasoning mind and the unconscious to accept that these thoughts and emotions are no longer what you intend to experience and express. Then replace them immediately with a desirable thought—lest the undesired ones fall back into the space you've created, like dry sand into a hole.

There is nothing truer than that the quality of thought which we entertain links certain externals in the outside world. This is the Law from which there is no escape. And it is this Law, this correlative of the thought with its object, that from time immemorial has led the people to believe in special providence.

—Helen Wilmans

Summary

- Thought is spiritual energy carried by the Law of Vibration.
- Thought is given vitality by the Law of Love.
- Thought takes form by the Law of Growth.
- The secret of thought's creative power is that it's a spiritual activity, part of Universal Mind.
- We may develop the faith, courage, and enthusiasm to accomplish by recognizing our spiritual nature—that the "I" of us is neither body nor mind but that which expresses as both.
- The secret to having Power is acting in service because we get what we give.
- The Silence is a physical stillness that is the first step to self-control, self-mastery.

LESSON FIVE

Thought Is Creative

AND NOW you reach lesson five. After studying this lesson carefully, you'll see that every conceivable force, object, or fact is the result of mind in action.

People are thinking now as they never thought before. As a result, this is a creative age, and the world is awarding its richest prizes to the thinkers. Mind is force, energy, and power. Matter is powerless, passive, and inert. Mind shapes and controls matter.

Mind in action is thought, and thought is creative. You can originate thought, and since thoughts are creative, you can create for yourself the things you desire. Every form that matter takes is nothing more than the expression of some preexisting thought.

But thought works no magic transformations. It obeys Natural Law. It sets in motion natural forces. It releases natural energies. It manifests in your conduct and actions, and these in turn act on your friends and acquaintances, and eventually on your whole environment.

Acting Consciously

The Law of Attraction is not bringing to us the things we like, the things we wish for, or the things someone else has; it brings us "our own," the things we've created by our thought processes, whether consciously or unconsciously. Unfortunately, many of us are creating these things unconsciously.

At least 90 percent of our mental life is unconscious, so those who fail to use this mental power live within very narrow limits. The unconscious can and will solve any problem for us if we know how to direct it; unconscious processes are always at work. The only question is: Are we simply to remain passive recipients of these activities, or are we going to consciously direct them?

The great fact is that the source of all life and all power is within. People, circumstances, and events may suggest need and opportunities, but the insight, strength, and power to answer these needs will always be found within.

We've found that the unconscious mind pervades every part of the physical body and is always capable of being directed or impressed by directives coming from the objective, more dominant portion of the mind. The unconscious mind pervading the body is largely the result of heredity, which is simply the accumulated response to all the environments of past generations.

Understanding this fact enables us to use our authority when we find some undesirable character trait manifesting. We can consciously use all our desirable characteristics while we remove our attention from—and so refuse to allow—any undesirable traits to manifest.

This mind pervading our physical body is not only the result of hereditary tendencies but is also the result of our home, business, and social environment, where countless thousands of impressions, ideas, prejudices, and similar thoughts have been received. Much of this has been received from others, the result of opinions, suggestions, or statements, and much of it is the result of our own thinking. But nearly all of it has been accepted with little or no examination or consideration.

An idea seemed plausible in the moment, so the conscious received it and passed it on to the unconscious, where it was taken up by the sympathetic nervous system and passed on to be built into our physical body. "What we think, we become."[18] This, then, is the way we're constantly creating and re-creating ourselves; we are today the result of our past thinking, and we will become what we are thinking today.

Building Our Mental Home

If any of us were building a home for ourselves, how careful we would be regarding the plans! We would study every detail; we'd watch the materials being used and select only the best of everything. And yet, how careless we are when it comes to building our mental home, which is infinitely more important than any physical home. Everything that can possibly enter into our lives depends upon the qualities of the material we use to construct our mental home.

What is this material? We've seen that it's the impressions we've accumulated in the past and stored away in our unconscious mind. If these impressions have been of fear, worry, care, or anxiety, or if they've been despondent, negative, or doubtful, then the walls we're building today will be framed in poor-quality lumber. They'll be mildewed and rotten and will bring us only more toil and care and anxiety. We'll forever be busy trying to patch it up and make it appear at least presentable.

18 Gautama, the Buddha.

But if we've stored away nothing but courageous thought; have been optimistic and positive; and have immediately thrown any kind of negative thought on the scrap pile, refusing to associate with it or to become identified with it in any way, what is the result? Our mental material is now the best kind; we can build any kind of structure we want, and we can make it any color we wish. We know that the foundation is firm, that the walls are solid and that will not crack, and that we have no fear, no anxiety concerning the future. There is nothing to cover, and there are no patches to hide.

These are psychological facts; there is no theory or guesswork about these processes. There's nothing secret about them. In fact, they're so plain that everyone can understand them. The thing to do is to have a mental housecleaning and to have this housecleaning every day, keeping our mental home free of distressing thought patterns. Mental, moral, and physical cleanliness are absolutely indispensable if we are to make progress of any kind. When this mental housecleaning has been completed, the material that's left will be suitable for making the kind of ideals or mental images we truly desire to realize.

Avoid counterfeits. Build firm foundations for your consciousness using materials that flow directly from Universal Mind, the Infinite Source, of which you are a part.

Our True Inheritance

You're probably familiar with the subject of heredity. Charles Darwin, Thomas Henry Huxley, and other biologists have piled evidence mountain-high that heredity is a law of progressive creation. Progressive heredity gives humans our erect stance, our modes of motion, our digestive organs, our blood circulation, our nerve force, our muscular force, our bone structure, and our host of other physical characteristics. All these constitute what may be called our human heredity, acquired from our ancestors.

There is, however, another form of heredity—one that scientists have not yet comprehended. It lies beneath and precedes all of their research. At the point where they throw up their hands, saying they can't account for what they see, this heredity is found. It's the benign force commanding all new creation. From Universal Mind, it flows directly into every being. It originates life, which the biologist has never done. It stands out among all forces supreme and unapproachable. No human heredity measures up to it.

This force, this Infinite Life, flows through you; it *is* you. Its doorways are the aspects of your consciousness. To keep these doors open is the secret of Power. Isn't it worth the effort?

There is a fine estate awaiting someone to claim it. Its broad acres, with abundant crops, running water, and fine timber, stretch as far as the eye can see. There's a mansion, spacious and cheerful, with rare pictures, a well-stocked library, rich curtains, and every comfort and luxury. All the heir has to do is claim this inheritance, take possession, and use the property. He or she must use it and not let it decay, for use is the condition on which it is held. To neglect it is to lose possession.

In the domain of mind and spirit, in the domain of practical power, such an estate is yours. You are the heir! You can claim your inheritance, and possess and use this rich estate. Power over circumstances is one of its fruits; health, harmony, and prosperity are assets on its balance sheet. It offers you poise and peace. It costs you only the labor of studying and harvesting its great resources. It demands no sacrifice except the loss of your limitations, your weaknesses. It clothes you with self-honor and puts a scepter in your hands.

Those who have come into possession of this inheritance are never quite the same again. They have a sense of power beyond anything they ever dreamed of. They can never again be timid, weak, vacillating, or fearful. They are permanently connected with Omnipotence. Something in them has been aroused; they suddenly discover that they possess a tremendous latent ability of which they had no idea before.

To gain this estate, three things are necessary:

1. You must earnestly desire it.
2. You must assert your claim.
3. You must take possession.

These rules are simple enough for everyone.

Applying the Principle

Power is from within, but we can't receive it unless we give it. The only way we can hold onto this inheritance is to use it.

We must use it because we are, in fact, channels through which Omnipotent Power is being brought forth into form.[19] Unless we give, the channel becomes blocked and we can receive no more. This is true on every plane of existence, in every field of endeavor, and in all walks of life. The more we give, the more we get.

The athlete who wishes to get stronger must make use of the strength he has, and the more he gives the more he will get. The financier who wishes to make money must make use of the money she has, for only by using it can she get more. The merchant who does not keep the goods going out will soon have none coming in. The business that fails to give competent service will soon lack customers. The attorney who fails to get results will soon lack

19 The Prayer of St. Francis is a commitment to be a channel of this Omnipotence. Some translations begin with "Lord, make me an instrument of Your peace; where there is hatred, let me sow love; where there is injury, pardon; where there is doubt, faith; where there is despair, hope; where there is darkness, light; and where there is sadness, joy."

clients. And so it goes everywhere; *increasing our power requires our proper use of the power already in our possession.*

The same thing that is true in these fields, and every other experience in life, is true of the power from which every other form of power emerges—spiritual power. Why? If spirit is all there is, then the ability to demonstrate any power, whether physical, mental, or spiritual, must depend on recognition of this fact. Take away the spirit from anything and what is left? Nothing.

All possession is the result of an attitude of mind that focuses on accumulation of wealth—what has been called "money consciousness." This is the magic wand that will enable you to receive the idea. It will formulate plans for you to execute, and you will find as much pleasure in the execution as in the satisfaction of attainment and achievement.

1. Go to your room.
2. Sit in the same seat, in the same position as you have so far.
3. Think of a place that you enjoy being in.
4. Make a complete mental picture of it; see the buildings, grounds, trees, friends, associations, everything complete.

At first, you'll find yourself thinking of everything under the sun except the ideal on which you're attempting to concentrate. But don't let that discourage you. Persistence will win, but persistence requires that you practice these exercises every day without fail.

Summary

- At least 90 percent of our mental life is unconscious.
- Few understand or appreciate the fact that this vast storehouse of unconsciousness is an activity they can consciously direct.

- The conscious mind received its governing tendencies through heredity, which means that it is the result of all the environments of all past generations.
- The Law of Attraction brings our "own" to us—that which we inherently are; the result of our past thinking, both conscious and unconscious.
- The secret of power is recognition of the omnipresence of Omnipotence originating from within.
- The possession of power is contingent on proper use of the power already in our possession.

LESSON SIX

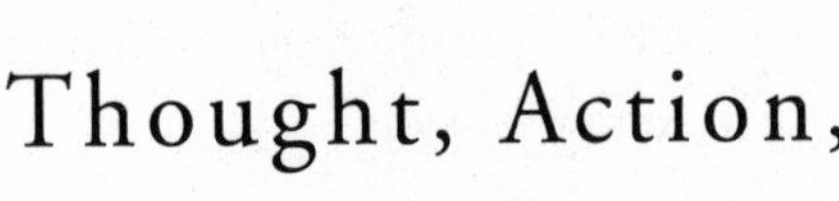

Thought, Action, and Effect

THE TWO great forms of human suffering are diseases of the body and mental anxiety. These are effects and may be readily traced to the infringement of some Natural Law, which was probably the result of partial knowledge of its working. But the clouds of darkness that symbolize this ignorance are beginning to roll away—and with them many of the miseries that result from inadequate information.

People are finally learning to place themselves in harmony with Universal Mind; they're learning the unity of all things. They're learning the basic methods and principles of thinking, and this is changing conditions and multiplying results. They're finding that circumstances and environment follow the trend of mental and spiritual progress. They find that growth follows knowledge, action follows inspiration, opportunity follows perception: always the spiritual first, then the transformation into the infinite and unlimited possibilities of achievement. As the individual is but the channel for the differentiation of the Universal, these possibilities are inexhaustible.

Universal Mind is so wonderful that it's difficult to understand its utilitarian powers, its possibilities, and its unlimited producing effects. We've found that this Mind is, not only all intelligence, but all substance. How, then, are we to bring it into the specific form—the particular effect—we desire?

This lesson introduces the most wonderful machine ever created—a machine by which you may create health, strength, success, prosperity, or any other experience you desire.

Thought is a product of Mind, and Mind is creative. This means that we can come into a harmonious relationship with the Universal, and our desires, needs, ideas, and thoughts will come into being, though we will not be "ruler" of the Universal, as this would not be a harmonious relationship. If you can comprehend that this is a scientific truth and one of the wonderful laws of Nature, it will be easier for you to get an understanding of the mechanism that is used to accomplish these extraordinary results.

The Ultimate Machine

Ask any electrician what the effect of electricity will be and he will reply with something like, "Electricity is energy in motion and its effect depends on the mechanism to which it is attached." It's this mechanism that determines whether we have heat, light, power, music, or any of the other marvelous demonstrations of power to which this vital energy has been harnessed.

What effect can be produced by thought? Thought is mind in motion (just as wind is air in motion and electricity is energy in motion), and its effect will depend entirely on the "mechanism to which it is attached." Here, then, is the secret of all mental power; *it depends entirely on the mechanism to which we attach it.*

What is this mechanism? Let's examine the wonders of this mechanism; perhaps we can get a better understanding of the various effects that it causes.

The human nervous system has been compared to an electric circuit: think of the nerve cell as the battery in which the force is originated and the white matter around it as insulated wires, carrying the current. It's through these channels that every impulse or desire is carried through the mechanism of our bodies. The spinal cord is the great sensory pathway by which messages are conveyed to and from the brain.

It is a beautifully constructed mechanism built around an electrical circuit generating an electrical field and transmitting information along its neural "wires." Every thought sets the brain cells in action—at first the body may fail to respond, but if the thought is sufficiently refined and concentrated, the substance of the body finally yields and expresses perfectly. Thus the mind can influence any part of the body, causing the elimination of any undesirable effect.

This then is the "Temple of the Living God" over which the individual "I" is given control. But this is by no means a new discovery; the Bible says exactly the same thing, and the language is just as plain and convincing: "Know ye not that ye are the temple of the living God?"[20] Jesus taught that God does not only live in the temple at Jerusalem, but "the kingdom of God is within."[21] Here, then, is the secret of the wonderful creative power of the world within.

You know something of radio, television, and the microwaves used for cell phones, by which space and time have become only

20 I Corinthians 6:19.

21 Luke 17:21.

figures of speech, but did you ever stop to think that the mechanism you have can transform the Universal and Omnipresent Power, which was invented by an inventor even greater than Edison or Tesla?

Now, beyond the body, there is the great mental field in which we live and move and have our being. This field is omnipotent, omniscient, and omnipresent and it responds to our desire in direct ratio to our purpose and faith. Thought is the process by which we may absorb the spirit of power and hold the result in our inner consciousness until it becomes a part of our ordinary consciousness. In order to receive any information, however, the receiver must be in tune with the transmitter; to be in tune with Eternal Truth we must possess poise and harmony within.

And our purpose must be in accordance with the Law of Our Being, which means it must be creative or constructive. If we infringe on the rights of others, we become moral thorns and find ourselves entangled at every turn of the road. Our success is contingent upon the highest moral ideal: "The greatest good to the greatest number." Aspiration, desire, and harmonious relations, constantly and persistently maintained, will accomplish results.

More, our outlook must be positive enough to generate sufficient power to bring our purpose into manifestation: "By bringing about a change in our outlook toward things and events, all phenomena can become sources of happiness."[22] You can see, then, that the greatest hindrance is erroneous ideas fixed in our unconscious minds.

So, people who look within instead of without can't fail to make use of these mighty forces which, in turn, will eventually determine their course in life and bring them into vibration with all that is best, strongest, and most desirable.

---

22 The Dalai Lama.

Think of the wonder of it all! Do you love music, flowers, literature, or are you inspired by the thought of ancient or modern genius? Remember, every beauty to which you respond must have its corresponding outline in your brain before you can appreciate it. There is not a single virtue or principle in the storehouse of Nature which the brain can't express.

At the same time, the brain is an embryonic world, ready to develop at any time as necessity may arise. Necessities are demands; demands create action, and actions bring about results. Individual development, like Universal development, occurs gradually, with an ever-increasing capacity and volume. Evolution is a process of constantly building new tomorrows out of our today.

The Power of Attention

Attention or concentration is probably the most important factor in the development of mental capacity. The possibilities of attention when properly directed are so startling that they would hardly appear credible to the uninitiated. The cultivation of attention is the distinguishing characteristic of every successful man or woman and is the very highest personal accomplishment that can be acquired.

The power of attention can be more readily understood by comparing it with a magnifying glass in which rays of sunlight are focused. They aren't particularly strong as long as the glass is moved about and the rays are directed from one place to another; but let the glass be held perfectly still with the rays focused on one spot, and the effect becomes immediately apparent.

It's the same with the power of thought; let power be dissipated by letting the thought bounce from one object to another, and no result is apparent; but focus this power through attention or concentration on any single purpose for any length of time and nothing becomes impossible.

Applying the Principle

Focused thought is a very simple remedy for a very complex situation, some will say. Those of you who have had no experience in concentrating the thought on a definite purpose or object should try it.

Choose any single object, and concentrate your attention on it with a definite purpose for ten minutes. Most likely, you cannot do it; the mind will wander a dozen times and it will be necessary to bring it back to the original purpose. Each time the effect will have been lost. At the end of the ten minutes, nothing will have been gained because you have not been able to hold your thought steadily to the purpose.

It is, however, through attention that you will finally be able to overcome obstacles of any kind that appear in your path, and the only way to acquire this wonderful power is by practice. Practice makes perfect, in this as in anything else.

To cultivate the power of attention:

1. Bring a photograph with you to the same seat in the same room in the same position as before.
2. Examine it closely for at least ten minutes. Note the expression of the eyes, the form of the features, the clothing, the way the hair is arranged. In fact, note every detail shown on the photograph carefully.
3. Now cover it and close your eyes. Try to see it mentally.
4. If you can see every detail perfectly and can form a good mental image of the photograph, you are to be congratulated; if not, repeat the process until you can.

This step is simply for the purpose of preparing the soil; in the next lesson we shall be ready to sow the seed. Through such exercises as these you'll finally be able to control your moods, your attitude—your consciousness.

That a man can change himself, improve himself, re-create himself, control his environment, and master his own destiny is the conclusion of every mind that is wide-awake to the power of right thought in constructive action.

—Christian Larsen

Summary

- The effects produced by electricity, including heat, light, power, and music, depend on the mechanism to which electricity is attached.
- The conditions and experiences we encounter are the result of the action and interaction of the individual mind upon the Universal.
- These conditions may be changed by changing the brain, which is the mechanism through which the Universal takes form.
- Conditions may be changed by the process we call thinking. Thoughts produce brain cells, and these cells respond to the corresponding thought in the Universal.
- The power of concentration is the highest personal accomplishment that can be acquired; it's the distinguishing characteristic of every successful man or woman.
- Concentration may be acquired by faithfully practicing the exercises in this system.
- Practice is important because it will enable us to control our thoughts, and since thoughts are causes and conditions are effects, controlling the cause also controls the effect.

LESSON SEVEN

Idealization, Visualization, Realization

EACH OF us has the option of depending on the human will with all its limitations and misconceptions, or we may access the potentialities of Infinity by making use of the unconscious mind. But to make use of the Omnipotent Power that is the unconscious mind, we have to practice with the conscious mind.

One method of consciously utilizing this Omnipotent Power, is visualization. Visualization is the process of making mental images from which the mold, model, or pattern of your future will emerge.

Make the pattern clear and make it beautiful; don't be afraid to make it grand. Remember that no limitation can be placed on you by anyone but yourself. You're not limited as to cost or material; draw on the Infinite for your supply. Construct it in your imagination; it will have to be there before it will ever appear anywhere else. Make the image clear and clean-cut, hold it firmly in the mind, and you will gradually and constantly bring the thing nearer to you. You can be what "you *will* to be."

This is another psychological fact that is well known, but unfortunately, just reading about it won't simply bring about any result you may have in mind; it won't even help you to form the mental image, much less bring it into manifestation. Work is necessary—labor, focused mental labor, the kind of effort few are willing to put forth.

The first step is idealization. You're sowing the seed, but before sowing any seed you want to know what the harvest will be. It's the most important step because it's the plan on which you are going to build.

Your plan must be solid; it must be permanent. The architect, when he plans a thirty-story building, has every line and detail pictured in advance. The engineer, when she plans a bridge to span a chasm, first ascertains the strength requirements of a million separate parts.

They see the end before a single step is taken; so you are to picture in your mind what you want. If you're not sure, return to your chair daily until the picture becomes plain. At first the general plan will be dim, but it will take shape. The outline will take form, then the details, and you'll gradually develop the ability to formulate plans that eventually materialize in the objective world. You'll come to know what the future holds for you.

Then comes the process of visualization. You must see the picture more and more completely: see the details, and, as the details begin to unfold, see the ways and means for bringing them into manifestation. One thing will lead to another.

Thought will lead to action, action will develop methods, methods will develop friends, and friends will bring about circumstances.

Finally, the *third step, realization*, will have been accomplished.

We all recognize that the universe must have been thought into shape before it ever could have become a material fact. And if we are willing to follow along the lines of the Great Architect of the universe, we shall find our thoughts taking material form, just as the universe took form. After all, it's the same Mind operating through the individual. There's no difference in kind or quality; the only difference is one of degree.

Visualizing

Visualization is a very different process from seeing; seeing is physical and is therefore related to the objective world, the world without; but visualization is a product of the imagination and is a product of the subjective mind, the world within. It therefore possesses the vitality of spirit; it will grow.

The architect visualizes her building; she sees it as she wants it to be. Her thought becomes a plastic mold from which the building will eventually emerge—a high one or a low one, a beautiful one or a plain one. Her vision takes form on paper, the necessary material is utilized, and eventually the building stands complete.

The inventor visualizes his idea in exactly the same manner. For instance, Nikola Tesla, one of the greatest inventors of all time, a man who brought forth the most amazing realities, always visualized his inventions before attempting to build them. He didn't rush to embody them in form and then spend his time in correcting defects. Having first built up the idea in his imagination, he held it there as a mental picture, observing its operation, then reconstructed and improved it by his thought. "In this way," he wrote in the *Electrical Experimenter,*

> I am enabled to rapidly develop and perfect a conception without touching anything. When I have gone so far as

> to embody in the invention every possible improvement I can think of and see no fault anywhere, I put into concrete the product of my brain. Invariably my device works as I conceived it should; in twenty years there has not been a single exception.

If you can conscientiously follow these directions, you will develop faith, the kind of understanding faith that William Blake referred to when he wrote "What is now proved was once only imagined."[23] You will then develop confidence, the kind of confidence that leads to endurance and courage. You will develop the power of concentration, allowing you to exclude all thoughts except the ones which are associated with your purpose. The law is that thought will manifest in form, and only one who knows how to be the divine thinker of his own thoughts can ever take a master's place and speak with authority.

Clarity and accuracy are obtained only by repeatedly "seeing" the image in mind. Each repeated viewing renders the image more clear and accurate than the preceding, and the outward manifestation will be clear and accurate in proportion to the image. You must build it firmly and securely in your mental world—the world within—before it can take form in the world without, and you can build nothing of value, even in the mental world, unless you have the proper material. When you have the material, you can build anything you wish; just make sure your material is of the highest quality. You can't make broadcloth from shoddy thread. This material will be brought out and fashioned by millions of silent mental workers into the form of the image you have in mind.

---

23 William Blake was an English poet, painter, and printmaker in the late eighteenth and early nineteenth centuries. While his work was largely unrecognized in his time, the fact that he was a proponent of imaginative freedom has made him a uniquely influential figure in popular culture today.

Think of it! You have over five million of these mental workers, ready and in active use—they're called brain cells. Besides this, you have another reserve force of at least an equal number, ready to be called into action at the slightest need. Your power to think, then, is almost unlimited, and this means that your power to create is practically unlimited. In addition to these millions of mental workers, you have billions of mental workers in the body, every one of which is endowed with sufficient intelligence to understand and act on any message or suggestion given. These cells are all busy creating and re-creating the body, but in addition to this, they're endowed with the ability to attract to themselves the substance necessary for perfect development.

They do this by the same law and in the same way that every form of life attracts to itself the necessary material for growth. The oak, the rose, and the lily all require certain material for their most perfect expression, and they secure it by silent demand, the Law of Attraction: the most certain way for you to secure what you require for your most complete development.

Make the mental image; make it clear, distinct, perfect. Hold it firmly. The ways and means will develop, supply will follow the demand, and you will be led to do the right thing at the right time and in the right way.

Earnest desire will bring about confident expectation, and this in turn must be reinforced by firm demand. These three cannot fail to achieve results, because the earnest desire is the feeling, the confident expectation is the thought, and the firm demand is the will, and, as we have seen, feeling gives vitality to thought and the will holds it steadily until the Law of Growth brings it into manifestation.

Isn't it wonderful that we have such tremendous power within ourselves, such transcendental faculties? Isn't it strange that we've always been taught to look for strength and power without? We've been taught to look everywhere but within, and whenever this power manifested in our lives, we were told that it was something supernatural.

There are many who understand this wonderful power and make serious and conscientious efforts to realize health, and other conditions, but they seem to fail. They don't seem able to bring the law into operation. The difficulty in nearly every case is that they are dealing with externals. *They want money, power, health, and abundance, but they fail to realize that these are effects that only come when the cause is found.*

The mechanism is perfect; it was created by the Master Architect who "doeth all things well," but unfortunately sometimes the operator (us) is inexperienced or inefficient. Practice and determination overcome this defect.

Those who give no attention to the world without, who seek only to ascertain the Truth and look only for wisdom, will find that this wisdom unfolds and discloses the source of all power, that it manifests in thought and purpose the external conditions desired. This Truth will express itself in noble purpose and courageous action.

Just create ideals; don't bother with external conditions. Make the world within beautiful and opulent, and the world without will express and manifest the conditions you have created within.[24] You will come into a realization of your power to create ideals, and these ideals will be projected into the world of effect.

For instance, consider a man who is in debt. He's continually thinking about the debt, concentrating on it, and as thoughts are causes, the result is that he not only fastens the debt closer to him but actually creates more debt. He is putting the great Law of Attraction into operation with the usual and inevitable result—focus on loss leads to greater loss.

---

24 This is Jesus's guidance: "Seek first the kingdom and all else will be added unto you" (Matthew 6:33).

What, then, is the correct principle? *Concentrate on the things you want, not on the things you do not want.* Think of abundance; idealize the methods and plans for putting the Law of Abundance into operation in your life. Visualize the conditions the Law of Abundance creates; this will result in manifestation.

If the law operates perfectly to bring about poverty, lack, and every form of limitation for those who are continually entertaining thoughts of lack and fear, it will operate with the same certainty to bring about conditions of abundance and opulence for those who entertain thoughts of courage and Power.

This is hard for many people. We're too anxious; we manifest anxiety, fear, distress; we want to do something, we want to help; we're like a child who has just planted a seed and goes every fifteen minutes to stir up the earth and see if the seed is growing. Of course, under such circumstances, the seed will never germinate, and yet this is exactly what many of us do in the mental world. We must plant the seed and leave it undisturbed, but this does not, by any means, imply that we are to sit down and do nothing! We will do more and better work than we've ever done before, new doors will open; all that's necessary is to have an open mind and a readiness to act when the time comes.

Thought force is the most powerful means of obtaining knowledge, and if concentrated on any subject, it will solve the problem. Nothing is beyond the power of human comprehension, but in order to harness thought force and make it do your bidding, work is required. Remember that thought is the fire that creates the steam that turns the wheel of fortune upon which your experiences depend.

Applying the Principle

Ask yourself a few questions and then reverently wait for the response. Do you now and then feel the self within you? Do you assert this self or do you follow the majority? Remember that majorities are always led; they never lead. It was the majority that fought, tooth and nail, against democracy, the computer, the cell phone, and every other advance or improvement ever suggested.

For your exercise in this lesson:

1. Visualize your friend; see him exactly as you last saw him; see the room, the furniture; now see his face.
2. Recall the conversation.
3. Now talk to him about some subject of mutual interest; see his expression change, watch him smile.
4. Arouse his interest now, and tell him a story of adventure; see his eyes light up with the spirit of fun or excitement.

Can you do all of this? If so, your imagination is good, and you are making excellent progress.

Summary

- Visualization is the process of making mental pictures.
- By holding the image or picture in mind, we can gradually but surely bring the thing nearer to us. We can be what we *will* to be.
- Idealization is a process of visualizing our ideal version of the plans that will eventually materialize in our objective world.
- Clarity and accuracy are necessary because "seeing" creates feeling, and feeling creates being: first the mental, then the emotional, then the illimitable possibilities of achievement.
- Each repeated "viewing" renders the image more accurate than the previous one.

- Brain cells secure the material for the construction of our mental image.
- The necessary conditions for bringing about the materialization of your ideal in the objective world are then secured by the Law of Attraction—the natural law by which all conditions and experiences are brought about.
- Three steps are necessary in order to bring this law into operation: earnest desire, confident expectation, and a firm demand.
- Many fail because they concentrate on loss, disease, and disaster. The law is operating perfectly by bringing the things they fear upon them.
- Concentrate on the ideals that you desire to see manifested in your life.

LESSON EIGHT

The Power of Imagination

THIS LESSON eliminates any idea of chance or fate and replaces it with an understanding of Universal Law.

The Law of Creation

The principle is this: you may freely choose what you think but the effect of your thought is governed by an immutable law. Isn't that a wonderful thought? To know that our lives are not subject to the variability of chance or whim? Our lives are governed by law. This stability is our opportunity because by complying with the law we can always be assured of achieving the desired effect.

Law makes the universe one grand song of Harmony. If it were not for law, the universe would be a Chaos instead of a Cosmos.

Here, then, is the secret of the origin of both good and evil; this is all the good and evil there ever was or ever will be.

Let me illustrate. Thought results in action. If your thought is constructive and harmonious, the result will be called good; if your thought is destructive or inharmonious, the result will be called evil.

There is, therefore, but one law, one principle, one cause, one Source of Power, and good and evil are simply words that were coined to describe the results of our compliance or noncompliance with this law.

The importance of this is well illustrated in the lives of Ralph Waldo Emerson and Thomas Carlyle—both famous philosophers in the mid-1800s. Emerson loved the good, and his life was a symphony of peace and harmony. Carlyle hated the bad, and his life was filled with discord and disharmony.

Here we have two grand men, each intent upon achieving the same ideal, but one makes use of constructive thought and is therefore in harmony with Natural Law; the other makes use of destructive thought and therefore brings upon himself discord of every kind and character.

It's evident, therefore, that we are to hate nothing, not even the "bad," because hatred itself is destructive, and we'll soon find that by entertaining any destructive thought we are planting seeds for the "wind" and setting ourselves up to reap the "whirlwind."

Thought is the creative principle of the universe and by its nature will combine with other similar thoughts. And, as the one purpose of life is growth, all principles underlying existence must contribute to give it effect. So thought, therefore, takes form and the Law of Growth eventually brings it into manifestation.

Managing Thought

The Law of Attraction will certainly and unerringly bring to you the conditions, environment, and experiences in life that correspond with your habitual, characteristic, predominant mental attitude. Not what you think once in a while when you are at your place of worship or spiritual retreat, or have just read a good book, but your predominant mental attitude is what counts. You cannot entertain weak, harmful, negative thoughts ten hours a day and expect to bring about beautiful, strong, and harmonious conditions by ten minutes of strong, positive, creative thought.

So, if we may freely choose what we think, but the result of our thought is governed by an immutable law that says any persistent line of thought must produce its result in our character, health, and circumstances, then we really want methods to substitute habits of constructive thinking for those which produce undesirable effects!

We all know that changing our thinking is by no means easy. Mental habits are difficult to control, but it can be done, and the way to do it is to begin at once to substitute constructive thought for destructive thought.

To begin with, form the habit of analyzing every thought. If it's necessary, if its manifestation in the objective will be a benefit, not only to yourself, but to all whom it may affect in any way, keep it; treasure it; it is of value; it is in tune with the Infinite; it will grow and develop and produce fruit many times over. On the other hand, it will be well for you to keep this quotation from George Matthews Adams in mind: "Learn to keep the door shut, keep out of your mind, out of your office, and out of your world every element that seeks admittance with no definite helpful end in view."

If your thoughts have been critical or destructive and have resulted in any discord or disharmony in your environment, it may be necessary for you to cultivate a new mental attitude that is conducive to constructive thought.

The Role of Imagination

The imagination can greatly assist in this process, as cultivating the imagination leads to the development of the ideal vision out of which your future will emerge.

The imagination gathers up the material by which the mind weaves the fabric in which your future is to be clothed. Imagination is the light by which we can penetrate new worlds of thought and experience. Imagination is the mighty instrument by which every discoverer, every inventor opened the way from precedent to experience. Precedent said, "It cannot be done," experience said, "It is done." Imagination is a plastic power, molding the things of sense into new forms and ideals. Imagination is the constructive form of thought which must precede every constructive form of action.

A builder cannot build a structure of any kind until he has first received the plans from the architect, and the architect must get them from his imagination.

The entrepreneur can't build a giant corporation to coordinate hundreds of smaller corporations and thousands of employees and utilize millions of dollars of capital until he has first created the entire work in his imagination.

Objects in the material world are as clay in the potter's hand; it's in the Master Mind that the real things are created, and by the use of the imagination that the work is done.

In order to cultivate the imagination it must be exercised. Exercise is necessary to cultivate mental muscle as well as physical muscle. It must be supplied with nourishment or it cannot grow.

Don't confuse imagination with fantasy or daydreaming, in which some people like to indulge. Daydreaming is a form of mental dissipation that can lead to mental disaster. Constructive imagination takes mental effort, considered by some to be the hardest kind of work, but, if done, it yields the greatest returns, for all the great things in life have come to men and women who had the capacity to think, to imagine, and so make their dreams come true.

Successful people make it their business to hold ideals of the conditions they wish to realize. They constantly hold in mind the next step necessary to the ideal for which they are striving. Thoughts are the materials with which they build, and the imagination is their mental workshop. Mind is the ever-moving force with which they connect with the people and circumstances necessary to build their success structure, and imagination is the matrix in which all great things are fashioned.

This creative power must not be confused with the Law of Growth, or evolution. Creation is the calling into existence of that which does not exist in the objective world. Evolution is simply the unfolding of potentialities involved in things that already exist.

If you've been faithful to your ideal, you'll hear the call when circumstances are ready to materialize your plans—and results will correspond in direct proportion with the steadfastness with which you hold on to your ideal. The steadily held ideal both determines and attracts the necessary conditions for its fulfillment.

This is how you may weave a garment of spirit and power into the web of your entire existence. This is how you may lead a charmed life and be forever protected from all harm. This is how you may become a positive force whereby conditions of opulence and harmony may be attracted to you. This is the idea that is gradually permeating the general consciousness and is largely responsible for the conditions of unrest which are seen nightly on the news.

Applying the Principle

In the last lesson, you created a mental image, you brought it from the invisible into the visible; this week I want you to take an object and follow it back to its origination, see what it really consists of. If you do this you will develop imagination, insight, perception, and sagacity. These come not by the superficial observation of the multitude but by a keen analytical observation that sees below the surface. Only a few know that the things they see are only effects and understand the causes by which these effects were brought into existence.

1. Take the same position as before.
2. Visualize a library.
3. See the beautiful building rising tall in the night. There appears to be no life anywhere about; all is silence. You know that the rooms and halls are hidden to your eye, but you know that the building is large. You know that during the day there are people inside, ready to spring to their appointed task instantly. You know that every department is in charge of able, trained, skilled librarians who have proven themselves competent to take charge of this marvelous storehouse of wisdom. You know that while it appears quiet, submissive, and innocent, it holds on its shelves the light of geniuses with which it educates multitudes of people. You know that it houses books containing countless pages, which, in turn, contain countless words; this—and much more—you can bring to mind with comparatively no effort whatever. But how did the library come to be where it is; how did it come into existence in the first place? You want to know all of this if you are a careful observer.
4. Now, follow the building's bricks through the great kilns, and see the thousands of men and women employed in their production. Go still further back and see the clay as it comes from the earth. See it loaded onto barges or train cars, see it moistened with water before being properly heated.
5. Go back even further to see the architect and engineers who planned the library.
6. Let the thought carry you back to the reasons for planning the library in this way. Perhaps someone from the local government gave the order to plan the building. You will see that you are now so far back that the library is something

intangible; it no longer exists physically; it is but a thought in the brain of the architect.

7. If the city council did hire the architect, whom does this local government represent? They represent you and me, so our line of thought begins with the library and ends with ourselves. And we find in this last analysis that our own thought is responsible for this and many other things that we seldom think of.

A little further reflection will develop the most important fact of all and that is, if someone had not discovered the need for this type of facility to house the precious written knowledge of centuries of men and women, many books would be lost and their ideas would be dust. The discovery that a sturdy structure made of four walls and a roof could not only shelter humans but also protect the craft of the written word was the start of foreward thinking, revolutionary sciences, and the advancement of the human race.

You will find exercises of this kind invaluable. When the thought has been trained to look below the surface—to trace back to the core—everything takes on a different appearance; the insignificant becomes significant; the uninteresting interesting. The things which we thought were of no importance are seen to be the only really vital things in existence.

Look to this day!
For it is life, the very life of life.
In its brief course lie all the verities
And realities of your existence;
The bliss of growth;
The glory of action;
The splendor of beauty;
For yesterday is but a dream,

And tomorrow is only a vision:
But today well lived
Makes every yesterday
A dream of happiness,
And every tomorrow a vision of hope.
Look well, therefore, to this day!

—Kalidasa (Sanskrit Poet)

Summary

- Imagination is a form of constructive thought—the light by which we penetrate new worlds of thought and experience. It is the mighty instrument by which every inventor or discoverer opened the way from precedent to experience.
- The cultivation of the imagination leads to the development of the ideal out of which your future will emerge.
- The imagination may be cultivated by exercise, but it must also be supplied with nourishment in order to live.
- Daydreaming is a form of mental dissipation, while imagination is a form of constructive thought which must precede every constructive action.
- Imaginative thought is the moving force with which successful men and women connect with the people and circumstances necessary to complete their plans.
- The ideal held steadily in mind attracts the necessary conditions for its fulfillment.
- A keen analytical observation results in the development of imagination, insight, perception, and sagacity, which lead to abundance and harmony.

LESSON NINE

Health, Wealth, and Love

ACTION IS the blossom of thought, and conditions are the result of action, so you always have in your possession the tools with which you will certainly and inevitably make or unmake yourself, and joy or suffering will be the reward.

All mistakes are actions taken in ignorance, so gaining knowledge and the power to create is the essence of growth and evolution. When people stop advancing their thoughts and ideals, their vital forces immediately begin to disintegrate and these changing conditions begin to show in their faces and bodies. In contrast, thought is the germ of humanity's conscious evolution; therefore, knowledge is the result of humanity's ability to think.

Recognizing and demonstrating knowledge constitutes Spiritual Power, and Spiritual Power is the power that lies at the heart of all things; it's the Soul of the universe. When you truly know that Mind is the only creative principle, that it is omnipotent, omniscient, and omnipresent, and that you can intentionally come into harmony with this Omnipotence through your personal power of thought, you will have taken a big step in the right direction.

The next step is to place yourself in position to receive this power. As it is omnipresent, it must be within you. We know that this is so because we know that all power is from within, but it must be developed, unfolded, cultivated. In order to do this we must be receptive, and this receptivity is acquired just as physical strength is gained: by exercise.

Changing Conditions By Changing Our Mind

If you wish to change conditions you must change your mind. Your whims, your wishes, your fancies, your ambitions may be thwarted at every step, but your inmost thoughts will be expressed just as surely as the plant springs from the seed.

Thoughts are causes, and conditions are effects; this is the origin of both good and evil. Thought is creative and will automatically correlate with its object. This is Universal Law at work—the Law of Attraction, the Law of Cause and Effect. Recognizing and applying this law will determine both beginning and end in every situation. It's the law which has lead people, in all ages and in all times, to believe in the power of Prayer. "As thy faith is, so be it unto thee" is simply another, shorter, and better way of stating it.

How then are we to change conditions? The reply is simple: by applying Universal Law.

We know that the Law of Cause and Effect are as absolute and undeviating in the hidden realm of thought as they are in the world of material things. So, if you are timid, vacillating, self-conscious, or if you're overanxious or harassed by thoughts of fear or impending danger, remember the physical principle that "two things cannot exist in the same place at the same time." Then, because exactly the same thing is true in the mental and spiritual world, your remedy is simply to substitute thoughts of courage, power, self-reliance, and confidence for those of fear, lack, and limitation. The positive thought will destroy the negative as certainly as light destroys darkness, and the results will be just as effective.

The easiest and most natural way to do this is to select an affirmation that seems to fit your particular case. Hold in mind the condition desired; affirm it as an already existing fact. The one replaces the other and then, through the Law of Growth, expands the space that the negative thought once filled. And, because whatever we repeat constantly becomes a part of ourselves, we are actually changing ourselves; we're making ourselves what we want to be.

The Three Essentials

Only three things can possibly be desired in the world without, and each of them can be found in the world within. The secret to finding them is simply to attach the proper "mechanism" to the Omnipotent Power Source to which everybody has access.

The three things which all humankind desires, and which are necessary for the highest expression and complete development, are health, wealth, and love. All will admit that health is absolutely essential; no one can be happy if the physical body is in pain. All will not so readily admit that wealth is necessary, but all must admit that a sufficient supply at least is necessary; and what would be considered sufficient for one would be considered absolute and painful lack for another. As Nature provides not only enough but abundantly, wastefully, lavishly, we realize that any lack or limitation is only the limitation which has been made by an artificial method of distribution.

Just about everybody will accept that Love is the third (or maybe some will say the first) essential for happiness. Those who possess all three—Health, Wealth, and Love—find their cup of happiness filled.

We have found that Universal Substance is everything, which means that it is all health, all wealth, and all love. We know that the mechanism whereby we can consciously connect with this Infinite Supply is in our thoughts. To think correctly is, therefore, to enter into the "Secret Place of the Most High,"[25] where all things are given to us.

What shall we think? If we know this, we shall have found the proper mechanism connecting us to "whatsoever things we desire." This mechanism may seem very simple, but read on; you will find that it is in reality the Master Key, the "Aladdin's lamp," if you please. It's the foundation, the imperative condition, the Absolute Law that *well-being comes from well-doing.*

The Truth

To think correctly and accurately, and to be connected with the Power Source, we must know the Truth.

To know the Truth—to be sure of it and confident in it—brings us satisfaction beyond compare. It's the only solid ground in a world of doubt, conflict, and danger. Knowing the Truth is the underlying principle in every business or social relation. It's the condition preceding every right action.

To know the Truth is to be in harmony with the Infinite and Omnipotent Power of Truth.[26] To know the Truth is, therefore, to

25 Genesis 1:26.

26 There is only one difference between "the Truth" and "Truth": Truth is an eternal principle, the ideal of which all truths are reflections. To know "the Truth" is to have the facts and be reasonably sure that no other explanation applies. To know, or be in harmony with Truth is to think and feel the thoughts of Universal Spirit.

connect with a power that is irresistible and sweeps away every kind of discord, disharmony, doubt, or error; "the Truth is mighty and will prevail."[27] The simplest mind can readily foretell the result of any action when he knows that it's based on Truth, but the mightiest intellect, the most profound and penetrating mind, hopelessly loses its way and can't even conceive of the possibilities that may result when his hopes are based on a premise he knows to be false.

Every action not in harmony with Truth, whether through ignorance or design, will result in discord and eventual loss in direct proportion to its extent and character.

How then are we to know the Truth so we can attach this mechanism and relate to the Infinite Power of Truth?

We're on the right track just as soon as we realize that Truth is the vital principle of Universal Mind and, as such, is omnipresent. No other thing or idea exists in its place.

For instance, if you seek perfect health, you must realize that the "I" in you is spiritual, that all spirit is one, and that wherever a part is, the Whole must be. *Every cell in the body must manifest the Truth as you see it.* If you see sickness, your cells manifest sickness; if you see perfection, they must manifest perfection.

Since the "I" is spiritual, it must then always be no less than perfect. The thought "I am whole, perfect, strong, powerful, loving, harmonious, and happy" is a logically sound statement. Thought is a spiritual activity, and spirit is creative; therefore, holding this thought in mind must necessarily bring about conditions in alignment with the thought. The affirmation is in strict accordance with Truth, and when Truth appears, every form of error or discord must necessarily disappear.

If you require wealth, realizing that the "I" in you is one with Universal Mind, which is all substance and is omnipotent, will assist you in bringing into operation the Law of Attraction. This

---

27 An old Latin proverb; *Veritas Magna est et pravelibit.*

law, in turn, will connect you with the forces of success and bring power and abundance into your experience in direct proportion with the character and purpose of your affirmation. Visualization is the mechanism: the thing visualized will manifest itself in form.

If you require love, realize that the only way to get love is by giving it; that the more you give, the more you will get; and that the only way you can give it is to fill yourself with it, until you become a magnet. This method was explained in another lesson.

Whoever has learned to bring the greatest spiritual truths in touch with the so-called "lesser things" of life has discovered the solution to every problem. We are always energized and made more thoughtful by approaching great ideas, great events, great natural objects, and great people. Approaching Abraham Lincoln is said to have felt like coming upon a mountain.

It's sometimes inspiring to hear from someone who has actually put these principles to the test—someone who has demonstrated them in their own life. A letter from Frederick Elias Andrews offers the following insight:

> I was about thirteen years old when Dr. T. W. Marsee, since passed over, said to my mother: "There is no possible chance, Mrs. Andrews. I lost my little boy the same way, after doing everything for him that it was possible to do. I have made a special study of these cases, and I know there is no possible chance for him to get well." She turned to him and said: "Doctor, what would you do if he were your boy?" And he answered, "I would fight; fight, as long as there is a breath of life to fight for."
>
> That was the beginning of a long drawn-out battle, with many ups and downs, the doctors all agreeing that there was no chance for a cure, though they encouraged and cheered us the best they could. But at last the victory

> came, and I have grown from a little, crooked, twisted, cripple, going about on my hands and knees, to a strong, straight, well-formed man.
>
> Now, I know you want the formula, and I will give it to you as briefly and quickly as I can.
>
> I built up an affirmation for myself, taking the qualities I most needed, and affirming for myself over and over again, "I am whole, perfect, strong, powerful, loving, harmonious, and happy." I kept up this affirmation, always the same, never varying, till I could wake up in the night and find myself repeating, "I am whole, perfect, strong, powerful, loving, harmonious, and happy." It was the last thing on my lips at night and the first thing in the morning.
>
> Not only did I affirm it for myself, but for others that I knew needed it. I want to emphasize this point.
>
> Whatever you desire for yourself, affirm it for others, and it will help you both. We reap what we sow. If we send out thoughts of love and health, they return to us like bread cast upon the waters; but if we send out thoughts of fear, worry, jealousy, anger, hate, etc., we will reap the results in our own lives.

It used to be said that the body is completely built-over every seven years, but some biologists now declare that we completely replace our cells every eleven months; so our bodies are really only eleven months old! If we continue to build the defects back into our bodies year after year, we have no one to blame but ourselves.

Clearly we are, each of us, the sum total of our own thoughts. So the question is, how do we entertain only the harmonious thoughts and reject the dissonant ones? At first we can't keep the unwanted thoughts from coming, but we can keep from entertaining them. The only way to do this is to *forget* them—which means, *get something for* them.

This is where the ready-made affirmation comes into play: when a thought of anger, jealousy, fear, or worry creeps in, just start your affirmation. The way to fight darkness is with light; the way to fight cold is with heat; the way to overcome evil is with good.

Some people put a lot of emphasis on denying the Truth of an idea. There is no help in such denials, however. Affirm the good, and the undesirable will vanish.

If at any time you feel you need anything, use this affirmation; it can't be improved upon: *I am whole, perfect, strong, powerful, loving, harmonious, and happy.* Use it just as it is; take it into the Silence with you until it sinks into your unconsciousness, and you can use it anywhere—in your car, at work, at home. This is one great advantage of spiritual methods; they're always available! Spirit is omnipresent, ever ready; all that is required is recognition of its omnipotence and a willingness, or desire, to become the recipient of its beneficent effects.

If our predominant mental attitude is one of power, courage, kindliness, and sympathy, we'll find that our environment will reflect back to us conditions corresponding to these thoughts.

Applying the Principle

Visualize a plant sprouting, growing, and blooming:

1. Consider a flower—the one you most admire—and bring it from the unseen into the seen.
2. Plant the tiny seed, water it, care for it, place it where it will get the direct rays of the morning sun. See the seed burst; it is now a living thing—something which has spirit and is beginning to search for the means of subsistence.
3. See the roots penetrating the earth, watch them shoot out in

all directions, and remember that they are living cells dividing and subdividing. They will soon number in the millions, each intelligent cell knowing what it wants and how to get it.

4. See the stem shoot forward and upward; watch it burst through the surface of the earth; see it divide and form branches; see how perfectly and symmetrically each branch is formed.
5. Visualize the leaves beginning to form and then the tiny stems, each one holding a tiny bud. As you watch, you see the bud grow and begin to unfold, and your favorite flower comes to view.
6. And now, if you will concentrate intently, you will become conscious of a fragrance; it's the fragrance of the flower as the breeze gently sways the beautiful creation which you have visualized.

When you're able to make your vision this clear and complete you'll be able to enter into the spirit of a thing; it will become very real to you.[28] You'll be learning to concentrate and the process will be the same, whether you are concentrating on health, a favorite flower, an ideal, a complicated business proposition, or any other aspect of life. Every success has been accomplished by persistent concentration upon the object in view.

Thought means life, since those who do not think do not live in any high or real sense. Thinking makes the man.

—A. Bronson Alcott

---

28 This is the basis for the Hindu and Buddhist meditation exercises that require long periods of focusing on a flower. The goal is to internalize the flower so that one can identify with it and evoke the image of its development at any time.

Summary

- The essential condition of all well-being is well-doing.
- The condition precedent to every right action is right thinking.
- The underlying condition necessary for effectiveness in every business transaction or social relation is to know the Truth.
- Through knowledge of the Truth, we can readily predict the result of any action that is based on a true premise, whereas the result of any action based upon a false premise can't even be conceived.
- We come to know the Truth through our realization that Truth is the vital principle of the universe and is therefore omnipresent.
- Truth is spiritual in nature, and applying Spiritual Truth is the secret solution to every problem.
- One great advantage of spiritual methods is that they're always available; the only requirements are: (1) recognition of the omnipotence of Spiritual Power, and (2) a desire to receive its beneficial effects.

LESSON TEN

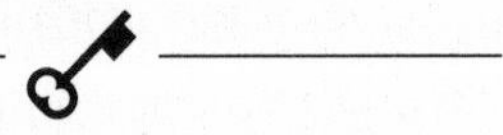

Cause and Effect

If you fully grasp the idea developed in this lesson—that nothing happens without a definite cause—you will know how to control any situation by bringing the appropriate causes into play. You'll be able to formulate your plans in accordance with exact knowledge. And when you achieve your goal, as you will, you'll know exactly why.

Thought

The ordinary person, with no definite knowledge of cause and effect, is governed by feelings or emotions. Such an individual thinks chiefly to justify actions taken or being considered. If he fails as a businessman, he says that luck is against him. If she dislikes music, she says that music is an expensive luxury. If he is a poor office worker, he says that he could succeed better at some outdoor work. If she lacks friends, she says she isn't properly appreciated.

These people never think their problem through to its core. In short, they don't know that every effect is the result of a certain specific cause. Instead they console themselves with explanations and excuses, thinking only in self-defense and not taking personal responsibility.

In contrast, someone who understands that there is no effect without an adequate cause thinks impersonally; they're not concerned with defending themselves or avoiding personal responsibility. Such people get down to the core fundamentals regardless of consequences. They're free to follow the trail of Truth wherever it may lead. They see the issue clear to the end and meet the requirements fully and fairly, and the result is that the world gives them all that it has to give: in friendship, honor, love, and approval. As Henry Drummond put it:

> In the physical world as we know it, there exists the organic and the inorganic. The inorganic of the mineral world is absolutely cut off from the plant or animal world; the passage is hermetically sealed. These barriers have never yet been crossed. No change of substance, no modification of environment, no chemistry, no electricity, no form of energy, no evolution of any kind can ever endow a single atom of the mineral world with the attribute of life.
>
> Only by the bending down into this dead world of some living form can those dead atoms be gifted with the properties of vitality; without this contact with life they remain fixed in the inorganic sphere forever.
>
> Huxley called this doctrine biogenesis ("life only from life") and said that it is victorious all along the line. Tyndall was compelled to say: "I affirm that no shred of trustworthy evidence exists to prove that life in our day has ever appeared independent of antecedent life."

> Physical law may explain the inorganic. Biology explains and accounts for the development of the organic, but concerning the point of contact science is silent. A similar passage exists between the natural world and the spiritual world—the point of contact is hermetically sealed on the natural side. The door is closed; no one can open it—no organic change, no mental energy, no moral effort, no material progress of any kind can enable any human being to enter the spiritual world.
>
> But as the plant reaches down into the mineral world and touches it with the mystery of life, so the Universal Mind reaches down into the human mind and endows it with new, strange, wonderful, and even marvelous qualities. All men or women who have ever accomplished anything in the world of industry, commerce, or art have accomplished because of this process.

With this impassable barrier between the organic and the inorganic, the only way matter can develop is to be impregnated with life. When a seed reaches down into the mineral world and begins to unfold and grow, the dead matter begins to live. A thousand invisible fingers begin to weave a suitable environment for the new arrival, and as the Law of Growth begins to take effect, we see the process continue until the lily finally appears.

In the same way, a thought is dropped into the Invisible Substance of Universal Mind—that substance from which all things are created—and as the thought takes root, the Law of Growth begins to take effect. Conditions and environment unfold as the objective form of our thought. This is how thought works as the connecting link between the Infinite and the finite, between the Universal and the individual.

Thought is an active, dynamic energy with the power to correlate with its object and bring it out of the Invisible Substance from which all things are created into the visible, or objective, world. This is the law by which and through which all things come into manifestation; it is the Master Key with which you are admitted into the Secret Place of the Most High and are given "dominion over all things."[29] With an understanding of this law you may "decree a thing and it shall be established unto thee."[30] You may finally understand that when "the doors of perception were cleansed, everything would appear to man as it is, infinite."[31]

It could not be otherwise; if Mind, or Soul, is the Universal Spirit, then the universe is simply the "body" or outward manifestation that the Universal Spirit has made for itself. We, as individualized Spirit, are creating the conditions for our growth in exactly the same way.

Spiritual Power

Humanity's knowledge of cause and effect regarding the laws governing electricity, chemical and nuclear reactions, and gravity enables us to plan courageously and execute fearlessly. These laws are called Natural Law because they govern in the physical world of matter and energy.

But all power is not physical power; there is also mental power, and there is moral and spiritual power.

Spiritual Power is superior because it exists on a level that contains the physical, mental, and moral powers. Through it,

---

29 Genesis 1:26.

30 Job 22:28.

31 William Blake.

humanity has discovered the physical laws by which the wonderful forces of Nature can be harnessed and made to do the work of hundreds and thousands of people. Spiritual Power has enabled humanity to discover laws whereby the effects of time and space have been annihilated (through, for example, television and the Internet), and the Law of Gravity can be overcome.

As the conversion of mineral form to living tissue requires the presence of life, the operation of this power depends on spiritual contact. In fact, in taking advantage of the wonderful possibilities opened up to us through its operation, we discover that we contribute nothing to its working. So we need to remember what one great teacher said: "An idea that is developed and put into action is more important than an idea that exists only as an idea."[32] We must take exactly the same position; we can do nothing to assist in the manifestation, we simply comply with the law, and the All-Originating Mind brings about the result—usually providing far more than we could ever imagine.

This shouldn't be too surprising: Abundance is everywhere in the universe; we see it on every hand. Everywhere we look, Nature is lavish, extravagant, even wasteful. Nowhere in any created thing is thrift observed; profusion is manifested in everything. The millions and millions of trees, flowers, plants, and animals; fruits and seeds; and the vast scheme of reproduction where the process of creating and re-creating is forever going on—all indicate the lavishness with which Nature provides.

That there is abundance for everyone is clear, but that many fail to participate in this abundance is also far too clear. The

32 Gautama, the Buddha.

reason for this is in their mental processes; they've not yet realized the universality of all substance, not yet understood that thought is the active principle connecting us to the things we desire.

The great error of the present day is the idea that we have to figure out how the Infinite can bring about a specific purpose or result. Nothing of this kind is necessary; the Universal Mind can be depended on to find the ways and means for bringing about any necessary manifestation. It depends only on our recognition of the potential powers of Spirit or Mind. We must, however, create the ideal, and this ideal must be complete in every detail if we are to have the result we desire.

We know that the laws governing electricity work in such a way that this invisible power can be controlled and used for our benefit and comfort in thousands of ways. We know that electricity carries messages around the world, that huge machines do its bidding, and that it illuminates practically the whole world. But we know, too, that if we consciously or ignorantly violate its law by touching a live wire, the result will be unpleasant and possibly disastrous.

A lack of understanding of the laws governing in the invisible world has the same result, and many people are suffering the consequences all the time.

It has been explained that the Law of Cause and Effect depends on a power circuit and this circuit can't be formed unless we operate in harmony with the law. How can we operate in harmony with the law unless we know what the law is?

We can know what the law is by study and observation.

The law is in operation everywhere; all Nature testifies to the operation of the law by silently, constantly expressing itself in growth. Where there is growth, there must be life; where there is life, there must be harmony. *Everything that lives is constantly attracting to itself the conditions and the supply it needs* for its most complete expression.

If your thought is in harmony with the creative principle of Nature, it's in tune with Infinite Mind and will form the circuit. The power will go out into your environment and will not return to you empty. Constructive thought must be creative but also harmonious, as this eliminates all destructive or competitive thought.

Still, it is possible for you to think thoughts that are not in tune with the Infinite, but the circuit will not be formed. What, then, is the result? What is the result when a generator produces electricity, the circuit is cut off, and there is no outlet? The generator stops.

It is exactly the same with you if you entertain thoughts that are not in accordance with the Infinite: there is no circuit. You are isolated; the thoughts cling to you, harass you, worry you, and finally bring about disease and possibly death. The physician may not diagnose the case exactly in this way, and may give it one of the many names that have been developed for the various ills that result from destructive thinking. The cause is the same nevertheless.

Wisdom, strength, courage, and all harmonious conditions are the result of power; all wealth is the offspring of power. Possessions are of value only as they confer power to achieve. Events are significant only as they affect the flow of power. All things are manifestations of various forms and degrees of power. And we have seen that all power is from within.

Likewise, every lack, limitation, or adverse circumstance is the result of weakness, and weakness is simply an absence of power; it comes from nowhere, it is nothing. The remedy then is simply to develop power, and this is accomplished in exactly the same manner that all power is developed: by exercise.

Applying the Principle

This exercise consists of applying your knowledge; knowledge will not apply itself. Abundance will not come to you out of the sky, neither will it drop into your lap. But a conscious realization of the Law of Attraction, along with the intention to bring it into operation for a specific purpose and the will to carry out this purpose, will bring about the materialization of your desire. If you are in business, it will increase and develop along regular channels, and new or unusual channels of distribution may be opened. When the law becomes fully operative, you will find that the things you seek are seeking you.

For your exercise this week:

1. Select a blank space on the wall or some other convenient spot in the room you've been using.
2. From where you usually sit, mentally draw a black, horizontal line about six inches long; try to see the line as plainly as though it were painted on the wall.
3. Now, mentally draw two vertical lines equal to the horizontal line at either end of the line so that they are perpendicular to it.
4. Draw another horizontal line connecting with the two vertical lines to form a square.
5. Try to see the square perfectly; when you can do so, draw a circle within the square.
6. Place a point in the center of the circle.
7. Draw the point toward you about 10 inches; you have a cone on a square base.
8. You will remember that your work was all in black; change it to white, to red, to yellow.

If you can do this, you are making excellent progress and will soon be able to concentrate on any problem you may have in mind.

> *When any object or purpose is clearly held in thought, its precipitation, in tangible and visible form, is merely a question of time. The vision always precedes and itself determines the realization.*
>
> —LILLIAN WHITING

Summary

- Wealth is the offspring of power; possessions are of value only as they confer power.
- The knowledge of cause and effect is available in the fact that it enables people to plan courageously and execute fearlessly.
- Life only originates in the inorganic world by the introduction of some living form. There is no other way.
- Because the Universal can manifest only through the individual, thought is the connecting link between the finite and the Infinite.
- Causation depends on a circuit; the Universal is the positive side of the battery of life, the individual is the negative, and thought forms the circuit.
- Many fail to secure harmonious conditions because they do not understand the law; there is no polarity; they have not formed the circuit.
- The remedy is a conscious recognition of the Law of Attraction with the intention of bringing it into existence for a definite purpose.

🗝 Thought will correlate with its object and bring it into manifestation because thought is a product of the spiritual "I," and spirit is the creative principle of the Universe.

A vivid thought brings the power to paint it; and in proportion to the depth of its source is the force of its projection.

—Ralph Waldo Emerson

LESSON ELEVEN

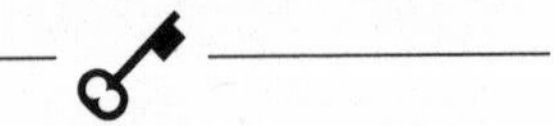

Answers from Nature

YOUR LIFE is governed by law—by actual, immutable principles that never vary. Law is in operation at all times, in all places. Fixed laws underlie all human actions. For this reason, those who control large corporations are able to determine with absolute precision just what percentage of every hundred thousand people will respond to any given set of conditions. They understand what effects certain causes will have.

We need to remember, however, that while every effect is the result of a cause, the effect in turn becomes a cause, which creates other effects, which in turn create still other causes. So when you put the Law of Attraction into operation, keep in mind that you are starting a train of causation for good or otherwise which may open endless possibilities.

We frequently hear from friends and neighbors "Something happened to me, but it wasn't my fault." "What do you mean I created this?" Too many of us fail to remember that our thought brings us relationships, conditions, and environment of a particular kind, which in turn lead to the conditions we complain about.

Inductive Reasoning and Faith

Inductive reasoning is a process of the objective mind by which we compare a number of separate instances with one another until we see the common factor that gives rise to them all. Induction proceeds by comparison of facts; it's the method of studying Nature that resulted in the discovery of the rule of law that has marked this epoch in human progress. The dividing line between superstition and knowledge, inductive reasoning has eliminated uncertainty from our lives and substituted law, reason, and certitude. It's the watchman at the gate mentioned in an earlier lesson.

Through this process, the world of the senses has been re-imagined. The sun was arrested in its course. The apparently flat earth was shaped into a ball and set whirling around it. Seemingly solid and inert matter was analyzed into active elements, and the universe was shown through telescopes and microscopes to be full of energy, motion, and life.

With these new understandings of the nature of the universe, we're compelled to wonder how its delicate patterns of organization are kept in order and repair.

First, we find polarity. On the one hand, poles with like forces repel each other or remain impenetrable to each other; this principle sets in place and distance stars, people, and fields of energy. On the other hand, as people with different qualities enter into partnership, so opposite poles attract each other. Elements with no property in common, like acids and gases, cling to each other in preference, and a general exchange is kept up between the surplus on one side and the demand on the other. Similarly, as the eye seeks and receives satisfaction from colors that are complementary to those it sees, so do need, want, and desire call forth, guide, and determine action.

Our privilege is to become conscious of the principle of polarity and to act in accordance with it.

For example, a paleontologist like Georges Cuvier sees a tooth belonging to an extinct species of animal. This tooth wants a body for the performance of its function, and it defines the particular body it needs with such precision that Cuvier was able to reconstruct the frame of this animal. Similarly, variations are observed in the orbit of Uranus. Celestial mathematician Urbain Leverrier discovered that a star was neded at a certain place to keep the solar system in order, and Neptune always appeared in the place and hour appointed. We see new species, stars, and planets discovered in the same way all the time. The instinctive wants of the animal and the intellectual wants of the paleontologist were similar to the wants of Nature and the wants of the mind of the astronomer, so they brought forth the results. On the one hand were the thoughts of an existence, on the other, an existence. A well-defined lawful want, therefore, furnishes the reason for the more complex operations of Nature.

Since humanity has recorded correctly the answers furnished by Nature, we've expanded our senses through science. Having placed our hands on the levers that move the earth, we're becoming conscious of a close, varied, and deep contact with the world without.

This contact is so deep that our wants and purposes are now as much at-one with the harmonious operations of the vast organization of Nature as the life, liberty, and happiness of the citizenry are identified with the structure of their government. We can see that our individual interests are protected by the country's defense systems, added to our own, and we may count on a continuous supply of necessities to the degree that our individual needs are felt steadily by the population. In the same way, our conscious citizenship in the republic of Nature keeps us secure from the annoyances of lesser agents through our alliance with greater powers. Through the laws of resistance or alignment working in mechanical and chemical agents, these powers distribute the labor to be performed between them and other people to protect and provide for us.

The method of inductive reasoning was given to us by Plato, but, because he worked without the evidence of its success, he could never find how the ideals he so admired became realities.[33] If Plato had seen modern photographs of the sun, or any of thousands of similar illustrations of what humanity accomplishes through inductive reasoning, he may well have envisioned a land where all manual, mechanical labor and repetition would be assigned to the powers of Nature. It would be a land where our wants are satisfied by purely mental operations set in motion by the will, and where the supply is created by the demand.

However distant that land may appear, inductive reasoning has taught people to make strides toward it and has surrounded us with benefits that are both rewards for past faithfulness and incentives for continued practice. Inductive reasoning also helps us concentrate and strengthen our faculties, providing solutions for individual as well as universal problems simply by operation of mind in the purest form.

The essence of this method, which is to believe that what is sought has been accomplished in order to accomplish it, is expanded on by Emanuel Swedenborg[34] in his writings. And it was Jesus who said, "What things soever ye desire, when ye pray, believe that ye receive them, and ye shall have them."[35]

---

33 Plato, who lived in Greece about 400 years BC, taught that everything we perceive with the senses is a "shadow" of its real, or ideal, form.

34 Swedenborg, the Royal Engineer of Sweden in the 1700s, became aware of a deeper reality, and his writings strongly influenced Goethe and Emerson.

35 Mark 11:24.

The difference in the tenses in this passage is remarkable: *we are first to believe that our desire has already been fulfilled; then its accomplishment will follow.* This is a concise direction for making use of the creative power of thought: impressing on the universal subjective Mind the particular thing that we desire as an already existing fact. This is thinking on the plane of the absolute and eliminating all consideration of conditions or limitation. When we do so we're planting a seed, which, if left undisturbed, will finally germinate and produce fruit.

To review: *inductive reasoning is the process of the objective mind by which we compare a number of separate instances with one another until we see the common factor that gives rise to them all.*

The recognition of the marvelous power possessed by the mind under proper conditions and the fact that this power can be used, directed, and applied to the solution of every human problem is of transcendental importance.

The effects of this thought process are seen in those fortunate people who effortlessly possess everything that others must acquire by toil; who never have a struggle with conscience because they always act correctly; who can never conduct themselves otherwise than with tact; who learn everything easily, complete everything they begin with a happy knack, and live in eternal harmony with themselves without ever experiencing difficulty or toil.

The fruit of this thought is what some people might call a "gift of the gods" but a gift that few as yet realize, appreciate, or understand. We see people in every country around the globe achieving results by a process they don't seem to understand themselves, which they usually call a "mystery." But our capacity to reason is given to us so we can discover the law by which these results are accomplished.

No One Formula for Truth

All Truth is the same, whether stated in modern scientific terms or in the language of apostolic times. Unfortunately, there are timid souls who can't see that the very universality of Truth requires various statements—that no one human formula will show every side of it.

Changing emphasis, new language, novel interpretations, and unfamiliar perspectives are not, as some suppose, signs of departure from Truth, but on the contrary, they are evidence that the Truth is being apprehended in some new relation to human needs and is becoming more generally understood.

Truth must be told to each generation and to every people in new and different terms, so that when Jesus said, "Believe that ye receive and ye shall receive," or when Blake said, "What is now proved was once only imagined,"[36] or when modern science says, "The Law of Attraction is the law by which thought links with its object, wherever that object may be located within or outside of space and time," each statement contains exactly the same Truth; the only difference is the form of presentation.

A New Era of Creative Power

We are standing on the threshold of a new era. Humanity has learned the secrets of mastery, and the way is being prepared for a new social order more wonderful than anything ever before dreamed of. The conflict of modern science with theology, the study of comparative religions, the tremendous power of new social movements—all of these are but clearing the way for the new order. They may have destroyed traditional forms that have become antiquated and impotent, but nothing of value has been lost. Rather, a new faith is being born—a faith that demands a new form of expression—and this faith is taking form in a

36 William Blake.

deep consciousness of power, evident in spiritual activity on every hand.

The spirit that sleeps in the mineral, breathes in the vegetable, moves in the animal, and reaches its highest development in the soul of humanity is Universal Mind, and it behooves us to span the gulf between being and doing, theory and practice, by demonstrating our understanding of the power which we have been given.

By far the greatest discovery of all the centuries is the creative power of thought. The importance of this discovery has been delayed in reaching popular awareness, but it has finally arrived. In every field of research the importance of this greatest-of-all-great discoveries is being demonstrated.[37]

What is the creative power of thought? It creates ideas, and these in turn objectify themselves by appropriating, inventing, observing, discerning, discovering, analyzing, ruling, governing, combining, and applying matter and energy into patterns that fit their mold. Thought can do this because it's an intelligent creative power.

Thought reaches its highest activity when plunged into its own mysterious depth, when it breaks through the limits of self, and it passes from truth to truth to the region of Eternal Light, where all that is, was, or ever will be melts into one grand harmony.[38] From this process of self-contemplation comes inspiration, or creative intelligence, which is undeniably superior to every element, force, or law of Nature because it can understand, modify, govern, and apply them to its own ends and purposes, and, therefore, possesses them.

---

37 The most famous illustration of this in physics is the "double slit" experiment, in which electrons show up as particles or waves depending on the presence of an observer.

38 This is the state of being that is called "Christ consciousness," "Buddha Nature," "No-thought," "Pure Awareness," or "samadhi." It's the ultimate goal of all meditation practices.

We all know many who have achieved the seemingly impossible, who have realized life-long dreams, who have changed everything including themselves. We've sometimes marveled at the demonstration of an apparently irresistible power, which seemed to be ever available just when it was most needed, but it is all clear now. All that is required is an understanding of certain fundamental principles and their proper application.

Wisdom begins with the dawn of reason, and reason is but an understanding of the knowledge and principles whereby we may know the true meaning of things. Wisdom, then, is illuminated reason, and this wisdom leads to humility, for humility is a large part of wisdom.

Applying the Principle

For your exercise in this lesson:

1. Concentrate on the Biblical quotation from earlier in this lesson: "What things soever ye desire, when ye pray, believe that ye receive them, and ye shall have them."
2. Notice that there is no limitation. "What things soever" is very definite and implies that the only limitation placed upon us is in our ability to think, to be equal to the occasion, to rise to the emergency, and to remember that faith is not a shadow but a substance that Blake noted "was once only imagined."

Summary

- Inductive reasoning is the process of the objective mind by which we compare a number of separate instances with each other until we see the common factor that gives rise to them all.

- This method of study has resulted in the discovery of a reign of law that, in turn, has marked an epoch in human progress.
- Need, want, and desire, in the largest sense, induce, guide, and determine action.
- As advocated by great teachers such as Jesus, Plato, and Swedenborg, the formula for the unerring solution of every individual problem is to believe that our desire has already been fulfilled; its accomplishment will then follow.
- In this process, we are thinking on the plane of the absolute and planting a seed which, if left undisturbed, will germinate and provide fruit.
- "What is now proved was once only imagined."
- The Law of Attraction is the law by which faith is brought into manifestation. It has eliminated the elements of uncertainty and caprice from human lives and substituted law, reason, and certitude.

LESSON TWELVE

The Law of Attraction

EVERY PURPOSE in life is best accomplished through a scientific understanding of the creative power of thought. Our power to think is infinite, consequently our creative power is unlimited. Understanding this, you can construct an ideal business, an ideal home, ideal friends, and an ideal environment. You are not restricted as to material or cost. Thought is omnipotent and has the power to draw on the infinite bank of Primary Substance for all that it requires. Infinite resources are, therefore, at your command.

There are three requirements for this creative process, and each one is absolutely essential. *You must first have the knowledge of your power; second, the courage to dare; third, the faith to do.*

The Importance of Concentration

We know that thought is building for us the thing we think of and is actually bringing it nearer, yet sometimes we find it difficult to banish fear, anxiety, or discouragement. These are powerful thought forces that send the things we desire further away, so we feel like the process is often "one step forward and two steps backward." The only way to keep from going backward is to keep going forward. Eternal vigilance is the price of success.

To do this, you must center your mind on a specific thought and hold it there, to the exclusion of all other thoughts. This is the power of concentration.

If you've ever looked through the viewfinder of a camera, you found that when the object was not in focus, the impression was indistinct and possibly blurred; but with the proper focus, the picture was clear and distinct. Similarly, unless you can concentrate on the object you have in view, you will have a hazy, indifferent, vague, indistinct, and blurred outline of your ideal, and the results will follow suit.

So your ideal must be sharp, clear-cut, and definite. To have one ideal today, another tomorrow, and a third next week is to scatter your forces and accomplish nothing; your result will be a meaningless and chaotic combination of wasted material.[39]

Unfortunately this is the result many are experiencing, and the cause is self-evident. If a sculptor started out with a piece of marble and a chisel and changed his ideal every fifteen minutes, what result could he expect? And why should you expect any different result in molding the greatest and most plastic of all substances—the only real Substance?

The result of this indecision and negative thought is often the loss of material wealth. Supposed independence, which required many years of toil and effort, suddenly disappears.

---

39 *In Conversations with God II*, Neale Donald Walsch asks God why he never seems to get what he wants. The answer is, "You keep changing your mind!"

That's when many people realize that money and property are not independence at all—*the only independence is found to be a practical, working knowledge of the creative power of thought.*

And this method works when you learn that the only real power that you can have is the power to adjust yourself to unchangeable principles.

You can't change the Infinite, but you can understand Universal Law. The reward of this understanding is the conscious realization of your ability to adjust your thought into alignment with Universal Thought, which is, by definition, omnipresent (everywhere) and omnipotent (all powerful). And the extent of your ability to focus, and cooperate with this Omnipotence, is the degree of your success in achieving your purpose.

Counterfeit Phenomena

The power of thought has many counterfeits, which may be fascinating but whose results are usually harmful instead of helpful. Of course, worry, fear, and all negative thoughts produce a crop after their kind; those who harbor thoughts of this kind must inevitably reap what they have sown.

There are also seekers who devour the so-called proofs and demonstrations obtained through spiritual experiences. Too often, they throw open their mental doors and soak themselves in the most poisonous currents that can be found in the psychic world. They don't seem to understand that becoming receptive and passive by draining themselves of all their own vital force is what enables them to bring about these vibratory thought forms.

There are also the *guru* worshippers who see a source of power in the materializing phenomena performed by adepts, forgetting, or never seeming to realize, that as soon as the will is withdrawn, the forms wither and the vibratory forces of which they are composed vanish.

Telepathy, or thought transference, has received considerable attention, but to the extent that it requires a passive mental state on the part of the receiver, the practice can also be harmful. A thought may be sent with the intention of hearing or seeing, but it will bring the penalty attached to the inversion of the creative principle involved.

In many instances, hypnotism can be dangerous to the subject as well as the operator. No one familiar with the laws governing the mental world would think of attempting to dominate the will of another, for by so doing, he will gradually (but surely) divest himself of his own power.

Understanding the Law of Attraction

All of these perversions of the principle have their temporary satisfaction and, for some, a keen fascination, but there is an infinitely greater fascination in a true understanding of the power of the world within. This is a power that increases with use; it's permanent instead of fleeting. It's a power that not only brings about the remedy for past error or the results of wrong thinking, but works as a preventative, protecting us from all manner and form of danger. It is an actual creative force building new conditions and a new environment.

The Law of Attraction is: thought will correlate with its object and bring forth in the material world the correspondence of the thing thought or produced in the mental world.

The combination of thought and love forms the irresistible force called the Law of Attraction, so the Law of Attraction is another name for love. This is an eternal and fundamental principle, inherent in all things—in every system of philosophy, in every religion, and in every science. There is no getting away from the Law of Love; the feeling that imparts vitality to thought is desire, and desire is love. *Thought impregnated with Love becomes invincible.*

Understanding this, we can see the absolute necessity of ensuring that every thought has the germ of Truth in it, so the law will only manifest good; only good can confer any permanent power. Thus, educated desire is the most potent means of bringing into action the Law of Attraction.

All Natural Law is irresistible; the Law of Gravity, the Law of Electricity, or any other law operates with mathematical precision. There is no variation; only the channel may be imperfect. If a bridge falls, we don't blame it on changes in the Law of Gravity. If a light fails us, we don't conclude that the laws governing electricity are no longer dependable. And if the Law of Attraction seems to be imperfectly demonstrated by an inexperienced or uninformed person, we are not to conclude that the greatest and most infallible law on which the entire system of creation depends has been suspended. We should rather conclude that a little more understanding of the law is required, for the same reason that the correct solution of a difficult problem in physics is not always readily and easily obtained.

Things are created in the mental or spiritual world before they appear as an action or event in the outer world. So, by the simple process of governing our thought today, we help create events that will come into our lives in the future—maybe even tomorrow.

Seeing these results of the operation of this marvelous Universal Law has caused people in all ages and all times to believe that there must be some personal being who responded to their petitions and desires, and manipulated events in order to comply with their requirements.

Instead, it's because Universal Mind is not only Intelligence; it is also Substance. It brings subatomic particles together by the Law of Attraction to form atoms; atoms in turn are brought together by the same law to form molecules; and molecules form objects. So we find that the Law of Love is the creative force behind every manifestation, not only of atoms but of worlds, of the universe—of everything that anyone can conceive.

Applying the Principle

The mind cannot comprehend an entirely new idea until a corresponding connection in the brain has been prepared to receive it. This explains why it's so difficult for us to appreciate or even receive an entirely new idea; we have no links in the brain capable of receiving it. We are therefore incredulous; we don't believe it.[40]

So if you haven't been familiar with the omnipotence of the Law of Attraction and the scientific method by which it can be put into operation, or if you haven't been familiar with the unlimited possibilities it opens to those who are enabled to take advantage of its resources, begin now to create the necessary links in the brain that will enable you to comprehend the unlimited powers which may be yours by cooperating with Natural Law.

This may be done by concentration or attention; intention governs attention. Power comes through peacefulness. Through concentration, all deep thoughts, wise speech, and mighty deeds are accomplished.

It's in the Silence that you get in touch with the omnipotent power of the Universal Mind from which all power is evolved. Whoever desires wisdom, power, or permanent success of any kind will only find it within, as an unfolding process. Some people lacking in experience may conclude that the Silence is very simple and easily attained. But only in Absolute Silence may one come into contact with Universal Mind, learn of the unchangeable law, and open the channels by which persistent practice and concentration lead to perfection.

This week go to the same room you've been using.

---

40 This concept is the basis for psychologist Wayne Dyer's book, *You'll See It When You Believe It.*

1. Take the same chair and sit in the same position as previously.
2. Be sure to relax: let go, both mentally and physically. Always do this; never try to do any mental work under pressure. See that there are no tense muscles or nerves—that you are entirely comfortable.
3. Concentrate on the statement: "You must first have the knowledge of your power; second, the courage to dare; third, the faith to do." If you concentrate upon the thought and if you give it your entire attention, you'll find a world of meaning in each sentence. You'll attract to yourself other thoughts in harmony with them, and you will soon grasp the full significance of the vital knowledge upon which you are concentrating.
4. Now realize your unity with Omnipotence.
5. Get in touch with this power; come into a deep and vital understanding, appreciation, and realization of the fact that your ability to think is your ability to act upon the Universal Mind and bring it into manifestation. Realize that it will meet any and every requirement, that you have exactly the same potential ability which any individual ever did have or ever will have. Each individual is but an expression or manifestation of the One, all are parts of the Whole. There is no difference in kind or quality; the only difference is one of degree.

Thought cannot conceive of anything that may not be brought to expression. He who first uttered it may be only the suggester, but the doer will appear.

—Woodrow Wilson

Summary

- Any purpose in life may be best accomplished through a scientific understanding of the spiritual nature of thought.
- Three requirements are absolutely essential: the knowledge of our power, the courage to dare, the faith to do.
- The practical working knowledge is secured by an understanding of Natural Law.
- The reward for this understanding is a conscious realization of our ability to adjust ourselves to unchanging principle.
- The degree to which we realize that we can't change the Infinite but must cooperate with it will indicate the degree of success with which we meet.
- The principle that gives thought its dynamic power is the Law of Attraction, which rests on vibration, which in turn rests upon the Law of Love. Thought impregnated with love becomes invincible.
- All Natural Law is irresistible and unchangeable and acts with mathematical precision; there is no deviation or variation.
- It sometimes seems difficult to find the solution to our problems in life for the same reason that it is sometimes difficult to find the correct solution to a mathematical problem: the operator is uninformed or inexperienced.
- It's impossible for the mind to grasp an entirely new idea because we have no corresponding vibratory connections in the brain capable of receiving the idea.
- Wisdom is secured by concentration; it unfolds from within.

LESSON THIRTEEN

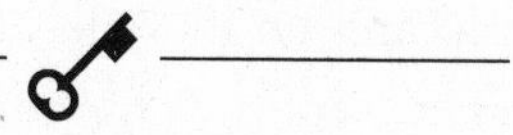

The Process

PHYSICAL SCIENCE is responsible for the marvelous age of invention in which we now live, but a new spiritual science is now emerging, whose possibilities no one can foretell.

Spiritual science has previously been the football of the uneducated, the superstitious, the mystical, but people are now interested in definite methods and demonstrated facts only.

We have come to know that thinking is a spiritual process; that vision and imagination preceded action and event, and that the day of the dreamer has come.

The following lines by Herbert Kaufman are interesting in this connection:

> They are the architects of greatness, their vision lies within their souls, they peer beyond the veils and mists of doubt and pierce the walls of unborn Time.

> The belted wheel, the trail of steel, the churning screw are shuttles in the loom on which they weave their magic tapestries. Makers of Empire, they have fought for bigger things than crowns and higher seats t han thrones. Your homes are set upon the land a dreamer found.
>
> The pictures on its walls are visions from a dreamer's soul. They are the chosen few—the blazers of the way. Walls crumble and Empires fall, the tidal wave sweeps from the sea and tears a fortress from its rocks. The rotting nations drop off from Time's bough, and only things the dreamers make live on.

This lesson explains why the dreams of the dreamer come true. It explains the Law of Cause and Effect by which dreamers, inventors, authors, and financiers bring about the realization of their desires. It explains the law by which the thing pictured in our mind eventually becomes our own.

Reasoning from the Facts

The classic scientific method is founded on measuring, observing, and repeating an experiment, a process that has helped to do away with superstition, precedent, and conventionality.

Historically, science has explained everyday facts by generalizing principles based on the exceptions. Thus the occasional eruption of a volcano provides evidence for the heat continually at work in the interior of the earth—to which the planet owes much of her configuration. Similarly, the occasional bolt of lightning reveals a subtle power constantly producing changes in the inorganic world. And, as dead languages now seldom heard were once ruling among the nations, so does a giant tooth in Siberia or a fossil in the depth of the earth not only bear record of the evolution of past ages but explains to us the origin of many of the hills and valleys we see today.

So, generalizing from the rare, the strange, or the exception has been the compass needle guiding all the discoveries of inductive science.

It's several hundred years since Francis Bacon[41] recommended this method of study, to which the developed nations owe most of their prosperity and much of their knowledge. Shifting humanity's attention from belief in the supernatural by surprising experiments, Bacon's method has purged minds from their narrow prejudices more effectively than the keenest satire and more successfully than the most forcible demonstration of ignorance ever could. It has encouraged inventiveness through the possibility of making useful discoveries available to all far more powerfully than any inspiring talk.

Bacon's method, or scientific method, has brought the spirit and intent of the great philosophers of Greece into effect. By new means of observation, it has gradually revealed wonders in the infinite space of astronomy, the microscopic egg of embryology, and the dim ages of geology. It has disclosed an order in the heartbeat that Aristotle's logic could never have unveiled, and reduced matter into formerly unknown elements that no scholarly analysis could ever force apart.

His method has lengthened life, mitigated pain, and extinguished diseases; it has increased the fertility of the soil. It has given new safety to the seafarer and spanned great rivers with bridges in forms unknown to our ancestors. It has guided the thunderbolt from Heaven to earth, lighting up night with

---

41 Sir Francis Bacon was a close associate of Queen Elizabeth I, around 1500 AD, and served in various capacities in her government. He was also a prolific reader, writer, and experimenter credited with setting forth the procedures we call "the scientific method."

the splendor of day. It has extended the range of human vision; it has multiplied the power of human muscles; it has accelerated motion; it has annihilated distance. It has facilitated conversation, correspondence, friendly activities, and dispatch of business. It has enabled men to descend into the depths of the sea, to soar into the air, to penetrate securely into the noxious recesses of the earth, and to walk on the moon.

This then is the true nature and scope of inductive reasoning. But the greater the success science has achieved, the more the teachings and example set by scientists convince us how important it is to observe carefully, patiently, accurately, and with all the instruments and resources at our command—the observed facts—before venturing to state general laws.

So, by the value we place on Truth and by our hope in a steady and universal progress, may we never permit a desire to please others' prejudice to cause us to neglect or mutilate unwelcome facts. May we thus be bold like Benjamin Franklin who, seeking to understand the direction of a spark drawn from an electric machine under every circumstance, used a kite to ask a cloud about the nature of lightning. Being sure how bodies fall, thanks to Galileo's observations, may we dare with Newton to ask the moon about the force that fastens it to the earth. Indeed, let's pay full attention to the most isolated, as well as the most frequent, phenomena.

Great quantities of material may be collected by observation, but these accumulated facts have very different values. And natural philosophy, the original term for what we now call "science," sifts the facts and ranks them, assigning the greatest importance to things we can't account for in our usual and daily observations of life.

If, then, we find that certain people seem to possess unusual power, what are we to conclude?

We may say it is not so, which is simply an acknowledgment of our lack of information, because every honest investigator admits that there are many strange and previously unaccountable phenomena constantly taking place.

Or we may say that they are the result of supernatural or divine interference, but a scientific understanding of Natural Law will convince us that there is nothing supernatural. Every phenomenon is the result of a definite cause, and the cause is Immutable Law or Principle, which operates with invariable precision whether the law is put into operation consciously or unconsciously.

We may say that we are on "forbidden ground," that there are some things that we should not know. This objection has been used against every advance in human knowledge. Every individual who ever advanced a new idea, whether Columbus, Darwin, Galileo, Emerson, or Einstein, was subjected to ridicule or persecution, so this objection should receive no serious consideration.

And we may carefully consider every fact brought to our attention so we can more readily discover the law on which it is based.

No matter what our method is, we will find that the principle of the creative power of thought will explain every possible condition or experience, whether physical, mental, or spiritual.

Constructive Thinking Requires Expansion

Thought is a spiritual activity and is therefore creative, but make no mistake: thought will create nothing significant unless it is consciously, systematically, and constructively directed. Herein is the difference between idle thinking, which is simply a dissipation of effort, and constructive thinking, which means practically unlimited achievement.

Thought will bring about conditions that correspond with our predominant mental attitude or feeling. So, if we fear disaster, since fear is a powerful form of thought, disaster will be the certain result of our thinking. Unfortunately, this form of thought frequently sweeps away the result of many years of toil and effort. Similarly, if we think, with feeling, of some form of material wealth, we may secure it. By concentrated thought, the required conditions will be brought about and the necessary effort will be put forth, which then results in bringing about the circumstances necessary to realize our desires.

But *we often find that when we secure the things we thought we wanted, they don't have the effect we expected*—that is, our satisfaction is only temporary, or possibly the effect is the reverse of what we expected.

What, then, is the most effective procedure? What are we to think to secure what we really desire?

What we all desire—what everyone is seeking—is happiness and harmony. If we can be truly happy we'll have everything the world can give. If we are happy ourselves, we can make others happy. But we can't be happy unless we have health, strength, congenial friends, a pleasant environment, and a sufficient supply of resources—not only to take care of our necessities but to provide for those comforts and luxuries that help us to expand our capacities.

This is in direct contrast to the old, orthodox way of thinking, based on the teachings of a powerful hierarchy, which was to be "a worm," satisfied with our portion, whatever we've been handed.

But the modern idea, based on direct interpretation of the ancient writings, is to know that the "Father and I are one," that we are "joint heirs,"[42] entitled to the best of everything because the "Father" is Universal Mind, the Creator, the Original Substance from which all things proceed.[43]

Now, admitting that this is all true in theory, that it has been taught for over two thousand years and is the essence of every sys-

42 Romans 8:17.

43 John 10:30.

tem of philosophy or religion,[44] how are we to make it practical in our lives? How are we to get actual, tangible results here and now?

We have found that everything we get comes to us by the Law of Attraction. A happy thought cannot exist in an unhappy consciousness; therefore, the consciousness must change, and, as the consciousness changes, all conditions necessary to meet the changed consciousness must gradually change in order to meet it.

So we must put our knowledge into practice; nothing can be accomplished any other way. An athlete may read books and lessons on physical training all his life, but unless he begins to give out strength by actual work he will never receive any strength. He will eventually get exactly what he gives, but he will have to give it first. It's exactly the same with us: we will get exactly what we give, but we have to give it first before it can return to us many times over.

Recognizing Omnipotence

Giving is simply a mental process. Because thoughts are causes and conditions are effects, giving out our thoughts of courage, inspiration, health, or help of any kind sets causes in motion to bring about their effects. We're projecting a thought into the Universal Substance from which all things are created.

This Universal Substance cannot be separated from Universal Mind, which is omnipresent, omnipotent, and omniscient. Are we

---

44 Other, non-Christian faiths use different terms for this same idea. For example, while the First Noble Truth of Buddhism is "Suffering exists" (more literally translated as "no thing ever fully satisfies"), the Second Noble Truth is "Suffering may be ended." Similarly, the "kingdom of Heaven" that Jesus taught about came from the Jewish teachings in which he was raised, and in the Jewish tradition, wealth and well-being are the result of living according to God's laws. Hindus use a variety of paths, or yogas, to achieve a state of being called "nirvana" or "sat-chit-ananda," which has been translated as "love-bliss-consciousness," and so forth.

to inform the Omniscient as to the proper channel to be used to materialize our demand? Can we, the finite, advise the Infinite?

This is the cause of failure, of every failure. Too many of us, too often, recognize the omnipresence of the Universal Substance but fail to appreciate the fact that this substance is not only omnipresent but is omnipotent and omniscient. Our thoughts may set events in motion that we know nothing about.

We can best achieve our intent by recognizing the infinite power and infinite wisdom of Universal Mind and letting go of the temptation to be concerned with "how."[45] In this way, we become a channel by which the Infinite can realize our desire. Recognition, therefore, brings about realization.

Applying the Principle

For your exercise in this lesson, make use of the principle:

1. Recognize the fact that you are a part of the Whole and that a part must be the same in kind and quality as the Whole; the only difference there can possibly be is in degree.
2. When this tremendous fact begins to permeate your consciousness, when you really come into a realization of the fact that you (not your body, not the small-minded ego of conceit, but the Great Self), the "I," the Spirit that thinks, is an integral part of the Great Whole, that it is the same in substance, quality, and kind, that the Creator could create nothing different from itself, then you'll also be able to say, "The Father and I are one," and you will come into an understanding of the beauty, the grandeur, the transcendental opportunities that are at your disposal.

45 This is what Jesus meant by "take no thought . . ." and "be not anxious . . ." in Matthew 6:23.

Increase in me that wisdom
Which discovers my truest interest,
Strengthen my resolution
To perform that which wisdom dictates.

—Benjamin Franklin

Summary

- The method by which natural philosophers (which is the old term for "scientists") obtain and apply their knowledge is through Bacon's scientific method, observing individual facts carefully, patiently, accurately, with all the instruments and resources at their command before stating any general laws, and not permitting any prejudice to neglect or mutilate unwelcome facts.
- When we learn of an established fact, we can be sure that it's the result of a definite cause and that this cause will operate with invariable precision.
- Facts that can't be accounted for by the usual daily observation of life are considered most important for explaining or developing new principles, and many of the laws of Nature have been discovered by generalizing from facts that are uncommon, rare, or strange, forming the exception.
- We may account for much of the strange and unexplained phenomena in our experience by the principle of the creative power of thought; it will explain the cause of every possible human condition, whether physical, mental, or spiritual.
- Our success in applying this principle depends on our recognizing the fact that the creative nature of thought puts us in touch with Infinite Power; we need not be concerned with how that Omnipotent Substance will manifest our desire.

LESSON FOURTEEN

Manifestation

Our study so far has demonstrated that thought is a spiritual activity, which is filled with a creative power. This does not mean that *some* thought is creative but that *all* thought is creative.

The conscious and unconscious are two phases of action in one mind. The relation of the unconscious to the conscious is similar to that between a weather vane and the atmosphere. Just as pressure of the atmosphere causes an action on the weather vane, so does the least thought entertained by the conscious mind produce action in your unconscious mind. And, as the weather vane responds to the amount, as well as the direction, of air pressure, the subconscious mind responds in exact proportion to the depth of feeling and intensity of the thought.

The Power of Denial

This same principle can work in a negative way, through the process of denial, or negation. If you negate the possibility of unsatisfactory conditions, you are withdrawing the creative power of your thought from these conditions. You are cutting them away at the root; you are sapping their vitality.

Remember that the Law of Growth governs every manifestation in the objective world, so a denial of unsatisfactory conditions will not bring about instant change. As a plant will remain visible for some time after its roots have been cut, gradually fading away and eventually disappearing, so the withdrawal of your thought from unsatisfactory conditions will gradually, but surely, terminate these conditions.

This is exactly opposite from the approach we would normally take and will have exactly the opposite effect. Most people concentrate intently upon unsatisfactory conditions, giving those conditions the energy necessary for vigorous growth.

All things have their origin in Mind, so all appearances are the result of thought. This means that *things have no origin or reality in themselves*. Since they're produced by thought, they can be erased by removing the energy of thought from them.

The Structure of the Universe

The Universal Energy in which all motion, light, heat, and color have their origin is not limited like the many effects it causes but is supreme over them all. This Universal Substance is the source of all power, wisdom, and intelligence. To recognize this Intelligence is to become acquainted with the knowing quality of Mind, and through it to bring the Universal Substance into harmony in our affairs.

This is something that most teachers of the physical sciences have not yet attempted—a field of discovery they haven't yet explored. In fact, few of the materialistic fields of study have even caught the first ray of this light. They don't seem ready to concede that wisdom is everywhere present just as power and substance are.[46]

Some will say, if these principles are true, why are we not demonstrating them? As the fundamental principle is obviously correct, why do we not get the desired results?

We do. The results we receive are in direct answer to our understanding of Universal Law and our ability to apply it. We secured no results from the laws governing electricity until someone formulated the law and showed us how to apply it.

This puts us in an entirely new relation to our environment, opening up possibilities previously undreamed of. Mind is creative, and the principle upon which this law is based is sound, legitimate, and inherent in the nature of things; but this Creative Power originates not in the individual but in the Universal, which is the source of all energy and substance. The individual is simply the channel for the distribution of this energy—the means by which the Universal produces the various combinations resulting in the formation of phenomena.

We know that scientists have resolved matter into an immense number of molecules; these molecules have been resolved into atoms; and the atoms have resolved into subatomic particles. The discovery of these particles in high vacuum glass tubes indicates conclusively that they fill all space, that they exist everywhere, that they are omnipresent. They fill all material bodies and occupy the

---

46 In the last decades of the twentieth century, three fields of study were addressing this possibility. Particle physicists, studying the infinitesimally tiny building blocks of matter and energy, came to see a pattern of order in their interactions that has led some to state that the universe is built by and on a pattern of order and intelligence; microbiologists have identified patterns of activity within cells that suggest that intelligence is at work in the chemical interactions within the cells; cyberneticians have defined the physical universe as structures built of patterns of matter, energy, and information.

whole of what we call empty space. This, then, is the Universal Substance from which all things proceed.

Subatomic particles would forever remain free in space unless directed where to go to be assembled into atoms and molecules, and this director is Mind.[47] A number of electrons revolving around a center of force constitutes an atom; atoms unite in absolutely regular mathematical ratios to form molecules; and these unite with each other to form a multitude of united compounds to build the universe.

The lightest known atom is hydrogen, and this is 1,800 times heavier than an electron, which is one of the larger subatomic particles. An atom of mercury is 300,000 times heavier than an electron. Electrons are pure negative energy, and as they have the same potential velocity as all other cosmic energy, such as heat and light, neither time nor space require consideration.

The manner in which the speed of light was ascertained is interesting. In 1676, the Danish astronomer Roemer, working with Christian Huygens, played an integral part in obtaining the calculations to figure out the speed of light by observing the eclipses of Jupiter's moons. When the earth was nearest to Jupiter, the eclipse appeared about eight and one-half minutes too soon for the calculations; when the earth was most remote from Jupiter, they were about eight and one-half minutes too late. Roemer concluded the reason to be that it required seventeen minutes for light from the planet to traverse the diameter of the earth's orbit, which measured the difference of the distances of the earth from Jupiter.[48] This calculation has since been verified, and it proves that light travels about 186,000 miles a second.

---

47 For a delightfully clear explanation of this, see "Dr. Quantum's" animated explanation of the role of the observer in the "double-slit" experiment on the DVD, *What the Bleep? Down the Rabbit Hole.*

48 These figures were documented in *Treatise on Light,* by Christian Huygens.

The Mind of the Cell

Subatomic particles manifest in the body as atoms, molecules, and cells. And cells possess Mind and Intelligence sufficient for them to perform their functions in the human physical anatomy. Every part of the body is composed of cells, some of which operate independently, others in communities. Some are busy building tissue, while others are engaged in forming the various secretions of toxins necessary for the body. Some act as carriers of material; others are the surgeons whose work it is to repair damage; others are scavengers, carrying off waste; others are constantly ready to repel invaders or other undesirable intruders of the germ family.

All these cells are moving for a common purpose, and each one is a living organism with enough Intelligence to enable it to perform its necessary duties. Each cell is also endowed with the intelligence to perpetuate its own life. To do so, it must secure adequate nourishment and exercise choice in the selection of such nourishment.

Each cell is born, reproduces itself, dies, and is absorbed. The maintenance of health and life itself depends upon the constant regeneration of these cells.

The mind contained in every cell of the body has been called the unconscious mind because it acts without our awareness to maintain the body. And, in our study, we've found that this unconscious mind is responsive to the will of the conscious mind.

Now, in mental as in natural science, experiments have established that our body is the reflection of the thoughts we have entertained during our lifetime. Thought is stamped on the face and form, as well as the character and environment; the unconscious mind of the cells has conformed to the thought in the conscious mind. This, then, is the scientific explanation for metaphysical healing and will enable anyone to understand the principle upon which this remarkable phenomenon rests.

Reflections

The objective world is controlled by an unseen and unexplained power, and the majority of people have personalized this power and called it God.

Let's explore this idea. Behind every effect there is a cause, and if we follow the trail to its starting point, we shall find the Creative Principle out of which the objective world grew—the permeating Essence or Principle of all that exists, the Infinite or Universal Mind.

Universal Mind, being infinite and omnipotent, has unlimited resources at its command, and when we remember that it is also omnipresent, we cannot escape the conclusion that each of us must be an expression or manifestation of that Mind.

Recognition and understanding of the resources of the unconscious mind will confirm that the only difference between the unconscious mind and the Universal Mind is one of degree. They differ only as a drop of water differs from the ocean. They are the same in kind and quality.

With the unconscious mind being the connecting link between Universal Mind and the conscious mind, is it not evident that the conscious mind can consciously suggest thoughts which the unconscious mind will put into action? And as the unconscious is one with the Universal, is it not evident that no limit can be placed upon its activities?

A scientific understanding of this principle will explain the wonderful results secured through Prayer. They're not brought about by any special dispensations of providence; on the contrary, they are the result of the operation of Natural Law. There is, truly, nothing either religious or mysterious about them.

Do you—can you—appreciate the value of this all-important fact? Do you realize that recognition of this tremendous fact places you in touch with Omnipotence?

Thought is the only reality, and conditions are just outward manifestations; as the thought changes, all outward or material conditions must change in order to be in harmony with their creator, which is thought. But the thought must be clear-cut, steady, fixed, definite, unchangeable; you cannot take one step forward and two steps backward, neither can you spend twenty or thirty years of your life building up negative conditions as the result of negative thoughts and then expect to see them all melt away as the result of fifteen or twenty minutes of right thinking.

Yet there are many who are not ready to enter into the action necessary to think correctly, even though it is evident that wrong thinking has brought failure.

If you enter into the work necessary to bring about a radical change in your life, you must do so deliberately, after giving the matter careful thought and full consideration, and then you must allow nothing to interfere with your decision.

This discipline, this change of thought, this mental attitude will not only bring you the material things necessary for your highest and best welfare but will bring health and harmonious conditions generally. If you wish harmonious conditions in your life, you must develop harmonious mental attitudes.

Your world without will be a reflection of your world within.

Applying the Principle

For your exercise in this lesson:

1. Concentrate on Harmony with all the focus and dedication that the word "concentrate" implies.
2. Focus so deeply, so earnestly, that you are conscious of nothing but harmony.
3. Remember, we learn by doing.

Reading these lessons will get you nowhere. It is in the practical application that the value consists.

Learn to keep the door shut, keep out of your mind and out of your world, every element that seeks admittance with no definite helpful end in view.

—George Matthew Adams

Summary

- The Universal Mind is the source of all wisdom, power, and intelligence.
- All motion, light, heat, and color have their origin in Universal Energy, which is one manifestation of Universal Mind.
- The creative power of thought originates in Universal Mind, so thought is Mind in motion.
- The human mind is the means by which the Universal produces the various combinations that result in the formation of phenomena.
- The power of each individual to think is our ability to act upon the Universal and bring form into manifestation.
- The basic form that the Universal takes is subatomic particles, which fill all space.
- All things have their origin in Mind.
- A change of thought results in a change in conditions.
- Harmonious mental attitudes result in harmonious conditions in life.

LESSON FIFTEEN

Metamorphosis

LESSON FIFTEEN will tell you more about the law under which we live. It will explain that these laws operate to our advantage; that all conditions and experiences that come to us are for our benefit; that we gain strength in proportion to the effort expended; and that our happiness is best attained through a conscious cooperation with Natural Law.

Thought, immaterial though it may be, is the matrix in which all the issues of life are shaped. Mind has been active in all fields during this prosperous new millennium, but it is to science that we must look for the thoughts that have shaped all thinking.

Jacques Loch, MD, PhD, a member of the Rockefeller Institute, reports the following:

> In order to obtain the material, potted rose bushes are brought into a room and placed in front of a closed

> window. If the plants are allowed to dry out, the aphids (parasites), previously wingless, change to winged insects. After the metamorphosis, the animals leave the plants, fly to the window, and then creep upward on the glass.

These tiny insects found that the plants on which they had been thriving were dead and that they could therefore secure nothing more to eat and drink from this source. The only method by which they could save themselves from starvation was to grow temporary wings and fly, which they did. Experiments such as these indicate that Omniscience as well as Omnipotence is omnipresent and that the tiniest living thing can take advantage of it in an emergency.

Experiencing the Law of Growth and Evolution

The laws under which we live are designed solely for our advantage. These laws are immutable and inescapable, but we can place ourselves in harmony with them to experience a life of comparative peace and happiness. Difficulties, disharmonies, and obstacles indicate that we are either refusing to give out what we no longer need or are refusing to accept what we need.

Growth is attained through an exchange of the old for the new, of the good for the better; it's a conditional reciprocal action, for each of us is a complete thought entity, and this completeness makes it possible for us to receive only as we give. This means we can't obtain what we desire if we cling to what we have.

We're able to consciously control our conditions as we sense the purpose of what we've attracted, and we're able to extract from each experience exactly what we require for further growth. Our ability to do this determines the degree of harmony or happiness that we attain.

The ability to manifest what we require for our growth increases as we reach higher levels and broader visions; the greater our ability to know what we require, the more certain we are to discern its presence, to attract it, and to absorb it.

Nothing can reach us except what is necessary for our growth. All conditions and experiences come to us for our benefit. Difficulties and obstacles will continue to come only until we absorb their wisdom and gather from them the essentials for further growth. And, since the principle that we reap what we sow is mathematically certain, we gain permanent strength exactly to the extent of the effort required to overcome the difficulties we encounter. This means that the inherent requirements of growth demand that we exert the greatest degree of attraction for what is perfectly in accord with us.

The Power of Words

The wonderful capacity to clothe thoughts in the form of words is what differentiates humanity from the rest of the animal kingdom. Words are the vessels in which thought is carried. They set the air in motion and reproduce our thought to others in the form of sound.

Words are thoughts and, because thoughts have power, our words will eventually embody themselves in the form they are given. Words may become mental palaces that will live forever, or they may become shacks that the first breeze will carry away. They may delight the eye as well as the ear; they may contain all knowledge. In them we find the history of the past as well as the hope of the future; they are living messengers from which every human and superhuman activity is born.

By use of the written word, we're able to look back over the centuries and see the stirring scenes by which we've come into our present inheritance. Through the written word, humanity has been able to come into communion with the greatest writers and thinkers of all time. The body of literature we possess today is not just the accumulation of human thought processes, but the expression of Universal Thought as it has been seeking to take form in the mind of humanity.

It is with words that we must express our thoughts, and if we're to make use of higher forms of Truth, we may use only such mental material as has been carefully and intelligently selected with this purpose in view.

It's evident that if we wish desirable conditions, we can afford to entertain only desirable thoughts. As words are only thoughts taking form, we must be especially careful to use nothing but constructive and harmonious language—words which, when finally crystallized into objective forms, will prove to our advantage.

We manifest more and more life as our thought becomes clarified and takes higher planes. This happens more easily as we use word pictures that are clearly defined and free of the ideas associated with lower planes of thought. However, we can't escape from the pictures we incessantly photograph in the mind, and photography of erroneous conceptions is exactly what is being done when we use language that doesn't support our well-being.

Thought may lead to action of any kind, but whatever the action, it is simply the thought attempting to express itself in visible form. This leads to the inevitable conclusion that if we wish to experience abundance in our lives, we can afford to think, speak, and write only abundance.

We know that Universal Thought has for its goal the creation of form, and we know that individual thought is likewise forever attempting to express itself in form. We know that the word is a thought form, and a sentence is a combination of thought forms. So if we wish our ideal to be beautiful or strong, we must see that the words we're using to create it are exact, and that they are put together carefully. Accuracy in building words and sentences is the highest form of architecture in civilization.

The Power of Principle

The beauty of the word consists in the beauty of the thought; the power of the word consists in the power of the thought; and the power of the thought consists in its vitality.

How shall we identify a vital thought? What are its distinguishing characteristics?

Love energizes thought and enables it to germinate. In order to possess vitality, therefore, thought must be impregnated with love. The Law of Attraction, or the Law of Love, for they are one and the same, will bring to each thought the necessary material for its growth and maturity. Love is a product of the emotions, so it's essential that the emotions be controlled and guided by reason so that they are harmonious with Universal Principle.

How shall we identify principle?

Look around. There is a principle of mathematics, but none of error; there is a principle of health, but none of disease; there is a principle of Truth, but none of dishonesty; there is a principle of light, but none of darkness; and there is a principle of abundance, but none of poverty.

How can we know that this is true? Because, if we apply the principle correctly, we can be certain of our results. Where there is health, there will be no disease. If we know the Truth we cannot be deceived. If we let in light there can be no darkness, and where there is abundance there can be no poverty.

These are self-evident facts, but the all-important Truth is this: a thought based on principle contains life and consequently takes root, slowly but certainly, to displace any negative thoughts. And negative thoughts, by their very nature, can contain no vitality.

But this is a truth that enables you to live in harmony, abundance, and peace. There can be no question; anyone who "is wise enough to understand"[49] will readily recognize that the creative power of thought makes him or her a master of destiny.

Applying the Principle

In the physical world, the Law of Compensation is this: "the appearance of a given amount of energy anywhere means the disappearance of the same amount somewhere else," and so we find that we can get only what we give. If we pledge ourselves to a certain action we must be prepared to assume the responsibility for the development of that action. The unconscious cannot reason; it takes us at our word. We have asked for something; we are now to receive it. We have made our bed; we are now to lie in it. The die has been cast, and the threads will carry out the pattern we have made.

For this reason, insight must be exercised so that the thoughts we entertain contain no mental, moral, or physical element that we do not wish objectified in our lives.

Insight is an aspect of the mind whereby we can examine facts and conditions at long range, a kind of human telescope. It enables us to understand the difficulties, as well as the possibilities, in any undertaking. Insight also enables us to be prepared for the obstacles that we might meet so we can overcome them before they can cause any difficulty. Insight enables us to plan to turn our thought and attention in the right direction, instead of into channels that can yield no possible return. Insight is absolutely essential for the development of any great achievement; with it we may enter, explore, and possess any mental field. Insight is a product of the world within and is developed in the Silence by concentration.

---

49 Jeremiah 9:12.

For your exercise in this lesson, concentrate on insight:

1. Take your accustomed position.
2. Focus your thought on the fact that to have knowledge of the creative power of thought does not mean to possess the art of thinking.
3. Let your thought focus on the fact that knowledge does not apply itself; that our actions are not governed by knowledge but by custom, precedent, and habit; that the only way we can get ourselves to apply knowledge is by a determined conscious effort.
4. Call to mind the fact that unused knowledge passes from the mind and that the value of the information is in the application of principle.
5. Continue this line of thought until you can formulate a definite program for applying this principle to your own particular problem.

Think truly, and thy thoughts
Shall the world's famine feed;
Speak truly, and each word of thine
Shall be a fruitful seed;
Live truly, and thy life shall be
A great and noble creed.

—Horatio Bonar

Summary

- Our ability to take what we need so we can grow and learn from each experience determines the degree of harmony we attain.

- Difficulties and obstacles occur when they are necessary for our wisdom and spiritual growth; they may be avoided by a conscious understanding of and cooperation with Natural Law.
- The principle by which thought manifests itself in form is the Law of Attraction.
- The Law of Love, which is the Creative Principle of the universe, imparts vitality to the thought, and the Law of Attraction brings the necessary substance to it by the Law of Growth.
- Desirable conditions are secured by entertaining only desirable thoughts.
- Undesirable conditions are brought about by thinking, discussing, and visualizing conditions of lack, limitation, disease, disharmony, or discord of any kind. This mental photography of erroneous conceptions is taken up by the unconscious, and the Law of Attraction inevitably crystallizes it into objective form. That we reap what we sow is scientifically exact.
- We overcome every kind of fear, lack, limitation, poverty, and discord by substituting principle for error.
- We recognize principle when we realize that Truth always destroys error, and that we don't have to work to keep the darkness out; all that is necessary is to turn on the light. The same principle applies to every form of negative thought.
- Many seem to think that knowledge will automatically apply itself, which is by no means true. Insight enables us to foresee the value of applying the knowledge we've gained.

LESSON SIXTEEN

The Cycle of Seven

To every man there openeth a way,
And the high soul climbs the high way,
And the low soul gropes the low;
And in between on the misty flats,
The rest drift to and fro.
But to every man there openeth
A high way and a low
And every man decideth
The way his soul shall go.

—JOHN OXENHAM

THE ACTIVITIES of the planets are regulated by a law of periodicity. Everything that lives has periods of birth, growth, blossoming, and maturity. These periods are governed by the Septimal Law, also known as the Law of Sevens.

The Law of Sevens governs the days of the week, the phases of the moon, and the harmonies of sound, light, heat, electricity, magnetism, and atomic structure. It governs the life of individuals and of nations, and it dominates the activities of the commercial world.

Life is growth, and growth is change, and each seven-year period takes us into a new cycle. The first seven years is the period of infancy. The next seven, the period of childhood, representing the beginning of individual responsibility. The next seven represents the period of adolescence. The fourth period marks the attainment of full growth. The fifth is the constructive period, when adults begin to acquire property, possessions, a home and family. The next, from thirty-five to forty-two, is a period of reactions and changes, and this in turn is followed by a period of reconstruction, adjustment, and recuperation, so as to be ready for a new cycle of sevens, beginning with the fiftieth year.[50]

There are many who think that the world is going through the same set of periods and is just about to pass out of the sixth period into the seventh period, the period of readjustment, reconstruction, and harmony; the period frequently referred to as the Millennium.[51]

Those familiar with these cycles will not be disturbed when things seem to go wrong, but they can apply the principle outlined in these lessons with the full assurance that a higher

---

50 Joan Borysenko provides an effective description of this process in *The Cycles of a Woman's Life.*

51 We have since experienced "Y2K," but the idea that we're in the process of moving through a huge change is still very much alive. At this writing, the focus is on "2012" and the many ancient prophecies (and modern computer models) that suggest that our current way of living, referred to as "the world," is coming to an end at that time.

law will invariably control all other laws and that through an understanding and conscious operation of spiritual laws, we can convert every seeming difficulty into a blessing.

Creating Wealth

Wealth is a product of labor. Capital is an effect, not a cause; a servant, not a master; a means, not an end. The most commonly accepted definition of wealth is that it consists of all useful and agreeable things that possess exchange value; it is recognized as exchangeable for some good or service. This exchange value is the predominant characteristic of wealth, and when we consider how small an addition having money in the bank is to the happiness of the possessor, we find that the true value consists in its exchange.[52] This exchange value makes it a medium for securing the things of real value with which our ideals may be realized.

Wealth, then, should never be desired as an end but simply as a means of accomplishing an end. Success is contingent upon a higher ideal than the mere accumulation of riches, and whoever aspires to such success must formulate an ideal to strive for. With such an ideal in mind, the ways and means can and will be provided, but the mistake must not be made of substituting the means for the end. There must be a definite fixed purpose, an ideal.

Prentice Mulford said: "The man of success is the man possessed of the greatest spiritual understanding, and every great

---

52 When this was written, U.S. dollars were based on the gold standard: there was a dollar's worth of gold in storage for every dollar bill printed. Today, the dollar bill is a "Federal Reserve Note." There is no gold or silver backing it, simply the promise of the Federal Reserve system to honor the paper as a dollar's worth of goods or services in exchange. This fact is encouraging the development of "local currencies" around the world to support local economies without being dependent on large corporations.

fortune comes of superior and truly spiritual power." Unfortunately, there are those who fail to recognize this power; they forget that Andrew Carnegie's mother had to help support the family when they came to America, that W. Averell Harriman's father was a poor clergyman with a salary of only $200 a year, that Sir Thomas Lipton started with only twenty-five cents, that Bill Gates slept on the sofa in his office for years, and that Steve Jobs started his business in his parents' garage. These men had no other power but their own to depend upon, and it did not fail them.

The power to create depends entirely upon spiritual power and there are three steps: idealization, visualization, and materialization.

The successful entrepreneur is more often than not an idealist who is always striving for higher and higher standards, and every successful entrepreneur depends exclusively upon this power. In the following interview in an article in *Everybody's Magazine*,[53] Henry M. Flagler, one of the founders of Standard Oil, admitted that the secret of his success was his power to see a thing in its completeness:

> "Did you actually envision to yourself the whole thing? I mean, did you, or could you, really close your eyes and see the tracks and the trains running? And hear the whistles blowing? Did you go as far as that?"
>
> "Yes."
>
> "How clearly?"
>
> "Very clearly."

Here we have a vision of the law; we see cause and effect, and we see that thought necessarily precedes and determines action.

53 *Everybody's Magazine* was in circulation from 1899 to 1929.

Managing Thought

If we are wise, we realize the tremendous fact that no arbitrary condition can exist—even for a moment—and that all human experience is the result of an orderly and harmonious sequence. The conditions we meet in the world without always correspond to the conditions in the world within. The subtle forces of thought constitute life as they crystallize in our daily moods.

Thought is moldable; it's the plastic material that we use to build images of our life. And, as in all other things, our ability to recognize it and use it properly is the necessary condition for attaining our desires. Acquiring premature wealth is therefore the forerunner of humiliation and disaster because we can't permanently retain anything we don't merit or haven't earned. The Law of Attraction requires that we be that which we wish to have.

How then should we determine what is to enter the world within ourselves?

Whatever enters the mind through the senses, or the objective mind, will impress the mind and result in a mental image that then becomes a pattern for the creative energies. These experiences are largely the result of environment, chance, past thinking, and other forms of negative thought, and must be subjected to careful analysis before being accepted.

On the other hand, *we can form our own mental images through our own inner processes of thought*, regardless of the thoughts of others, regardless of exterior conditions, regardless of environment of every kind. It is by the exercise of this power that we can control our own destiny, body, mind, and soul.

Exercise of this power takes our fate out of the hands of chance and lets us consciously make the experiences we desire. When we consciously realize a condition, that condition will eventually manifest in our lives. Therefore, to control thought is to control circumstances, conditions, environment, and destiny.

How then are we to control thought; what's the process?

To think is to a create thought, but the result of the thought will depend on its form, its quality, and its vitality.

- The form of a thought depends on the mental images from which it emanates: the depth of the impression, the predominance of the idea, the clarity of the vision, and the intensity of the image.
- The quality depends on the material of which the mind is composed; if this material has been woven from thoughts of vigor, strength, courage, determination, the thought will possess these qualities.
- And finally, the vitality depends on the feeling with which the thought is imbued.

If the thought is constructive, it will possess vitality; it will have life, it will grow, develop, expand. It will be creative; it will attract to itself everything necessary for its complete development. If the thought is destructive, it will have within itself the germ of its own dissolution; it will die, but in the process of dying, it will bring sickness, disease, and every other form of discord.

We call this "evil," and when we bring it upon ourselves, some of us are disposed to attribute our difficulties to a power outside ourselves. But the only power is Omnipotent Mind, being neither good nor bad; it simply is. Our ability to bring it into form is our ability to manifest good or evil. Good and evil therefore are not entities; they're simply words we use to indicate the result of our actions, and these actions are, in turn, determined by the character of our thought.

If our thought is constructive and harmonious, we manifest what is called good; if it is destructive and discordant, we manifest what is called evil.

Visualization

If you desire to visualize a different environment, the process is simply to hold the ideal qualities of your new environment in mind until your vision has been made real. Give no thought to the "how" in terms of persons, places, or things; these have no place in the absolute; the environment you desire will contain everything necessary; the right persons and the right things will come at the right time and in the right place.

It's sometimes difficult to see how character, ability, attainment, achievement, environment, and destiny can be controlled through the power of visualization, but this is a scientifically determined fact.[54] You can see that what we think determines the quality of mind and that the quality of mind in turn determines our ability and mental capacity, and you can easily understand that an improvement in our ability will naturally be followed by an increase in abundance and a greater control of circumstances. You will then see that Natural Law works in a perfectly harmonious manner; everything seems to "just happen." If you need evidence of this fact, simply compare results of your efforts in your own life when your actions were prompted by high ideals versus times when you had selfish or ulterior motives in mind. You will need no further evidence.

We can only see what already exists in the objective world, but *what we visualize already exists in the spiritual world,* and this visualization is a substantial token of what will one day appear in the objective world, if we are faithful to our thoughts. So, if you

---

54 Dennis Waitley, who participated in the research at NASA and in the Olympics, has summarized this research nicely in Rhonda Byrne's *The Secret.*

wish to manifest any desire, form a mental picture of success in your mind by consciously visualizing your desire; in this way you will externalize it in your life.

The reasoning for this is not difficult; visualization is a form of imagination. It forms impressions on the mind; these impressions in turn form concepts and ideals; and these concrete thoughts in turn become the plans from which Universal Mind, the Master Architect, will weave the future.

Visualization must, of course, be directed by the will. If we are to visualize exactly what we want, we must be careful not to let the imagination run riot. Imagination is a good servant but a poor master; unless controlled, it may easily lead us into all kinds of speculations and conclusions that have no basis or foundation in fact whatever. Every kind of plausible opinion is liable to be accepted without any analytical examination, and the inevitable result is mental chaos.

We must, therefore, build our mental images only on ideas that are known to be scientifically true. Subject every idea to a searching analysis and accept nothing that is not scientifically correct.

When you do this you will attempt nothing but what you know you can carry out, and success will crown your efforts; this is farsightedness. It's much the same as insight and is one of the great secrets of success in all-important undertakings.

Applying the Principle

For your exercise in this lesson:

1. Bring yourself to realize the important fact that harmony and happiness are states of consciousness and do not depend upon the possession of things—that things are effects and come as a consequence of correct mental states.

2. Concentrate on the idea that, if we desire material possessions of any kind, our chief concern should be to acquire the mental attitude that will bring about the desired result. This mental attitude is brought about by a realization of our spiritual nature and our unity with the Universal Mind, which is the substance of all things.

The right mental attitude will bring about everything that is necessary for our complete enjoyment; this is correct, scientific thinking. When we succeed in bringing about this attitude it is comparatively easy to realize our desire as an already accomplished fact; we shall have found the Truth, which frees us from every lack or limitation of any kind.

A man might frame and let loose a star, to roll in its orbit, and yet not have done so memorable a thing before God as he who lets a golden-orbed thought to roll through the generations of time.

—HENRY WARD BEECHER

Summary

- Wealth depends on an understanding of the creative nature of Thought.
- Wealth's true value consists on its exchange value.
- Success depends on spiritual power.
- This power depends on use; use determines its existence.
- We take our fate out of the hands of chance by consciously realizing the conditions that we desire to see manifested in our lives.

- Thinking, then, is the great business of life.
- This is so because thought is spiritual and therefore creative. To consciously control thought is therefore to control circumstances, conditions, environment, and destiny.
- The source of all evil is destructive thinking.
- The source of all good is correct, scientific thinking.
- Correct, scientific thinking is a recognition of the creative nature of spiritual energy and our ability to control it.

The greatest events of an age are its best thoughts.
It is the nature of thought to find its way into action.

—John Bovee Dods

LESSON SEVENTEEN

Concentration and Desire

THE KIND of deity that someone worships, consciously or unconsciously, indicates the wisdom of the worshipper.

Ask one religious group, and they will describe to you a powerful chieftain of a glorious tribe. Ask another group of God, and they will tell you of a god of fire, a god of water, a goddess of earth, wind, water, and spirit. Ask the Israelites of God, and they will tell you of the God of Moses, who ruled His people by coercive measures, hence the Ten Commandments. Ask Wiccans and they will tell you of a dual god that is both man and woman, Lord and Lady; every person sees a god they can relate to.

The so-called heathen made "graven images" of their gods, whom they were accustomed to worship, but among the wisest, at least, these images were but the visible symbols with which people were enabled to mentally concentrate on the qualities that they desired to externalize in their lives.

We of the twentieth century worship a God of love in theory, but in practice we make for ourselves "graven images" of wealth, power, fashion, custom, and conventionality. We "fall down" before them and worship them. We concentrate on them and so they are externalized in our lives.

As you master the contents of lesson seventeen you won't mistake the symbols for the reality; you'll be interested in causes rather than effects. You will concentrate on the realities of life and so will not be disappointed by the results.

The Power of Concentration

We are told that humanity has "dominion over all things."[55] This dominion is established through Mind. The Highest Principle, by reason of its superior essence and qualities, necessarily determines the circumstances, aspects, and relation of everything with which it comes in contact, so thought controls every principle beneath it. The vibrations of mental forces are the finest and consequently the most powerful in existence.

To those who understand the transcendent nature of mental force, the pursuit of physical power becomes insignificant.

We usually perceive the universe through the lens of the five senses, and from these experiences we create conceptions of the outer world as having the same characteristics as ourselves. But true conceptions are based on spiritual insight. This insight requires a link with Mind, which is only secured when the conscious mind is continuously concentrated in a given direction.

Sadly, the average person has no conception of the meaning of concentration. Continuous concentration means an even, unbroken flow of thought that is patient, persistent, persevering,

55 Genesis 1:26.

and well-regulated. This requires control of the mental and physical being. All modes of consciousness, whether mental or physical, must be under control.

Such concentration leads to intuitive perception and immediate insight into the nature of the object concentrated upon. So all great discoveries are the result of long-continued investigation. The science of mathematics requires years of concentrated effort to master it, and the greatest science—that of Mind—is revealed only through concentrated effort.

Concentration is much misunderstood; there's an idea of effort or activity associated with it, when just the contrary is necessary. An actor's greatness lies in the fact that he forgets himself in the portrayal of his character, becoming so identified with it that the audience is swayed by the realism of the performance. This will give you a good idea of true concentration; you should be so interested in your thought, so engrossed in your subject, as to be aware of nothing else.

All knowledge is the result of concentration of this kind. Through it the secrets of Heaven and earth have been discovered; the mind becomes a magnet by which the desire to know draws the knowledge, irresistibly attracts it, and makes it our own. People center their minds on the problems of life, and the result is the vast and complex social order in which we live. The astronomer centers his mind on the stars and they give forth their secrets; the geologist centers his mind on the construction of the earth and we have geology. So it is with all things.

Most people cry "to have" but never cry "to be." They fail to understand that they can't have one without the other, that they must first find the "kingdom" before they can have the "things added." Momentary enthusiasm is of no value; the goal is reached only with unbounded self-confidence.

So the kind of desire we're talking about is largely unconscious. While conscious desire rarely realizes its object when the latter is out of immediate reach, unconscious desire arouses the latent faculties of the mind, and difficult problems seem to solve themselves. By concentration, the unconscious mind may be aroused and brought into action in any direction and made to serve us for any purpose.

Desire added to concentration will wrench any secret from Nature. *All mental discovery and attainment are the result of desire plus concentration*; desire is the strongest mode of action; the more persistent the desire, the more authoritative the revelation.

Psychologists have come to the conclusion that there is but one sense—the sense of feeling—and that all other senses are but modifications of this one sense. This would explain why feeling is the very fountainhead of power, why the emotions so easily overcome the intellect, and why we must put feeling into our thought if we wish results. *Thought with feeling is the irresistible combination.*

Developing Power

All of us are dynamos, but a dynamo of itself is nothing; an engine must work the dynamo. Then it's useful and its energy can be definitely concentrated. The mind is an engine whose power is undreamed; thought is an omni-working power. It is the ruler and creator of all form and all events occurring in form. This means that physical energy is nothing in comparison with the omnipotence of thought because thought enables man to harness all other natural power.

Thought acts in vibration; vibration reaches out and attracts the materials to build with. There's nothing mysterious about the power of thought; concentration simply means that consciousness can be focalized to the point where it becomes identified with the object of its attention. As food absorbed is the essence of the body, so the mind absorbs the object of its attention and gives it life and being.

So concentration is not merely thinking thoughts but transmuting these thoughts into internal experience. Spiritual Truth is therefore the controlling factor; it enables you to reach the point where you can easily translate thought into character and consciousness.

The spirit of initiative and originality is developed through persistence and continuity of mental effort, so weakness is the only barrier to mental attainment. If you've failed to accomplish your mental goals, attribute your weakness to temporary physical limitations or mental uncertainties and try again; ease and perfection are gained by repetition. The mind may place the ideal a little too high and fall short of the mark; it may attempt to soar on untrained wings and, instead of flying, fall to earth. But, as the child learning to walk knows, that's no reason for not making another attempt. The primary need is to strengthen the mind so that it rises superior to the distractions and wayward impulses of instinctive life, and wins mastery in the conflict between the higher (reasoning) and lower (instinctive) self.

The mind appreciates the value of higher things when it realizes great thoughts and it experiences the great emotions that correspond with great thoughts. The intensity of one moment's earnest concentration and the intense longing to become and to attain such experiences may take you further than years of slow, "normal," forced effort. It unfastens the prison bars of unbelief, weakness, impotence, and self-belittlement, and you come into a realization of the joy of overcoming.

Remember that fundamentally the unconscious Intelligence is omnipotent; there is no limit to the things that can be done when it is given the power to act. Your degree of success is determined by the nature of your desire. If your desire is in harmony with Natural Law or Universal Mind, it will gradually emancipate the mind and give you invincible courage.

Every obstacle conquered and every victory gained will give you more faith in your power, and you'll have greater ability to win. Your strength is determined by your mental attitude; if this attitude is one of success and is permanently held with an unswerving purpose, you will attract to you the things you silently demand from the invisible domain.

As we keep a thought in mind, it will gradually take tangible form. A definite purpose sets causes in motion that go out into the invisible world and find the material necessary to serve your purpose.

Intuition

When you concentrate on some matter of importance, help will also come in the nature of information that leads to success: your intuitive power will be turned on.

Intuition arrives at conclusions without the aid of experience or memory and often solves problems that are beyond the grasp of reasoning power. It often comes with a suddenness that is startling, revealing the Truth we seek so directly that it seems to come from a higher power.

To cultivate and develop your intuition, you must first recognize and appreciate this gift; if the intuitive awareness is given a royal welcome when it comes, it will come again. The more cordial the welcome, the more frequent its visits will become. If it is ignored or neglected, however, it will make its visits few and far between.

Intuition usually comes in the Silence; great minds seek solitude frequently, and it is here that all the larger problems of life are worked out. For this reason every professional who can afford it has a private office, where he or she will not be disturbed. If you can't afford a private office, at least find somewhere where you can be alone a few minutes each day to train thought along lines which will enable you to develop that invincible power which is necessary to achieve.

The Heart of Things

Thought ordinarily leads outwardly in evolutionary directions, but it can be turned within where it will take hold of the basic principles of things, the heart of things, the spirit of things. When you get to the heart of things, it is comparatively easy to understand and command them. This is because the spirit of a thing is the thing itself—the vital part of it, the real substance. The form is simply the outward manifestation of the spiritual activity within.

You may be pursuing the symbols of power instead of power itself. You may be pursuing fame instead of honor, riches instead of wealth, position instead of servitude. In either event you will find that they turn to ashes just as you overtake them.

Premature wealth or position cannot be retained because it has not been earned; we get only what we give, and those who try to get without giving always find that the Law of Compensation is relentlessly bringing about an exact equilibrium. The push has usually been for money and other mere symbols of power, but with an understanding of the true source of power, we can afford to ignore the symbols. We conform to Spiritual Truth by being the quality rather than merely possessing its sign. As someone with a large bank account finds it unnecessary to carry lots of coins, so someone who has found the true source of power is no longer interested in its shams or pretensions.

Applying the Principle

For your exercise, do your best to concentrate using the method outlined in this lesson; let there be no conscious effort or activity associated with your purpose.

1. Relax completely; avoid any thought of anxiety about your intended results. Remember that power comes through peace.
2. Let the thought dwell upon your object until it is completely identified with it—until you are conscious of nothing else. If you wish to eliminate fear, concentrate on courage; if you wish to eliminate lack, concentrate on abundance; if you wish to eliminate disease, concentrate on health.

Always concentrate on the ideal as an already existing fact; this is the germ cell, the life principle that goes forth guide, direct, and bring about the necessary relation, which eventually manifests in form.

Thought is the property of those only who can entertain it.

—Ralph Waldo Emerson

Summary

- The true method of concentration is to become so identified with the object of your thought that you are aware of nothing else.
- The result of this method is the ignition of invisible forces that irresistibly bring about conditions corresponding with your thought; concentration develops the powers of perception, wisdom, intuition, and sagacity.
- The controlling factor in this method of thought is Spiritual Truth because the nature of our desire must be in harmony with Natural Law.

- Through this method of concentration, thought is transmuted into character, and character is the magnet drawing forth all that is needed to create the environment of the individual.
- The mental element is the controlling factor in every commercial pursuit because Mind is the ruler and creator of all form and all events occurring in form.
- Intuition is superior to reason because it doesn't depend on experience or memory, frequently bringing the solution to our problems by methods we know nothing about.
- The symbols of reality often turn to ashes just as we overtake them because the symbol is only the outward form of the spiritual activity within. Unless we can possess the spiritual reality, which means to "be" rather than merely to "have," the form disappears.

LESSON EIGHTEEN

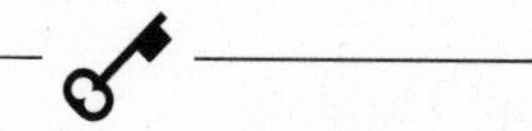

The Value of Belief

In order to grow we must obtain what is necessary for our growth. This is brought about through the Law of Attraction.

Think for a moment, what would a man be if he were not a friend, partner, husband, father, or brother? What would a woman be if she were not a friend, partner, wife, mother, or sister? What if you were not participating in the social, economical, political, or religious world? You would be nothing but an abstract, theoretical ego. You exist, therefore, only in relationship with other people and with society as a whole. This set of relationships constitutes your environment and defines your being.[56]

So the individual is simply the differentiation of the one Universal Mind "which lighteth every man that cometh into the

56 Physicist Dana Zohar presents the quantum mechanical basis for this in her books, *The Quantum Self* and *The Quantum Society.*

world,"[57] and our so-called individuality or personality consists of nothing but the manner in which we relate with the whole, which we call our environment, and which is shaped by the Law of Attraction.

Lesson eighteen, which follows, has something more to say concerning this important law.

A New Way of Thinking

A change is occurring in humanity's thinking. This change, silently transpiring in our midst, is more important than any shift the world has undergone since the Renaissance, which began in Italy in the late 1400s and transformed all of western Europe over the next three centuries. The whole world is on the eve of a new consciousness, a new power, and a new realization of the resources within the self.

Science has made such vast discoveries, has revealed such an infinity of resources, has unveiled such enormous possibilities and such unsuspected forces, that scientists are more and more hesitant to declare certain theories to be firmly established or to deny other theories as absurd or impossible.

The last centuries have seen the most magnificent material progress in history. The present century will produce the greatest progress in mental and spiritual power. The blinders of tradition are being lifted off of humanity, and as the last limiting vestiges of materialism are released, human thought is being liberated; Truth is appearing, fully formed, before an astonished multitude.

As a result, a new civilization is being born: old assumptions, with their associated customs, creeds, and cruelty are passing; a new paradigm based on vision, faith, and service is taking their place.

---

57 John 1:9.

The whole world is on the eve of a new consciousness, a new power, and a new realization within the self. In the process, physicists have analyzed matter into molecules, molecules into atoms, and atoms into energy, and now they're suggesting that intelligence underlies the pattern of energy.

At the beginning of the twentieth century, Sir Ambrose Fleming, in an address before the British Royal Society, said, "In its ultimate essence, energy may be incomprehensible by us except as an exhibition of the direct operation of that which we call Mind or Will." Today, particle physicist Amit Goswami calls the universe, "Self-Aware," suggesting that an all-pervading Intelligence underlies all of physical reality and brings it into form. [58]

So this Mind is the sustaining, energizing, all-pervading Spirit of the universe. Every living thing must be sustained by this Omnipotent Intelligence, and we find the difference in individual lives to be largely measured by the degree of this Intelligence that they manifest. Greater intelligence places the animal in a higher scale of being than the plant, and human beings higher than the animal. Increased use of Omnipotent Intelligence is indicated by the power of the individual to control action and thus to intentionally adjust to the environment. This adjustment consists in nothing other than the recognition of an existing order in Universal Mind, for *Mind will obey us precisely in proportion as we first obey it.*

The Power of Thought

Recognition of Natural Law has made it possible for humanity to radically modify our environment: to annihilate the effects of time and space, to soar in the air, and to make iron float. And the greater the degree of Universal Intelligence we manifest, the

58 *The Self-Aware Universe* by Amit Goswami, professor emeritus, Department of Physics, University of Oregon.

greater will be our recognition of Natural Law and the greater will be the power we possess.

Recognition of the self as an individualization of this Universal Intelligence enables us to control other forms of intelligence not yet at this level of self-recognition. These beings do not know that Universal Intelligence permeates all things, ready to be called into action, responsive to every demand. They are therefore in bondage to the laws of their own being.

Thought is creative; this creative power, however, originates not in the individual but in the Universal, which is the source and foundation of all energy and substance. The individual is simply the channel for distribution.

We are the means by which the Universal produces the various combinations of energy and substance that result in the formation of phenomena. They are formed through varying rates of motion, or frequencies of vibration, in the primary substance following certain numerical ratios according to the Law of Vibration. And thought, being vibratory action, is the invisible link by which the individual comes into communication with the Universal, the finite with the Infinite, the seen with the Unseen. Thought is the magic by which the human is transformed into a being who thinks and knows and feels and acts—and participates in the creation of the universe.

As the proper apparatus has enabled the eye to discover an infinite number of galaxies millions of miles away, so, with the proper understanding, humans have been enabled to communicate with Universal Mind, the source of all power.

The understanding usually developed is nothing more than a "belief," which means nothing at all. The only belief that is of any value to anyone is a belief that has been put to the test and demonstrated to be a fact; then it's no longer a belief but has become a living Truth.

The understanding put forth here has been put to the test by hundreds of thousands of people and has been found to be the Truth in exact proportion to the usefulness of the apparatus which they used. No one would expect to locate stars hundreds of millions of miles away without a sufficiently strong telescope, so science is continually engaged in building larger and more powerful telescopes, and is continually rewarded by additional knowledge of the heavenly bodies. And so it is with understanding; people are continually making progress in the methods they use to come into communication with Universal Mind and its infinite possibilities.

Universal Mind manifests itself in the objective, through the Law of Attraction, in the affinity that each atom has for every other atom in infinite degrees of intensity.

Only through this principle of combining and attracting are things brought together. This principle is universal and is the way that intention is carried into effect. Likewise, on the mental plane, like attracts like and mental vibrations respond only to the extent of their vibratory harmony.

It's clear, therefore, that thoughts of abundance will respond only to similar thoughts; the wealth of the individual is seen to be what he or she inherently is. Affluence within is therefore the secret of attraction for affluence without. The ability to produce is found to be the real source of wealth of the individual. This is why people who have their heart in their work are certain to meet with unbounded success. They will give and continually give; and the more they give, the more they will receive.

Thought is the energy. The Law of Attraction brings it into operation, and it eventually manifests in abundance. Universal Mind is substance in equilibrium. It is differentiated into form only by our power to think. Thought is the dynamic phase of Mind.

What do the great financiers, the entrepreneurs, the politicians, the great attorneys, the inventors, the physicians, the authors, the artists, and the musicians—what do each of these people contribute to the sum of human happiness but the power of their thought?

Power depends on consciousness of power. Unless we use it, we lose it, and unless we are conscious of it, we can't use it. The use of this power depends upon attention; the degree of our attention determines our capacity for the acquisition of knowledge, which is another name for power.

Applying the Principle

Knowledge has long been held to be the distinguishing mark of genius. The cultivation of knowledge depends on attention, and even attention can and should be practiced. The reward of attention is growing interest. Attention and interest have a reciprocal relationship: the greater the interest, the greater the attention; the greater the attention, the greater the interest, and therefore, the greater the knowledge, action, and reaction. Begin by paying attention, and before long you will have aroused interest. This interest will attract more attention, and this attention will produce more interest, and so on. This is how to cultivate the power of attention.

For your exercise in this lesson, concentrate upon your Power to create.

1. Relax as before.
2. Seek insight and perception; try to find a logical basis for the faith that lives in you.
3. Let the thought dwell on the fact that the physical being lives and moves and has its being in air, the sustainer of all organic life—that we must breathe to live.[59]

---

59 Even fish need the primary component of air—oxygen—to live; their gills separate it from the water. Only certain forms of bacteria and a few other life forms that live near heat vents at the bottom of the ocean can survive without it.

4. Then let the thought rest on the fact that the Spiritual Being also lives and moves and has its substance in a similar but subtler energy that we depend on for life. Allow yourself to experience this Energy flowing in and through your being with each breath.

As in the physical world, no life assumes form until after a seed is sown, and no higher fruit than that of the parent stock can be produced. So, in the spiritual world, no effect can be produced until the seed is sown, and the fruit will depend upon the nature of the seed. The results you achieve depend on your perception of law in the Mighty Domain of Causation, the highest evolution of human consciousness.

There is no thought in my mind but it quickly tends to convert itself into a power and organizes a huge instrumentality of means.

—Ralph Waldo Emerson

Summary

- Individual lives are measured by the degree of Intelligence they manifest.
- The law by which the individual may control other forms of intelligence is recognition of the self as an individualization of the Universal Intelligence.
- Creative power originates in the Universal.
- The Universal creates form by means of the individual.
- The connecting link between the individual and the Universal is thought.

- The principle by which the means of existence is carried into effect is the Law of Love, which is brought into expression by the Law of Growth.
- The Law of Growth depends on reciprocal action. The individual is complete at all times, and this makes it possible to receive only as we give.
- We give and receive thought through Mind, which is Universal Substance in equilibrium and which is constantly being differentiated in form by what we think.

LESSON NINETEEN

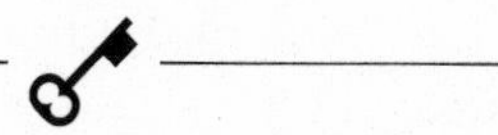

Matter Is Changing

FEAR IS a powerful form of thought. It paralyzes the nerve centers and muscular system, and redirects the circulation of the blood, so that fear affects the entire being—body, brain, and nerve.

Of course the way to overcome fear is to become conscious of power. But what is this mysterious vital force we call power? We don't know, but then, neither do we know what electricity is. All we do know is that by conforming to the requirements of the law by which electricity is governed, it will be our obedient servant; it will light our homes and our cities, run our machinery, and serve us in many useful capacities.

It's the same with the Vital Force. Although we don't know what it is, and possibly may never truly know, we do know that it is a primary energy manifesting through living bodies and that, by complying with the laws and principles by which it is governed, we can open ourselves to a more abundant inflow of its energy and thus express the highest possible degree of mental, moral, and spiritual effectiveness.

This lesson tells of a very simple way to develop this Vital Force. If you put the information into practice, you'll soon develop the sense of power that has always been the distinguishing mark of genius.

Ultimate Cause

The search for Truth is no longer a haphazard venture but a systematic process, logical in its operation.

In seeking Truth we are seeking Ultimate Cause. We know that every human experience is an effect, so if we may ascertain the cause, and find that this cause is one we can consciously control, the effect—the experience—will be within our control also.

Human experience will then no longer be at the mercy of fate; we will not be children of fortune but of destiny. Fate and fortune will be controlled as readily as a captain controls his ship or an engineer his train. All things are finally resolvable into the same element and so are translatable, one into the other, always in relation and never in opposition to one another.

In the physical world there are innumerable distinctions between all these things. There are sizes, colors, shades, or ends to all things. There's a North Pole and a South Pole, an inside and an outside, a seen and an unseen, but these names merely place extremes in contrast. The two extremes are, not separate entities, but are two parts or aspects of the Whole.

In the mental world we find the same law. We speak of knowledge and ignorance, but ignorance is just a lack of knowledge and is therefore found to be simply a way to describe the absence of knowledge; it has no principle in itself.

In the world of morals we again find the same law; we speak of good and evil, but good is a reality, something tangible, while evil is found to be simply a negative condition, the absence of good. Evil is sometimes thought to be a very real condition, but it has no principle, no vitality, no life; we know this because it can always be destroyed by good; just as light destroys darkness and Truth destroys error, so evil vanishes when good appears. There is, therefore, but one principle in the moral world.

We find exactly the same law existing in the spiritual world; we speak of Mind and matter as two separate entities, but clearer insight makes it evident that there is but one operative principle, and that is Mind. Matter is forever changing. Mind is the real and the eternal; we know that, in the eons of time, a hundred years is actually like a day.

Matter and Energy

If we stand in any large city and look at the many magnificent buildings with all their conveniences of modern civilization, we may remember that not one of them was there just over a century ago. And if we could stand on the same spot a hundred years from now, in all probability we would find that few of them remain. In the animal kingdom, we find the same Law of Change. Millions and millions of animals come and go, with life spans of a few years. In most of the plant world, the change is still more rapid: many plants and nearly all grasses come and go in a single year. When we consider the inorganic, we expect to find something more substantial, but as we gaze on the apparently solid continent, we are told that it floats on a sea of magma; we see the giant mountain and are told that the place where it now stands was once a lake; and as we stand in awe before the great cliffs in the Yosemite Valley, we can easily trace the path of the glaciers that carved them.

We are in the presence of continual change, and we know that this change is the evolution of Universal Mind, the grand process through which all things are continually being created. So we come to know that matter is just a form that Mind takes and is therefore simply a condition of Mind. Matter, therefore, has no principle; Mind is the only principle.

We have come to know that Mind is the only principle operating in the physical, mental, moral, and spiritual world. We also know that this Mind is static, at rest, and that our ability to think is our ability to act upon Universal Mind to convert it into dynamic mind, or mind in motion.

But human beings cannot think without the fuel that comes from having eaten, and so we find that even a spiritual activity such as thinking cannot be converted into sources of pleasure and profit except by making use of material means. It requires energy of some kind to collect electricity and convert it into a dynamic power; it requires the rays of the sun to give the necessary energy to sustain plant life; it also requires energy to enable the individual to think and thereby act upon Universal Mind.

Whether or not you know that thought is constantly and eternally taking form, forever seeking expression, the fact remains that if your thought is powerful, constructive, and positive, it will be plainly evident in the admirable state of your health, your business, and your environment. If your thought is weak, critical, destructive, and negative, it will manifest in your body as fear, worry, and nervousness, in your finances as lack and limitation, and in your environment as discord.

All things represent certain forms and degrees of power. A knowledge of cause and effect as shown by the laws governing steam, electricity, chemistry, and gravity enables people to plan courageously and to execute fearlessly.

These laws are called natural laws because they govern the physical world, but all power is not physical power; there is also mental power, and there is moral and spiritual power.

What are our schools, our universities, but mental powerhouses, places where Mental Power is being developed? As there are many mighty powerhouses supplying power to machinery in huge factories, where raw material is collected and converted into the necessities and comforts of life, so mental powerhouses collect raw material and develop it into a power which is infinitely superior to all the forces of Nature.

What is this raw material being collected in these thousands of mental powerhouses all over the world and then being developed into a power that is evidently controlling every other power? In its static form it is Mind—in its dynamic form, it is thought.

Thought power is superior because it exists on a higher level, and because it has enabled man to discover the law by which these wonderful forces of Nature can be harnessed and made to do the work of hundreds and thousands of people. It has enabled humanity to discover laws annihilating the effects of time and space, overcoming the Law of Gravity.

Thought is the Vital Force or Energy that has, over the last half-century, brought about a world that would be absolutely inconceivable to someone living only seventy-five or one hundred years ago. If such results have been achieved by organizing these mental powerhouses in seventy-five years, what may we expect in another fifty years?

The substance from which all things are created is infinite in quantity. We know that light travels at the rate of 186,000 miles per second, we know that there are stars so remote that it takes light billions of years to reach us, we know that such stars exist in all parts of the heavens. We know, too, that this light, as substance, is universally present.

How, then, does it manifest in form? Consider electricity: we connect opposite poles of zinc and copper in a battery, which creates an electric current that flows from one pole to the other.

This same process is repeated in every polarity, and if we wish to change the form of manifestation, we must change the polarity. This is the principle of causation at work.

Applying the Principle

For your exercise in this lesson:

1. Sit in your chair.
2. Concentrate; become so absorbed in the object of your thought that you are aware of nothing else, and *do this a few minutes every day*. You take the necessary time to eat in order that the body may be nourished; why not take the time to assimilate your mental food?
3. Let the thought rest on the fact that appearances are deceptive.

The earth is not flat, neither is it stationary; the sky is not a dome; the sun does not move; the stars are not small specks of light; and matter, which was once supposed to be fixed, has been found to be in a state of perpetual flux. Try to realize that the day is fast approaching—its dawn is now at hand—when our current understandings and modes of thought and action must be adjusted to our rapidly increasing knowledge of the operation of Eternal Principle.

Silent thought is, after all, the mightiest agent in human affairs.

—William Ellery Channing

Summary

- Extremes are designated by distinctive names, such as inside and outside, top and bottom, light and dark, good and bad, but they're not separate entities; they are parts or aspects of one Whole.
- The one creative principle in the physical, mental, and spiritual world is Universal Mind, the Eternal Energy, from which all things proceed.
- We are related to this creative principle by our ability to think: Thought is the seed, which results in action, and action results in form.
- Form depends on the rate of vibration in substance; the rate of vibration may be changed by mental action, which, in turn, depends on polarity, the action and reaction between the individual and the Universal.
- Creative energy originates in the Universal, but the Universal can manifest only through the individual because the Universal is static and requires energy to start it in motion.

LESSON TWENTY

Balance in the Universe

FOR MANY years there has been ongoing discussion as to the origin of evil. Theologians have told us that God is Love and that God is Omnipresent. If this is true, there is no place where God is not. Where, then, is evil, Satan, or Hell?

Let's trace the reasoning:

- God is Spirit.
- Spirit is the Creative Principle of the universe, creating all form.
- Men and women are created in the image and likeness of God, with dominion over other life forms.
- Men and women are, therefore, spiritual beings.
- Spirit's only activity is to think.

- Thinking is therefore a creative process.
- All form is therefore the result of the thinking process.
- The destruction of form must also be a result of the thinking process.
- Fictitious representations of form are the result of the creative power of thought, which we experience in hypnotism.
- Apparent representations of form are the result of the creative power of thought, which we experience in spiritualism.
- Invention, organization, and constructive work of all kinds are the result of the creative power of thought, which we experience in applying the Master Key.
- When the creative power of thought is manifested for the benefit of humanity, we call the result good.
- When the creative power of thought is manifested in a destructive manner, we call the result evil.
- So good and evil are simply words coined to indicate the nature of the result of the creative process.

Thought necessarily precedes and predetermines action; action precedes and predetermines condition; conditions are the result or effect of thought, which is, by definition, a spiritual activity. Lesson twenty will throw more light on this important subject.

Activating the Spirit Within

The spirit of a thing is that thing; it is by definition fixed, changeless, and eternal. The spirit of you is your life, your individuality, the basis for your manifest form; it is—you. Without the spirit you would be nothing.

Spirit becomes active through your recognition of it and its possibilities. You may have all the wealth on the planet, but unless you recognize it and make use of it, it has no value. It's the same with your spiritual wealth: unless you recognize it and use it, it will have no value. The one and only condition of spiritual power is use, or recognition.

You're dealing with the magical power of thought and consciousness all the time. What results can you expect so long as you remain oblivious to the power in your control?

So long as you don't see it, you limit yourself to superficial conditions and make yourself a pack horse for those who *do* recognize their power—those who know that, unless we are willing to think, we shall have to work; that the less we think the more we have to work, and the less we get for our work.

It's important to remember that this principle is unchangeable, as all principles are changeless; if this were not so, it wouldn't be reliable. This stability of Mind is your opportunity: you are its active attribute, the channel for its activity. The Universal can only act through the individual.

When you begin to perceive that the Essence of the Universal is within yourself—*is you*—you begin to feel your power. It's the fuel that fires the imagination, lights the torch of inspiration, energizes thought, and enables you to connect with all the invisible forces of the universe. This is the power that enables you to plan fearlessly and execute masterfully.

Perfect power relies on a perfect understanding of the principles, forces, methods, and combinations at work in our minds, with a perfect understanding of our relationship to Universal Mind.

But understanding will come only in the Silence: the condition required for all great purposes. Imagination is the workshop in which your ideal is to be visualized.

So, because a perfect understanding of the nature of this power is the first condition for its manifestation, visualize the entire process of creation over and over again to make it available for your use whenever an occasion requires it—only then may we have the inspiration of the omnipotent Universal Mind on demand at any time.

We can fail to recognize this world within, but it will still be the basic fact of all existence; and when we learn to recognize it, not only in ourselves but in all people, events, things, and circumstances, we shall have found the "Kingdom of Heaven" which we are told is within us.[60]

Our distress is a result of the operation of exactly the same principle; the principle is unchangeable, its operation is exact; there is no deviation. If we think lack, limitation, or discord, we shall find their fruits on every hand; if we think poverty, unhappiness, or disease, the thought messengers will carry the summons as readily as any other kind of thought, and the result will be just as certain. If we fear a coming calamity, we shall be able to say with Job, "the thing I feared has come upon me."[61] If we think unkindly or ignorantly, we shall attract to ourselves the results of our ignorance. This power of thought, if understood and correctly used, is the greatest labor-saving device ever dreamed of; but if not understood or improperly used, the result will most likely be disastrous.

You may use thought constructively or destructively, but the Immutable Law will not allow you to plant a thought of one kind and reap the fruit of another. You are free to use this marvelous creative power as you will, but you must understand and accept the consequences.

This is the danger of what is called "will power." There are those who seem to think that by force of will or action they can coerce this law; that they can sow seed of one kind and use will power make it bear fruit of another. But the fundamental principle of creative power is in the Universal, so forcing things to happen the way we want by the power of the individual is eventually doomed to fail.

---

60 Luke 17:21.

61 Job 3:25.

It antagonizes the very power that it seeks to use because the individual is attempting to coerce the Universal, putting the finite in conflict with the Infinite—a conflict that must inevitably be lost.

Inspiration—The Breath of Life

Our permanent well-being will be best developed by our conscious cooperation with the continuous forward movement of the Great Whole. With the help of this unlimited power we can confidently undertake things that seem impossible, because this power is the secret of all inspiration, all genius.

To become inspired means to get off the beaten path and out of the rut because extraordinary results require extraordinary means. Inspiration implies power; to understand and apply the method of inspiration is to become superhuman.

Remember, thought is creative vibration, and the quality of the conditions created will depend totally on the quality of our thought; we can't express powers we don't possess. We must "be" before we can "do," and we can "do" only to the extent to which we "are"; and what we "are" depends on what we "think" and "feel." To do more, then, we must *become* more.

Inspiration is the art of self-realization. It's the art of adjusting the individual mind to that of Universal Mind—the art of harnessing all power; the art of bringing the formless into form. Inspiration is the art of becoming a channel for the flow of Infinite Wisdom, the art of visualizing perfection, the art of realizing the omnipresence of Omnipotence.

Understanding and appreciating the fact that Infinite Power is omnipresent—that it is in the infinitely small as well as the infinitely large—enables us to absorb its essence. The further understanding that this power is spirit and therefore indivisible, enables us to appreciate its presence at all points at the same time. Thus, when we recognize the unity of all things and *feel* that the source of all power is within, we tap the Source of Inspiration. Our understanding of these facts, at first intellectually and then emotionally, enables us to drink deeply from this well of Infinite Power. An intellectual understanding is not enough in itself; the emotions must be brought into action—thought without feeling is ineffective. Both are required.

Inspiration is from within; the Silence is necessary to experience it. The senses must be stilled, the muscles relaxed, repose cultivated. When you have come into a sense of poise and power you will be ready to receive whatever inspiration or wisdom may be necessary for the development of your purpose.

Do not confuse these methods with those of a medium; they have nothing in common. Your business in life is to understand and command these invisible forces instead of letting them command or rule you.

We can live more abundantly every time we breathe if we consciously breathe with that intention. The *if* is a very important condition, as our intention controls our attention, and without attention you can achieve only the results everyone else achieves—a supply equal to the demand. In order to secure a larger supply your demand must be increased, and as you consciously increase the demand the supply will follow—you'll find yourself coming into a larger and larger supply of life, energy, and vitality.

The reason for this isn't hard to understand, but it's another of those vital mysteries of life that aren't generally appreciated. If you make it your own, you'll find it one of the wonderful realities of life.

We are told that "In Him we live and move and have our being,"[62] and we are told that what is called "Him" is Spirit and

62 Acts 17:28.

Love, so that every time we breathe, we breathe in this Life, Love, and Spirit. This is also called Prana, Pranic Energy, or Chi, and we could not exist a moment without it. It is the Cosmic Energy; it is the life of the solar plexus.

This "breath of life" is the essence of the "I am." It is pure "Being" or Universal Substance, and our conscious unity with it enables us to localize it and thus exercise the powers of this creative energy. Every time we breathe, we fill our lungs with air and at the same time revitalize our body with this Prana, which is Life itself. So, every time we breathe, we have the opportunity of making a conscious connection with all life, all intelligence, and all substance. If you're aware of your relationship and oneness with this principle that governs the universe, and if you understand the simple method that brings you to consciously identify yourself with it, you may free yourself from disease and from lack or limitation of any kind. In fact, it enables you to breathe the "breath of life."

Applying the Principle

For your exercise in this lesson:

1. Go into the Silence and concentrate on the fact that the statement, "In Him we live and move and have our being" is literally and scientifically exact: you *are* because that Spirit we call "Him" *is* in all things. And if spirit is Omnipresent Spirit it must be in you. Spirit is all in all.
2. Recognize that "He" is the totality of Spirit and you are made in "His image and likeness." The only difference between that spirit and your spirit is one of degree—a part must be the same in kind and quality as the Whole.

When you can realize this clearly you will have found the secret of the creative power of thought; you will have found the origin of both good and evil; you will have found the secret of the wonderful power of concentration; you will have found the key to the solution of every problem—whether physical, financial, or environmental.

> *The power to think, consecutively and deeply and clearly, is an avowed and deadly enemy to mistakes and blunders, superstitions, unscientific theories, irrational beliefs, unbridled enthusiasm, fanaticism.*
>
> —Frank Channing Haddock

Summary

- Power is conditional upon recognition and use.
- Recognition is awareness.
- The true business of life is scientific thinking. It enables us to adjust our thought processes to the will of Universal Mind, which is the basic fact of all existence. In other words, it's to cooperate with Natural Law.
- We align our thoughts with the will of Universal Mind by developing a perfect understanding of the principles, forces, methods, and combinations of Mind.
- Inspiration is the art of realizing the omnipresence of Omniscience.
- Our experience depends upon the quality of our thought because what we do depends on what we are, and what we are depends on what we think.
- All lack, limitation, disease, and discord is due to the operation of the same Immutable Law; the Law operates relentlessly and is continually bringing about conditions that will match the thought that originated or created them.

LESSON TWENTY-ONE

Prepare for Success

In this lesson, you will find that one of the secrets of success, one of the methods of organizing victory, as well as one of the accomplishments of the Master Mind is to think big thoughts. You will also find that everything we hold in our conscious mind for any length of time becomes impressed upon our unconscious mind and so becomes a pattern that the creative Eternal Energy will weave into our life and environment. This is the secret of the wonderful power of Prayer.

Prayer

We know that the universe is governed by Creative Law, that for every effect there must be a cause, and that the same cause, under the same conditions, will invariably produce the same effect. Consequently, if Prayer has ever been answered, it will always be answered if the proper conditions are complied with.

This must be true, otherwise the universe would be a chaos instead of a cosmos. The answer to Prayer must be subject to Law, and the Creative Law is definite, exact, and scientific, just like the laws governing gravity and electricity. An understanding of this law takes the foundation of religion out of the realm of superstition and credulity and places it upon the firm rock of scientific understanding.

But, unfortunately, comparatively few people know how to pray.

Most people understand that there are laws governing electricity, mathematics, and chemistry, but for some inexplicable reason, it never seems to occur to them that there are spiritual laws which are also definite, scientific, and exact, and operate with Immutable Precision.

The real secret of power is awareness of power. Universal Mind is unconditional; therefore, the more aware we become of our unity with Mind, the less aware we shall become of conditions and limitations. And as we become emancipated or freed from conditions, we come into a realization of the unconditional Universal. We become free!

As soon as we become aware of the inexhaustible power in the world within, we begin to draw on this power, and develop and apply the greater possibilities that this awareness has opened. This happens because *whatever we become aware of in our conscious mind is invariably manifested in the objective world.*

This is because the Infinite Mind, which is the source from which all things proceed, is one and indivisible, and each individual is a channel through which this Eternal Energy is being manifested. *Our ability to think is our ability to act upon this Universal Substance, and what we think is what is created in the objective world.*

The result of this discovery is nothing less than marvelous; it means that Mind is extraordinary in quality, limitless in quantity, and contains possibilities without number. To become conscious of this power is to become a "live wire," just like placing an ordinary wire in contact with a wire that is charged. Universal Mind is the live wire; it carries power sufficient to meet every situation that may arise in the life of every individual. *When the individual mind touches the Universal, it receives all the power it requires*; this is the world within. All power is contingent upon our recognition of this world, and the more fully aware we become of our unity with the Source, the greater our power will be to control and master every condition.

Large ideas have a tendency to eliminate all smaller ideas, so *it's a good practice to hold ideas large enough to counteract and destroy any small or undesirable tendencies*. This will remove any petty and annoying obstacles from your path. You also become aware of a larger world of thought, thereby increasing your mental capacity, as well as placing yourself in a position to accomplish something of greater value.

This is one of the secrets of success and one of the accomplishments of the Master Mind. The Universal Mind, or Master Mind, thinks big thoughts. The creative energies of Mind find no more difficulty in handling large situations than small ones. Mind is just as much present in the infinitely large as in the infinitesimally small.

When we realize these facts concerning Mind, we understand how we may bring to our lives any condition by creating the corresponding conditions in our consciousness. We find that *our lives are simply the reflection of our predominant thoughts, our mental attitudes.*

Our predominant thought or mental attitude is a magnet, and the Law of Attraction is that "like attracts like;" consequently the mental attitude will invariably attract such conditions as correspond to its Nature. This mental attitude forms our personality and is composed of the thoughts in our own mind; so *if we wish to change our conditions, we simply need to change our thought.* This will in turn change our mental attitude, which will change our personality, which will then change the persons, things, and conditions or experiences we meet in life. Thus, through the Law of Attraction, we meet in the world without conditions that correspond to our world within.

Every thought creates an impression on the brain, and these impressions create mental tendencies, which create character, ability, and purpose. The combined action of character, ability, and purpose becomes our mental attitude, which, in turn, determines the experiences we meet in life.

It's not easy to change our mental attitude, but by persistent effort it may be accomplished. Our mental attitude is patterned after the mental images photographed in the brain. If you don't like the pictures, destroy the negatives and create new ones; impress on the mind a perfect picture of the desire you wish to experience and continue to hold the picture in your mind until your results are obtained. This is the art of visualization.

If the desire requires determination, ability, talent, courage, power, or any other spiritual faculty, these are necessary components for your picture. Build them in; they are the feeling that combines with thought and creates the irresistible magnetic power to draw the things you require to you. They give your picture life, and life means growth. As soon as it beings to grow, the result is practically assured.

Don't hesitate to aspire to the highest possible attainments in anything you may undertake, for the powers of Mind are always ready to assist a purposeful will seeking to crystallize its highest aspirations into acts, accomplishments, and events.

The formation of a habit illustrates how these forces operate. We do something, then we do it again and again and again until it becomes easy and perhaps almost automatic. The same rule applies to breaking any and all bad habits; we stop doing a thing, and then avoid it again and again until we are entirely free from it. And if we do fail now and then, we should by no means lose hope, for the Law is absolute and invincible and counts every effort and every success, even though our efforts and successes may be intermittent.

There's no limit to what this Creative Law can do for you! Dare to believe in your own idea! Remember that Nature is plastic to the ideal; *think of the ideal as an already accomplished fact.*

The real battle of life is one of ideas; it's being fought by the few against the many. On the one side is the constructive and creative thought, on the other side the destructive and passive thought. The creative thought is dominated by an ideal; the passive thought is dominated by appearances. Both sides are supported by science, literature, and expediency.

On the creative side are people who spend their time in front of computers or over microscopes and telescopes, side by side with those who lead the commercial, political, and scientific world. On the negative side are scholars who spend their time investigating law and precedent, preachers who mistake theology for religion, politicians who mistake might for right, and all the millions who seem to prefer precedent to progress—who are eternally looking backward instead of forward, who see only the world without and know nothing of the world within.[63]

In the last analysis, everyone will have to take their place on one side or the other; they will have to go forward or go back. There is no standing still in a world where all is motion; it's the attempt to stand still that gives sanction and force to the arbitrary and unequal codes of law.

That we are in a period of transition is evident in the unrest apparent everywhere. The dawn of a new era necessarily declares that the existing order of things cannot remain much longer.

63 This could easily be a description of the situation Jesus faced: the Pharisees and the Temple focused on precedent, while he offered understanding of creative processes of Mind in the world within.

The issue between the old regime and the new, the crux of the problem, is a question in the minds of the people as to the nature of the universe. As long as the people regard the Cosmic Power as nonhuman and alien to humanity, it will be comparatively easy for a supposedly privileged class to rule by divine right, in spite of every protest of social sentiment. When the people realize that the transcendent force of Spirit, or Mind, of the Cosmos, is within each individual, it will be possible to frame laws that consider the liberties and rights of the many instead of the privileges of the few.

The real interest of democracy is therefore to exalt, emancipate, and recognize the divinity of the human spirit—to recognize that all power is from within and that no human being has any more power than any other human being, except such as some may willingly delegate to another.

The Divine Mind is Universal Mind; it makes no exceptions, it plays no favorites; it does not act through sheer caprice or from anger, jealousy, or wrath; neither can it be flattered, cajoled, or moved by sympathy or petition to supply anyone with some need that he or she thinks is necessary for happiness—or even existence.

The Divine Mind makes no exceptions to favor any individual. Whoever understands and realizes humanity's unity with the Universal Principle will appear to be favored because that person will have found the source of all health, all wealth, and all power.

Applying the Principle

For your exercise in this lesson:

1. Concentrate on the Truth.
2. Try to realize that the Truth shall make you free; that is, nothing can permanently stand in the way of your perfect

success when you learn to apply the scientifically correct thought methods and principles.

3. Realize that you are externalizing in your environment your inherent soul potencies.
4, Realize that the Silence offers an ever-available and almost unlimited opportunity for awakening the highest conception of Truth.

Try to comprehend that Omnipotence itself is Absolute Silence; all else is change, activity, limitation. Silent concentration is therefore the true method of reaching, awakening, and then expressing the wonderful potential power of the world within.

The possibilities of thought training are infinite, its consequence eternal, and yet few take the pains to direct their thinking into channels that will do them good, but instead leave all to chance.

—ORISON SWETT MARDEN

Summary

- The real secret of power is consciousness of power because whatever we become consciously aware of is invariably manifested in the objective world and is brought forth into tangible expression.
- The source of this power is Universal Mind, from which all things proceed, and which is One and indivisible.
- This power is manifested through the individual; each individual is a channel through which this energy is being differentiated into form.

- Our ability to think is our ability to act on this Universal Energy, and what we think is what is produced or created in the objective world.
- This discovery opens unprecedented and limitless opportunity.
- We may eliminate imperfect conditions by becoming conscious of our unity with the source of all power.
- The Master Mind thinks big thoughts, holding ideas large enough to counteract and destroy all petty and annoying obstacles.
- Experiences come to us through the Law of Attraction, formed from the substance of the universe based on our predominant mental attitude.
- The issue between the old regime and the new thinking is a question of the nature of the universe: the old regime regards the Cosmic Power as nonhuman and alien to humanity, justifying privilege for a few; the new recognizes the divinity of the individual, and seeks the true democracy of humanity, with equal justice for all.

LESSON TWENTY-TWO

Planting the Seeds

In lesson twenty-two, you will find that thoughts are spiritual seeds which, when planted in the unconscious mind, have a tendency to sprout and grow, but unfortunately their fruit is often not to our liking. The primary manifestation of life and how you may get in touch with it is explained in this lesson.

Health and Disease

As food, water, and air are the only things needed for the construction of cells, it would seem that the problem of prolonging life indefinitely would not be a very difficult one. Yet many people are overwhelmed by physical discomfort and illness.

To understand this, we need to understand that life processes are carried on by two distinct methods: first, taking up and making use of nutritive material necessary for constructing cells; second, breaking down and excreting the waste material and toxic substances. All life is based on these constructive and destructive activities.

The second, or destructive, activity is, with rare exception, the cause of disease and aging: waste material and toxins accumulate, blocking vessels and saturating tissues. These in turn lead to symptoms of inflammation, dislocation, weakening of joints and tissues, and sometimes deterioration of bone and other tissue. These symptoms may be localized, or they may affect the whole system.

The problem, then, in the healing of disease is to increase the inflow and distribution of vital energy throughout the system. And, as we have discovered in earlier lessons, this can only be done by eliminating thoughts of fear, worry, care, anxiety, jealousy, hatred, and every other destructive thought, as these manifest in the body in ways that tend to tear down and destroy the nerves and glands that control the excretion and elimination of poisonous waste matter, blocking the flow of energy.

However carefully grown and prepared, nourishing foods and supplements cannot bestow life because these, being material objects, are manifestations and so are inferior to life.

But when we realize that our present character, our present environment, our present ability, and our present physical condition are all the result of past methods of thinking, we begin to have some conception of the healing process.

If the state of our health is not all that could be desired, let's first examine our thinking. Remember that every thought produces an impression on the mind; every impression is a seed that sinks into the unconscious and forms a tendency; the tendency will be to attract other similar thoughts, and these will manifest in conditions.

If these thoughts contain germs of disease, the harvest will be sickness, decay, weakness, and failure. So the questions to ask are always, “What are we thinking?” “What are we creating?” “What is the result?”

If there’s any physical condition to change, visualization will be effective. Make a mental image of physical perfection and hold it in the mind until it is absorbed by the consciousness. Many have eliminated chronic ailments in a few weeks by this method, and thousands have overcome and destroyed all manner of ordinary physical disturbances by this method in a few days—sometimes in a few minutes.

The mind exercises this control over the body through the Law of Vibration. We know that every mental action is a vibration, and we know that all form is simply a mode of motion, a rate of vibration. Change the rate of vibration and you change the nature, quality, and form. Therefore, a change in a given vibration immediately modifies every atom in the body; every living cell is affected, and a biochemical change is made in every group of cells.

We can change the vibration and so produce any condition we desire to manifest in our bodies; we are all using this power every minute. The trouble is that most of us are using it unconsciously and are thus producing undesirable results.

The challenge is to use it intelligently to produce only desirable results. This shouldn’t be difficult because we all know what produces pleasant vibrations in the body and what produces unpleasant, disagreeable sensations.

All we need to do is consult our own experience. When our thought has been uplifted, progressive, constructive, courageous, noble, kind, or in any other way desirable, we have set in motion vibrations that brought about certain results. When our thought has been filled with envy, hatred, jealousy, criticism, or any of the other thousands of forms of discord, vibrations were set in motion that brought about results of a different nature.

Each of these rates of vibration, if kept up, crystallize in form. In the first case, the result would be mental, moral, and physical health, and in the second case, discord, disharmony, and disease.

How does this work? The objective mind has certain effects on the body that are readily recognized. Someone says something that strikes you as ludicrous and you laugh, possibly until your whole body shakes, which shows that thought has control over the muscles of your body. Maybe someone says something that excites your sympathy and your eyes fill with tears, which shows that thought controls the glands of your body. Or someone says something that triggers your anger and the blood mounts to your cheeks, which shows that thought controls the circulation of your blood. But as these experiences are all the results of the action of your objective mind over the body, the results are of a temporary nature; they soon pass, and leave the situation as it was before.[64]

Now, see how the action of the unconscious, subjective mind over the body differs. You receive a wound and thousands of cells begin the work of healing at once; in a few days or a few weeks the work is complete. You may even break a bone, but no surgeon on earth can weld the tissue together; surgeons can only set the bone in place for you. The subjective mind will immediately begin the process of welding the parts together, and in a short time the bone is as solid as it ever was. You may swallow poison; the subjective mind will immediately discover the danger and make violent efforts to eliminate it. You may become infected; the subjective will at once commence

64 These processes are the result of increases in "messenger" chemicals called neuropeptides, which microbiologist Candace Pert calls "molecules of emotion" in her book by that title. Very effective explanations and illustrations of their operation may be found in the film, *What the Bleep Do We Know?*

to build a wall around the infected area and destroy the infection by absorbing it in the white blood cells that it supplies for the purpose.

These processes of the subjective mind usually proceed without our personal knowledge or direction, and as long as we don't interfere, the result is perfect. But these millions of repair cells are intelligent and respond to our thought. So they are often paralyzed and rendered impotent by our thoughts of fear, doubt, and anxiety. Under these conditions, they're like an army of workers, ready to start an important piece of work, but every time they get started, a strike is called or plans are changed until they finally get discouraged and give up.

Healing

The way to health is founded on the Law of Vibration, and this law is brought into operation by the mind in the world within. Our world of power is within, and if we are wise, we won't waste time and effort trying to deal with effects as we find them in the world without, which is only an external reflection. Instead, we will always find the cause in the world within; by changing the cause, we change the effect.

Every cell in your body is intelligent and will respond to your direction. The cells are all creators and will create the exact pattern that you give them. Therefore, when perfect images are placed before the subjective mind, the creative energies in the cells will build a perfect body.

This means that, if we wish the body to manifest health, strength, and vitality, these must be our predominant thoughts. We now know how to make any physical change in the body we desire, because we know that practically no limit can be placed on our ability to bring ourselves into harmony with Natural Law, which is omnipotent.

Mind's influence and control over the body is coming to be more and more generally understood, and many physicians are now giving the matter their earnest attention. However, Dr. Albert T. Shofield, who wrote several earlier books on the subject, points out the mainstream medical field's lack of attention to this when he says:

> The subject of mental therapeutics is still ignored in medical works generally. In our physiologies no references [are] made to the central controlling power that rules the body for its good, and the power of the mind over the body is seldom spoken of.[65]

No doubt many physicians treat diseases that originate in mental processes wisely and well. What I contend is that the knowledge they display was neither taught at school nor learned from a book but is intuitive and empirical, and this is not as it should be. The power of "mental therapeutics," or "healing with the mind" would ideally be taught in every medical school and in-patient education programs as well.

There can be no doubt that few patients are aware of how much they can do for themselves. What the patient can do for himself—the forces he can set in motion—are as yet unknown. It is likely that they're far greater than most imagine and will undoubtedly be used more and more. For now, mental healing processes may be directed by the patient: calming the mind in excitement; arousing feelings of joy, hope, faith, and

65 "Mental therapeutics, as Shofield uses the term, means the use of the mind to establish and maintain a healthy body. "Mind healing" or "faith healing" were popular across much of the United States during the late nineteenth century and are still used in Christian Science, Pentecostal, and New Thought churches. They were based on essentially the same methods described here.

Love; motivating for exercise; and diverting the thoughts from the ailment.[66]

Applying the Principle

For your exercise in this lesson:

1. Concentrate on Tennyson's beautiful lines "Speak to Him, thou, for He hears, and spirit with spirit can meet, Closer is He than breathing, and nearer than hands and feet."
2. Try to realize and feel that when you do "Speak to Him," you are in touch with Omnipotence. This realization and recognition of Omnipresent Power will quickly destroy any and every form of sickness or suffering, replacing it with harmony and perfection.
3. Then remember that there are those who seem to think that sickness and suffering are sent by God. Follow this thought to its logical end; understand that, if so, every physician, every surgeon, and every nurse is defying the will of God, and hospitals and mental health institutions are places of rebellion instead of houses of mercy. Of course, this quickly reasons itself into an absurdity, but there are many who still cherish the idea.
4. Consider the fact that, until recently, theologians have been trying to teach about an impossible Creator—one who created beings capable of sinning and then allowed them to be eternally punished for such sins. Follow this thought and see

66 Herbert Benson and Joan Borysenko at Harvard Medical Center and Jon Kabat-Zinn at the University of Massachusetts Medical Center have directed extensive studies on the use of relaxation and visualization in reducing symptoms. Also, the biofeedback research pioneered by Elmer and Alyce Green offers many useful insights and methods. These and similar studies are outlined in *Calm Healing: Methods for a New Era in Medicine*, by Robert Bruce Newman and Ruth L. Miller.

that the necessary outcome of such extraordinary ignorance was to create fear and obedience instead of love.

5. Now realize that this is ancient propaganda, and that some theologians are redefining their belief systems, appreciating the ideal person, made in the image and likeness of God—creative, blessed by the indwelling presence of the Holy Spirit.[67]

As you do so, you will more readily appreciate the all-originating Mind that forms, upholds, sustains, originates, and creates all there is.

All are but parts of one stupendous whole, whose body Nature is and God the soul.

—Charles F. Haanel

Summary

- Sickness may be eliminated by placing ourselves in harmony with Omnipotent Natural Law.
- We do this through the realization that humans are spiritual beings and that this spirit must necessarily be perfect.
- A conscious recognition of this perfection—first intellectually, then emotionally—brings about a manifestation of this perfection.
- This occurs because thought is spiritual and therefore

67 The work of Emma Curtis Hopkins and Thomas Troward in the nineteenth century, of Charles Fillmore, Emmet Fox, and Ernest Holmes in the mid-twentieth century, and of Matthew Fox and Neale Donald Walsch in the late twentieth century, along with more esoteric writings such as *Conversations With God* and *A Course in Miracles*, all point to this shift in theology.

creative. It links with its object and brings it into manifestation through the Law of Vibration, which states that a higher rate of vibration governs, modifies, controls, changes, or destroys a lower rate of vibration.

- There are literally millions of people in the United States who make use of this system of mental healing in one form or another (and obviously many more worldwide).
- True science and true religion are twin sisters; where one goes, the other necessarily follows.

LESSON TWENTY-THREE

Success in Service

In this lesson, you will find that money weaves itself into the entire fabric of our very existence; that the Law of Success is service; that we get what we give, and for this reason, we should consider it a great privilege to be able to give.

We have found that thought is the creative activity behind every constructive enterprise. We can, therefore, give nothing of more practical value than our thought.

Creative thought requires attention, and the power of attention is, as we have found, superhuman.

Attention develops concentration and concentration develops Spiritual Power, which is the mightiest force in existence.

This is the science embracing all sciences. It's the art, above all arts, relevant to human life. In the mastery of this science and this art, there is opportunity for unending progression. Perfection in this is not acquired in six days, six weeks, or even in six months. It is the labor of life. To not go forward is to go backward.

Desire is the attractive force that sets the current in motion, and fear is the great obstacle by which the current is stopped or reversed and turned away from us. Fear is just the opposite from money consciousness; it is poverty consciousness. And since the law is unchangeable and we get exactly what we give, if we fear, we get what we feared.

We Get What We Give

It's inevitable then, that the entertainment of positive, constructive, and unselfish thoughts would have a far-reaching effect for good. Compensation is the keynote of the universe. Nature is constantly seeking equilibrium. Where something is sent out, something must be received to fill the vacuum.

Because of this rule, you cannot fail to profit in proportion to your effort when using this method. Money consciousness is an attitude of mind, the open door to the arteries of commerce, and the receptive attitude. Money weaves itself into the entire fabric of our very existence; it engages the best thought of the best minds. We make money by making friends, and we enlarge our circle of friends by making money for them, by helping them, by being of service to them.

The law of success then is service, and this in turn is built on integrity and justice. Anyone who is not at least fair in intention is simply ignorant. Such a person has misunderstood the fundamental law of all exchange; his goal is impossible, and he will surely lose. He may not know it and he may think he is winning, but he is doomed to certain defeat. He cannot cheat the Infinite. The Law of Compensation will demand of him an eye for an eye and a tooth for a tooth.

A generous thought is filled with strength and vitality, but a selfish thought contains the germs of dissolution; it will disintegrate and pass away. Great financiers are simply channels for the distribution of wealth; enormous amounts come and go, but it would be as dangerous to stop the output as it would be to stop the income; both ends must remain open. So, our greatest success will come as we recognize that it's giving is as essential as receiving.

The forces of life are composed of our thoughts and ideals, and these in turn are molded into form. Our problem is to keep an open mind, to constantly reach out for the new, to recognize opportunity, to be interested in the race rather than the goal because the pleasure is in the pursuit rather than the possession.

You can make a money magnet of yourself, but to do so, you must first consider how you can make money for other people. If you have the necessary insight to perceive and utilize opportunities and favorable conditions, as well as recognize values, you can put yourself in position to take advantage of them. Your greatest success will come as you are able to assist others, however. What benefits one must benefit all.

When we recognize the Omnipotent Power that is the source of all supply, we adjust our consciousness to this supply in such a way that it constantly attracts all that it needs; we find that the more we give the more we get.[68]

Giving in this sense implies service. The banker gives his money, the merchant gives her goods, the author gives his thought, the worker gives her skill. All have something to give, but the more they can give the more they get, and the more they get the more they are able to give.

Successful entrepreneurs get much because they give much. They think; they're seldom the people who let someone else do

---

68 When this book was written, a loaf of bread cost a nickel. Today it costs $2 to $3. So a "half a million" then would be 40–50 times that much in today's dollars, or around $25 million.

their thinking for them. They want to know how results are to be secured; you must show them. When you can do this, they will furnish the means by which hundreds or thousands may profit, and in proportion, as those others are successful, the financier will be successful. Morgan, Rockefeller, Carnegie, Warren Buffet, and Bill and Melinda Gates did not get rich because they *lost* money for other people; on the contrary, it's because they made money for other people that they became the wealthiest people in the wealthiest country on the globe.

The average person accepts the ideas of others and repeats them in very much the same way as a parrot. This docile attitude on the part of a majority, who are perfectly willing to let a few people do all their thinking for them, is what enables a few people to usurp all the avenues of power and hold the millions in subjection in a great many countries.

Creative thinking requires attention.

The power of attention is called concentration, which is directed by the will. For this reason, we must refuse to concentrate on or think of anything except the things we desire. Many people are constantly concentrating upon sorrow, loss, and discord of every kind. But, as thought is creative, this concentration inevitably leads to more loss, more sorrow, and more discord. How could it be otherwise? On the other hand, when we meet with success, gain, or any other desirable condition, we naturally concentrate on the effects of these things and thereby create more. And so it follows that much leads to more—the rich get richer.

Spirit Works in Business

How to use our understanding of this principle in business is well expressed by an associate of mine.[69]

---

69 A personal story of Charles F. Haanel.

> Spirit, whatever else it may or may not be, must be considered as the Essence of Consciousness, the Substance of Mind, the reality underlying Thought. And as all ideas are phases of the activity of Consciousness, Mind, or Thought, it follows that in Spirit, and in it alone, is to be found the Ultimate Fact, the Real Thing, or Idea.

Having admitted this, doesn't it seem reasonable that a true understanding of Spirit and its laws of manifestation would be the most practical thing that a practical person can hope to find? Doesn't it seem certain that if the practical people of the world realized this fact, they would "fall all over themselves" getting to where they might obtain knowledge of such spiritual things and laws? These people are not fools; they need only grasp this fundamental fact to move toward the essence of all achievement.

Let me give you a concrete example. I know a man in Chicago whom I had always considered to be quite materialistic. He had made several successes in life and also several failures. The last time I talked with him he was practically "down and out." It looked as if he had reached the end of his rope, for he was well into middle age, and new ideas came slower and less frequently to him than in former years.

In essence, he said to me: "I know that all things that 'work out' in business are the result of Thought; any fool knows that. Just now, I seem to be short on thoughts and good ideas. But if this 'All-Mind' teaching is correct, it should be possible for the individual to attain a direct connection with Infinite Mind; and in Infinite Mind there must be the possibility of all kinds of good ideas that a man of my courage and experience could put to practical use in the business world and so make a big success. It looks good to me and I am going to look into it."

This was several years ago. The other day I heard of this man again. Talking to a friend, I said: "What has come of our old friend X? Has he ever gotten on his feet again?" The friend looked at me in amazement. "Why," said he, "don't you know about X's great success? He is the Big Man in the '__________ Company' (naming a concern which has made a phenomenal success during the last eighteen months and is now well known, by reason of its advertisements from one end of the country to another and also abroad). He is the man who supplied the *big idea* for that concern. Why, he's about a half-million to the good and is moving rapidly toward the million mark; all in the space of eighteen months."

I had not connected this man with the enterprise mentioned, although I knew of the wonderful success of the company in question. Further investigation has shown that the story is true and that the above stated facts are not exaggerated in the slightest.

Now, what do you think of that? To me, it means that this man actually made the "direct connection" with Infinite Mind—Spirit—and, having found it, he set it to work for him. He "used it in his business."

Does this sound unbelievable or outrageous? I hope not; I don't mean it to be so. Take away the implication of divine personality, or magnified human nature, from the concept of the the Infinite, and what you have left is the concept of an Infinite Presence of Power, the Essence of which is Consciousness—in fact, at the last, it is Spirit. As this man also, in the final analysis, must be considered a manifestation of Spirit, there is nothing sacrilegious in the idea that he, being Spirit, should so harmonize himself with his Origin and Source—that he would be able to manifest at least a minor degree of its power. All of us do this, more or less, when we use our minds in the direction of Creative Thought. This man did more; he went about it in an intensely practical manner.

I have not consulted him about his procedure, though I intend to do so at the first opportunity. I'm sure he not only drew upon the Infinite Supply for the ideas he needed (and which formed the seed of his success), he also used the Creative Power of Thought in building for himself an ideal pattern of what he hoped to manifest in material form, adding to it, changing it, improving its detail from time to time—proceeding from the general outline to the finished detail. I consider this to be the case, not only from my memory of our conversation a few years ago, but also because I have found the same thing to be true in the cases of other prominent men who have made similar manifestation of Creative Thought.

Those who may shrink from this idea of employing the Infinite Power to aid someone in his work in the material world should remember that if the Infinite objected in the least to such a procedure the thing could never happen. The Infinite is quite able of taking care of itself.

Spirituality is quite practical, very practical, *intensely* practical. It teaches that Spirit is the reality, the Whole, and that matter is but plastic stuff, which Spirit is able to create, mould, manipulate, and fashion. So spirituality is the most practical thing in the world—the only really and absolutely practical thing there is!

Applying the Principle

This week:

1. Concentrate on the fact that a human being is not a body with a spirit but a spirit with a body, and that it is for this reason that our desires are incapable of any permanent satisfaction in anything not spiritual. Money is, therefore, of no value except to bring about the conditions we desire, and these conditions are necessarily harmonious.

2. Harmonious conditions require sufficient supply, so if there appears to be any lack, we should realize that the idea or soul of money is service. As this thought takes form, channels of supply will be opened, and you will have the satisfaction of knowing that spiritual methods are entirely practical.

We have discovered that premeditated, orderly thinking for a purpose matures that purpose into fixed form, so that we may be absolutely sure of the result of our dynamic experiment.

—Francis Larimer Warner

Summary

- The Law of Success is service.
- We may be of the most service when we have an open mind and are interested in the race rather than the goal, in the pursuit rather than possession.
- A selfish thought contains the germs of its dissolution.
- Our greatest success is achieved by recognizing the fact that it's just as essential to give as to receive.
- Entrepreneurs frequently achieve great success because they do their own thinking.
- The great majority of people in every country remain the docile and apparently willing tools of the few because they let the few do all their thinking for them.
- The effect of concentrating our attention on sorrow and loss is more sorrow and more loss.
- The effect of concentrating on gain is more gain.
- This is the only principle that is ever used, or ever can be used

in business there is no other principle. The fact that it may be used unconsciously does not alter the fact.

Success is an effect, not a cause, and if we wish to secure the effect, we must ascertain the cause, idea, or thought by which the effect is created.

Nurture your mind with great thoughts; to believe in the heroic makes heroes.

—BENJAMIN DISRAELI

LESSON TWENTY-FOUR

The Master Key

IN THIS chapter, you will find lesson twenty-four, your final lesson of this course.

If you've practiced each of the exercises a few minutes every day, as suggested, you will have found that you can get out of life exactly what you wish by first putting into life that which you wish, and you will probably agree with the student who said: "The thought is almost overwhelming, so vast, so available, so definite, so reasonable, and so usable!"

The fruit of this knowledge could be called a gift of the gods; it's the Truth that makes us free—not only free from every lack and limitation but free from sorrow, worry, and care. And this Law doesn't care who you are; it makes no difference what your habit of thought may have been; the way has been prepared by others.

If you're inclined to be religious, the greatest religious teacher the world has ever known made the way so plain that all may follow. If your mental bias is toward physical science, the Law will operate with mathematical certainty. If you're inclined to be philosophical, Plato or Emerson may be your teacher, but in any case, you may reach degrees of power to which it's impossible to assign a limit.

An understanding of this principle is the secret for which the ancient alchemists vainly sought because it explains how gold in the mind may be transmuted into gold in the heart and in the hand.

When scientists first put the sun in the center of the solar system and sent the earth spinning around it, there was immense surprise and consternation. The whole idea was self-evidently false; nothing was more certain than the movement of the sun across the sky, and anyone could see that it descended behind the western hills and sank into the sea. Scholars raged and scientists rejected the idea as absurd, yet the evidence has finally carried conviction in the minds of all.

We speak of a bell as a "sounding body," yet we know that all the bell can do is produce vibrations in the air. When these vibrations come to the eardrum at the rate of sixteen cycles per second, they cause a sound to be heard in the mind. It's possible for the mind to hear vibrations up to the rate of 38,000 vibrations per second. Beyond this, all is silence again, so we know that the sound is not in the bell, it's in our own mind.

We speak and even think of the sun as "giving light." Yet we know it's simply radiating energy in the form of particles moving through space at the rate of four hundred trillion a second, causing what we call light. So the only light existing is the sensation caused by the motion of these particles against the retina of the eye.

As the frequency increases, the light changes color, each change being caused by shorter and more rapid vibrations. So although we speak of the rose as being red, the grass as being green, or the sky as being blue, we know that the colors exist only in our minds and are the sensations experienced by us as the result of the vibrations of light waves. And, when the vibrations are slowed to less than four hundred trillion a second, they no longer affect us as light but as heat.

It's clear, therefore, that we can't depend on the evidence of the senses for our information concerning the reality of things; if we did we would believe that the sun moved, that the world was flat instead of round, and that the stars were bits of light instead of vast suns.

From Theory to Practice

Metaphysics consists in knowing the Truth about yourself and the world in which you live. The whole theory and practice of any metaphysical system depends on knowing that in order to express and experience harmony, you must think harmony; in order to experience and express health you must think health; and in order to express and experience abundance you must think abundance. To do this requires that you reverse the evidence of the senses.

When you come to know that every form of disease, sickness, lack, and limitation is simply the result of wrong thinking, you will have come to know "the Truth which shall make you free." You will see how mountains may be moved. If these mountains consist only of doubt, fear, distrust, or other forms of discouragement, they are nonetheless real and need not only to be moved but to be "cast into the sea."

Your real work consists in convincing yourself of the Truth of these statements. When you have succeeded in doing so, you'll have no difficulty thinking the Truth, and as has been shown, Truth will manifest itself.

Those who heal diseases by mental methods have come to know this Truth; they demonstrate it in their lives and the lives of others daily. They know that life, health, and abundance are omnipresent, filling all space and time, and they know that those who allow disease or lack of any kind to manifest have not yet understood this great law.

As all conditions are thought creations and therefore entirely mental, disease and lack are simply mental conditions in which the person fails to perceive the Truth. *As soon as the error is removed, the condition is removed.*

The method for removing this error is to go into the Silence and know and *feel* Truth. As all mind is one Mind, you can do this for yourself or anyone else. If you've learned to form mental images of desired conditions, this will be the easiest and quickest way to achieve your result. If you haven't learned to form these images, you can achieve your results by reasoning out and convincing yourself of the Absolute Truth of your statement.

Remember, and this is one of the most difficult as well as most wonderful statements to grasp, that *no matter what the difficulty is, no matter where it is, no matter who is affected, you have no patient but yourself*; you have nothing to do but to convince yourself of the Truth of that which you desire to see manifested.

This is an exact scientific statement in accordance with every system of metaphysics in existence, and no permanent results are ever secured in any other way. Every form of concentration, forming mental images, argument, and suggestion are all simply methods by which you are enabled to realize the Truth.

If you intend to help someone, to destroy some form of lack, limitation, or error, don't think about the person you wish to help; the intention to help them is entirely sufficient, as this puts you in mental touch with the person. Then drive out of your own mind any belief of lack, limitation, disease, danger, difficulty, or whatever the trouble might be. As soon as you have succeeded in doing this, the result will have been accomplished, and that person will be free.

But remember that thought is creative, so every time you allow your thought to rest on any inharmonious condition, you must realize that such conditions are apparent only, they have no reality. Spirit is the only reality, and it can never be less than perfect.

All thought is a form of energy, a rate of vibration, but a thought of Truth is the highest rate of vibration known, and consequently, it destroys every form of error in exactly the same way that light destroys darkness. No form of error can exist when Truth appears, so your entire mental work consists in understanding the Truth. This will enable you to overcome every form of lack, limitation, or disease.

Truth is not the result of logical training or of experimentation or even of observation; it's the product of a developed consciousness. We can't get an understanding of the Truth from the world without; the world without is only relative. Truth is Absolute. We must, therefore, find it in the world within. To train the mind to see only Truth is to express and experience only real conditions, and our ability to do this is an indication of our progress.

The Absolute Truth is that the "I" is perfect and complete. The real "I" is spiritual and can therefore never be less than perfect; it can never have any lack, limitation, or disease. Genius does not originate in the molecular motion of the brain; it's inspired by the spiritual "I," which is one with Universal Mind. Our ability to recognize this unity is the cause of all inspiration, all genius. These results are far-reaching and will have their effect upon generations to come; they are the pillars of fire, marking the path that millions follow.

Truth within the mind of a ruler or leader manifests in that leader's life and actions and his or her influence upon social forms and progress. Your life, your actions, and your influence in the world will depend upon the degree of Truth which you're able to perceive, for Truth will not manifest in creeds but in conduct. Truth manifests in character, and our character is an expression of our religion, which is the body of what to us is Truth. It's also evident in the nature of our possessions.

If people complain about the drift of fortune in their life, they're as unjust to themselves as if they denied a rational and irrefutable Truth. Our environment and the innumerable circumstances and accidents of our lives already exist in our unconscious personality, which attracts to itself the mental and physical materials that resonate with its nature. So our future is being determined from our present, and if there should be apparent injustice in any aspect of our personal life, we must look within for the cause and try to discover the mental "fact" that is responsible for the outward manifestation.

This is the Truth that makes you free, and the conscious knowledge of this Truth enables you to overcome every difficulty. The conditions you meet in the world without are invariably the result of the conditions in the world within; therefore, it follows with scientific certainty that, by holding the perfect ideal in mind, you can bring about ideal conditions in your environment.

If you see only the incomplete, the imperfect, the relative, the limited, such conditions will manifest in your life; but if you train your mind to see and realize the spiritual ego, the "I" which is forever perfect and complete, then only harmonious, wholesome, and healthful conditions will be manifested.

Since thought is creative and Truth is the highest and most perfect thought that anyone can think, to think Truth is to create what is true. When Truth comes into being, the false appearance must cease to be.

Universal Mind is the totality of all mind in existence. Spirit is Mind because Spirit is Intelligence. The difficulty is to realize that Mind is not individual. It's omnipresent; it exists everywhere. In other words, there is no place where it is not. This is what we mean when we say it is Universal.

People have, up until now, generally used the word "God" to indicate this Universal, creative principle; but the word "God" does not convey the right meaning. Most people understand this word to mean some being outside of themselves, but the fact is exactly contrary to this; it is our very life. Without it, we would be dead. We would cease to exist. The minute the spirit leaves the body, we are as nothing. Therefore, Spirit is really all there is of us.

Now, Spirit's only activity is the power to think. And because Spirit is creative, thought must be creative. This Creative Power is impersonal, and your ability to think is your ability to control it and make use of it for the benefit of yourself and others.

When you have realized, understood, and appreciated the Truth of this statement, you will have come into possession of the Master Key. But remember that only those who are wise enough to understand, broad enough to weigh the evidence, firm enough to follow their own judgment, and strong enough to maintain the self-discipline may enter the door of Heaven and partake of its riches.

From now on, you'll be able to realize that this truly is a wonderful world and that you are a wonderful being. Many people are awakening to knowledge of the Truth, and as fast as they wake up and come to this knowledge, they begin to realize that "the doors of perception are cleansed, every thing [is] appear[ing] to man as it is, infinite."[70] They find that splendor exists for those who find themselves in the Promised Land. They will have crossed the river of judgment and will arrive at the point of discrimination between

70 William Blake.

the true and the false, and they will find that all they ever willed or dreamed is but a faint reflection of the dazzling reality.

Though an inheritance of acres may be bequeathed,
an inheritance of knowledge and wisdom cannot.
The wealthy man may pay others for doing his work
for him, but it is impossible to get his thinking done
for him by another or to purchase any kind of self-culture.

—SAMUEL SMILES

Summary

- The theory and practice of every system of metaphysics in existence depends on knowledge of the Truth concerning yourself and the world in which you live.
- This Truth is that the real "I," or ego, is spiritual and can therefore never be less than perfect.
- The method of destroying any form of error is to absolutely convince yourself of the Truth concerning the condition you wish to see manifested.
- The Universal Mind in which "we live and move and have our being" is one and indivisible, so it's just as possible to help others as to help ourselves.
- Universal Mind, the totality of all Mind in existence, is omnipresent; it exists everywhere. There is no place without it. It is, therefore, within us. It is the world within. It is our spirit, our life.
- Universal Mind is spiritual and consequently creative. It seeks to express itself in form.

- Our ability to think is our ability to act on the Universal Mind and bring it into manifestation for our benefit and for the benefit of others.
- Thinking is clear, decisive, calm, deliberate, sustained thought with a definite end in view.
- When you think in this way, you will also be able to say, "It is not I that doeth the works, but the 'Father' that dwelleth within me, He doeth the works." You will come to know that the "Father" is Universal Mind and that "He" does really and truly dwell within you. In other words, you will come to know that the wonderful promises made in the Bible are fact, not fiction, and can be demonstrated by anyone having sufficient understanding.

Temples have their sacred images, and we see what influence they have always had over a great part of mankind; but, in truth, the ideas and images in men's minds are the invisible powers that constantly govern them; and to these they all pay universally a ready submission.

—Jonathan Edwards

ORIGINAL TEXT

FOREWORD

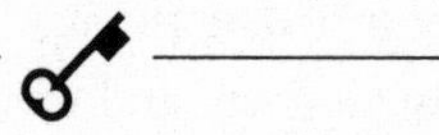

Nature compels us all to move through life. We could not remain stationary however much we wished. Every right-thinking person wants, not merely to move through life like a sound-producing, perambulating plant, but to develop—to improve—and to continue the development mentally to the close of physical life.

This development can occur only through the improvement of the quality of individual thought and the ideals, actions, and conditions that arise as a consequence. Hence a study of the creative processes of thought and how to apply them is of supreme importance to each one of us. This knowledge is the means whereby the evolution of human life on earth may be hastened and uplifted in the process.

Humanity ardently seeks the "Truth" and explores every avenue to it. In this process it has produced a special literature, which ranges the whole gamut of thought from the trivial to the sublime—up from Divination, through all the Philosophies, to the final, lofty Truth of the "Master Key."

The Master Key is here given to the world as a means of tapping the great Cosmic Intelligence and attracting from it that which corresponds to the ambitions and aspirations of each reader.

Every thing and institution we see around us, created by human agency, had first to exist as a thought in some human mind. Thought therefore is constructive. Human thought is the spiritual power of the cosmos operating through its creature, man. The Master Key instructs the reader how to use that power and use it both constructively and creatively. The things and conditions we desire to become realities we must first create in thought. The Master Key explains and guides the process.

The Master Key teaching has hitherto been published in the form of a correspondence course of twenty-four lessons, delivered to students one per week for twenty-four weeks. The reader, who now receives the whole twenty-four parts at one time, is warned not to attempt to read the book like a novel but to treat it as a course of study and conscientiously to imbibe the meaning of each part—reading and rereading one part only per week before proceeding to the next. Otherwise the later parts will tend to be misunderstood, and the reader's time and money will be wasted.

Used as thus instructed, the Master Key will make of the reader a greater, better personality, and equip him with a new power to achieve any worthy personal purpose and a new ability to enjoy life's beauty and wonder.

—F. H. Burgess

INTRODUCTION

Some men seem to attract success, power, wealth, and attainment, with very little conscious effort; others conquer with great difficulty; still others fail altogether to reach their ambitions, desires, and ideals. Why is this so? Why should some men realize their ambitions easily, others with difficulty, and still others not at all? The cause cannot be physical, else the most perfect men, physically, would be the most successful. The difference, therefore, must be mental—must be in the mind; hence Mind must be the creative force, must constitute the sole difference between men. It is Mind, therefore, which overcomes environment and every other obstacle in the path of men.

When the creative power of thought is fully understood, its effect will be seen to be marvelous. But such results cannot be secured without proper application, diligence, and concentration. The student will find that the laws governing in the mental and spiritual world are as fixed and infallible as in the material world. To secure the desired results then, it is necessary to know the law and to comply with it. A proper compliance with the law will be found to produce the desired result with invariable exactitude. The student who learns that power comes from within, that he is weak only because he has depended on help from outside, and who unhesitatingly throws himself on his own thought will instantly right himself, stand erect, assume a dominant attitude, and work miracles.

It is evident, therefore, that he who fails to fully investigate and take advantage of the wonderful progress which is being made in this last and greatest science will soon be as far behind as the man who would refuse to acknowledge and accept the benefits which have accrued to mankind through an understanding of the laws of electricity.

Of course, Mind creates negative conditions just as readily as favorable conditions, and when we consciously or unconsciously visualize every kind of lack, limitation, and discord, we create these conditions; this is what many are unconsciously doing all the time.

This law as well as every other law is no respecter of persons but is in constant operation and is relentlessly bringing to each individual exactly what he has created; in other words, "Whatsoever a man soweth that shall he also reap."

Abundance, therefore, depends upon a recognition of the laws of abundance and the fact that Mind is not only the creator but the only creator of all there is. Certainly nothing can be created before we know that it can be created and then make the proper effort. There is no more electricity in the world today than there was fifty years ago, but until someone recognized the law by which it could be made of service, we received no benefit; now that the law is understood, practically the whole world is lit by it. So it is with the Law of Abundance; it is only those who recognize the law and place themselves in harmony with it who share in its benefits.

The scientific spirit now dominates every field of effort; relations of cause and effect are no longer ignored.

The discovery of a region of law marked an epoch in human progress. It eliminated the element of uncertainty and caprice in men's lives, and it substituted law, reason, and certitude.

Men now understand that for every result there is an adequate and definite cause; when a given result is desired, they seek the condition by which alone this result may be attained.

The basis upon which all law rests was discovered by inductive reasoning, which consists of comparing a number of separate instances with one another until the common factor which gives rise to them all is seen.

It is this method of study to which the civilized nations owe the greater part of their prosperity and the more valuable part of their knowledge; it has lengthened life, mitigated pain, spanned rivers, brightened the night with the splendor of day, extended the range of vision, accelerated motion, annihilated distance, facilitated intercourse, and enabled men to descend into the sea and ascend into the sky. What wonder then that men soon endeavored to extend the blessings of this system of study to their method of thinking, so that when it became plainly evident that certain results followed a particular method of thinking, it only remained to classify these results.

This method is scientific, and it is the only method by which we shall be permitted to retain that degree of liberty and freedom which we have been accustomed to look upon as an inalienable right. People are safe at home and in the world only if national preparedness means such things as a growing surplus of health, accumulated efficiency in public and private business of whatever sort, continuous advance in the science and art of acting together, and the increasingly dominant endeavor to make all of these and all other aspects of national development center and revolve about ascending life, single and collective, for which science, art, and ethics furnish guidance and controlling motives.

The Master Key is based on absolute scientific truth and will unfold the possibilities that lie dormant in the individual and teach how they may be brought into powerful action, to increase the person's effective capacity, bringing added energy, discernment, vigor, and mental elasticity. The student who gains an understanding of the mental laws which are unfolded will come into the possession of an ability to secure results hitherto undreamed of and rewards hardly to be expressed in words.

It explains the correct use of both the receptive and active elements of the mental nature and instructs the student in the recognition of opportunity; it strengthens the will and reasoning powers and teaches the cultivation and best uses of imagination, desire, emotions, and intuitional faculty. It gives initiative, tenacity of purpose, wisdom of choice, intelligent sympathy, and thorough enjoyment of life on its higher planes.

The Master Key teaches the use of Mind Power—true Mind Power—not any of the substitutes and perversions; it has nothing to do with hypnotism, magic, or any of the more or less fascinating deceptions by which many are led to think that something can be had for nothing.

The Master Key cultivates and develops the understanding which will enable you to control the body and thereby the health. It improves and strengthens the memory. It develops insight—the kind of insight which is so rare, the kind which is the distinguishing characteristic of every successful business man, the kind which enables men to see the possibilities as well as the difficulties in every situation, the kind which enables men to discern opportunity close at hand, for thousands fail to see opportunities almost within their grasp while they are industriously working with situations which under no possibility can be made to realize any substantial return.

The Master Key develops mental power which means that others instinctively recognize that you are a person of force, of character—that they want to do what you want them to do; it means that you attract men and things to you; that you are what some people call "lucky" and "things" come your way, that you have come into an understanding of the fundamental laws of Nature and have put yourself in harmony with them; that you are in tune with the Infinite; that you understand the Law of Attraction, the natural laws of growth, and the psychological laws on which all advantages in the social and business world rest.

Mental power is creative power. It gives you the ability to create for yourself; it does not mean the ability to take something away from someone else. Nature never does things that way. Nature makes two blades of grass grow where one grew before, and Mind Power enables men to do the same thing.

The Master Key develops insight and sagacity, increased independence, the ability and disposition to be helpful. It destroys distrust, depression, fear, melancholia, and every form of lack, limitation, and weakness, including pain and disease; it awakens buried talents and supplies initiative, force, energy, and vitality; it awakens an appreciation of the beautiful in art, literature, and science.

It has changed the lives of thousands of men and women by substituting definite principles for uncertain and hazy methods—and principles for the foundation upon which every system of efficiency must rest.

Elbert Gary, the chairman of the United States Steel Corporation, said, "The services of advisors, instructors, efficiency experts in successful management are indispensable to most business enterprises of magnitude, but I deem the recognition and adoption of right principles vastly more important."

The Master Key teaches right principles and suggests methods for making a practical application of the principles; it differs from every other course of study. It teaches that the only possible value which can attach to any principle is in its application. Many read books, take home study courses, and attend lectures all their lives without ever making any progress in demonstrating the value of the principles involved. The Master Key suggests methods by which the value of the principles taught may be demonstrated and put in actual practice in the daily experience.

There is a change in the thought of the world. This change, silently transpiring in our midst, is more important than any which the world has undergone since the downfall of paganism.

The present revolution in the opinions of all classes of men, the highest and most cultured of men as well as those of the laboring class, stands unparalleled in the history of the world.

Science has of late made such vast discoveries, revealed such an infinity of resources, and unveiled such enormous possibilities and such unsuspected forces that scientific men more and more hesitate to affirm certain theories as established and indubitable or to deny certain other theories as absurd or impossible, and so a new civilization is being born; customs, creeds, and cruelty are passing; vision, faith, and service are taking their place. The fetters of tradition are being melted off from humanity, and as the dross of materialism is being consumed, thought is being liberated and truth is rising full-orbed before an astonished multitude.

The whole world is on the eve of a new consciousness, a new power, and a new realization of the resources within the self. The last century saw the most magnificent material progress in history. The present century will produce the greatest progress in mental and spiritual power.

Physical science has resolved matter into molecules, molecules into atoms, atoms into energy, and it has remained for Sir Ambrose Fleming, in an address before the Royal Institution, to resolve this energy into Mind. He says: "In its ultimate essence, energy may be incomprehensible by us except as an exhibition of the direct operation of that which we call Mind or Will."

Let us see what are the most powerful forces in Nature. In the mineral world everything is solid and fixed. In the animal and vegetable kingdom it is in a state of flux, forever changing, always being created and re-created. In the atmosphere we find heat, light, and energy. Each realm becomes finer and more spiritual as we pass from the visible to the invisible, from the coarse to the fine, from the low potentiality to high potentiality. When we reach the invisible we find energy in its purest and most volatile state.

And as the most powerful forces of Nature are the invisible forces, so we find that the most powerful forces of man are his invisible forces, his spiritual force; the only way in which the spiritual force can manifest is through the process of thinking. Thinking is the only activity which the spirit possesses, and thought is the only product of thinking.

Addition and subtraction are therefore spiritual transactions; reasoning is a spiritual process; ideas are spiritual conceptions; questions are spiritual searchlights and logic; argument and philosophy are spiritual machinery.

Every thought brings into action certain physical tissue, parts of the brain, nerve, or muscle. This produces an actual physical change in the construction of the tissue. Therefore, it is only necessary to have a certain number of thoughts on a given subject in order to bring about a complete change in the physical organization of a man.

This is the process by which failure is changed to success. Thoughts of courage, power, inspiration, and harmony are substituted for thoughts of failure, despair, lack, limitation, and discord, and as these thoughts take root, the physical tissue is changed and the individual sees life in a new light. Old things have actually passed away; all things have become new; he is born again, this time born of the spirit; life has a new meaning for him; he is reconstructed and is filled with joy, confidence, hope, energy. He sees opportunities for success to which he was heretofore blind. He recognizes possibilities which before had no meaning for him. The thoughts of success with which he has been impregnated are radiated to those around him, and they in turn help him onward and upward. He attracts to himself new and successful associates, and this in turn changes his environment; by this simple exercise of thought, a man changes not only himself but his environment, circumstances, and conditions.

You will see—you must see—that we are at the dawn of a new day; the possibilities are so wonderful, so fascinating, so limitless as to be almost bewildering. A century ago any man with a Gatling gun could have annihilated a whole army equipped with the implements of warfare then in use. So it is at present. Any man with a knowledge of the possibilities contained in the Master Key has an inconceivable advantage over the multitude.

It is my privilege to share with you the Master Key System. Would you bring into your life more power? Get the power consciousness. More health? Get the health consciousness. More happiness? Get the happiness consciousness. Live the spirit of these things until they become yours by right. It will then become impossible to keep them from you. The things of the world are fluid to a power within man by which he rules them.

You need not acquire this power. You already have it. But you want to understand it; you want to use it; you want to control it; you want to impregnate yourself with it so that you can go forward and carry the world before you.

Day by day as you go on and on, as you gain momentum, as your inspiration deepens, as your plans crystallize, and as you gain understanding, you will come to realize that this world is no dead pile of stones and timber but that it is a living thing! It is made up of the beating hearts of humanity. It is a thing of life and beauty.

It is evident that it requires understanding to work with material of this description, but those who come into this understanding are inspired by a new light, a new force; they gain confidence and greater power each day; they realize their hopes and their dreams come true; life has a deeper, fuller, clearer meaning than before.

And now, chapter one.

ONE

The World Within

THAT MUCH gathers more is true on every plane of existence and that loss leads to greater loss is equally true. Mind is creative, and conditions, environment, and all experiences in life are the result of our habitual or predominant mental attitude. The attitude of Mind necessarily depends upon what we think. Therefore, the secret of all power, all achievement, and all possession depends upon our method of thinking.

This is true because we must "be" before we can "do," and we can "do" only to the extent which we "are," and what we "are" depends upon what we "think."

We cannot express powers that we do not possess. The only way by which we may secure possession of power is to become conscious of power, and we can never become conscious of power until we learn that all power is from within. There is a world within—a world of thought and feeling and power; of light and life and beauty—and, although invisible, its forces are mighty. The world within is governed by Mind. When we discover this world we shall find the solution for every problem, the cause for every effect; and since the world within is subject to our control, all laws of power and possession are also within our control.

The world without is a reflection of the world within. What appears without is what has been found within. In the world within may be found infinite Wisdom, infinite Power, infinite Supply of all that is necessary, waiting for unfoldment, development, and expression. If we recognize these potentialities in the world within, they will take form in the world without. Harmony in the world within will be reflected in the world without by harmonious conditions, agreeable surroundings, the best of everything. It is the foundation of health and is essential to all greatness, all power, all attainment, all achievement, and all success. Harmony in the world within means the ability to control our thoughts and to determine for ourselves how any experience is to affect us. Harmony in the world within results in optimism and affluence; affluence within results in affluence without.

The world without reflects the circumstances and the conditions of the consciousness within. If we find wisdom in the world within, we shall have the understanding to discern the marvelous possibilities that are latent in this world within, and we shall be given the power to make these possibilities manifest in the world without. As we become conscious of the wisdom in the world within, we mentally take possession of this wisdom, and by taking mental possession we come into actual possession of the power and wisdom necessary to bring into manifestation the essentials necessary for our most complete and harmonious development.

The world within is the practical world in which the men and women of power generate courage, hope, enthusiasm, confidence, trust, and faith, by which they are given the fine intelligence to see the vision and the practical skill to make the vision real. Life is an unfoldment, not an accretion. What comes to us in the world without is what we already possess in the world within. All possession is based on consciousness. All gain is the result of an accumulative consciousness. All loss is the result of a scattering consciousness. Mental efficiency is contingent upon harmony; discord means confusion; therefore, he who would acquire power must be in harmony with Natural Law.

We are related to the world without by the objective mind. The brain is the organ of this mind, and the cerebro-spinal system of nerves puts us in conscious communication with every part of the body. This system of nerves responds to every sensation of light, heat, odor, sound, and taste. When this mind thinks correctly, when it understands the truth, when the thoughts sent through the cerebro-spinal nervous system to the body are constructive, these sensations are pleasant, harmonious.

The result is that we build strength, vitality, and all constructive forces into our body, but it is through this same objective mind that all distress, sickness, lack, limitation, and forms of discord and inharmony are admitted to our lives. It is therefore through the objective mind, by wrong thinking, that we are related to all destructive forces.

We are related to the world within by the subconscious mind. The solar plexus is the organ of this mind; the sympathetic system of nerves presides over all subjective sensations, such as joy, fear, love, emotion, respiration, imagination, and all other subconscious phenomena. It is through the subconscious that we are connected with the Universal Mind and brought into relation with the infinite constructive forces of the universe. It is the coordination of these two centers of our being, and the understanding of their functions, which is the great secret of life. With this knowledge, we can bring the objective and subjective minds into conscious cooperation and thus coordinate the finite and the infinite. Our future is entirely within our own control. It is not at the mercy of any capricious or uncertain external power.

All agree that there is but one principle or consciousness pervading the entire universe, occupying all space, and being essentially the same in kind at every point of its presence. It is all powerful, all wisdom, and always present. All thoughts and things are within itself; it is all in all. There is but one consciousness in the universe able to think; and when it thinks, its thoughts become objective things to it. As this consciousness is omnipresent, it must be present within every individual; each individual must be a manifestation of that Omnipotent, Omniscient, and Omnipresent Consciousness.

As there is only one consciousness in the universe that is able to think it necessarily follows that your consciousness is identical with Universal Consciousness, or, in other words, all Mind is one mind. There is no dodging this conclusion. The consciousness that focuses in your brain cells is the same consciousness which focuses in the brain cells of every other individual. Each individual is but the individualization of the Universal, the Cosmic Mind. Universal Mind is static or potential energy; it simply is. It can manifest only through the individual, and the individual can manifest only through the Universal. They are one.

The ability of the individual to think is his ability to act on the universal and bring it into manifestation. Human consciousness consists only in the ability of man to think. Mind in itself is believed to be a subtle form of static energy, from which arises the activity called "thought," which is the dynamic phase of Mind. Mind is static energy, thought is dynamic energy—the two phases of the same thing. Thought is therefore the vibratory force formed by converting static Mind into dynamic Mind. As the sum of all attributes are contained in Universal Mind, which is omnipotent, omniscient, and omnipresent, these attributes must be present at all times in their potential form in every individual. Therefore, when the individual thinks, the thought is compelled by its nature to embody itself in an objectivity or condition which will correspond with its origin.

Every thought therefore is a cause and every condition an effect; for this reason it is absolutely essential that you control your thoughts so as to bring forth only desirable conditions.

All power is from within and is absolutely under your control; it comes through exact knowledge and by the voluntary exercises of exact principles. It should be plain that when you acquire a thorough understanding of this law and are able to control your thought processes, you can apply it to any condition; in other words, you will have come into conscious cooperation with Omnipotent Law, which is the fundamental basis of all things. Universal Mind is the life principle of every atom which is in existence; every atom is continually striving to manifest more life; all are intelligent, and all are seeking to carry out the purpose for which they were created.

A majority of mankind lives in the world without; few have found the world within, and yet it is the world within that makes the world without. It is therefore creative, and everything which you find in your world without has been created by you in the world within. This system will bring you into a realization of power which will be yours when you understand this relation between the world without and the world within. The world within is the cause, the world without the effect; to change the effect you must change the cause. You will at once see that this is a radically new and different idea; most men try to change effects by working with effects. They fail to see that this is simply changing one form of distress for another. To remove discord, we must remove the cause, and this cause can be found only in the world within.

All growth is from within. This is evident in all Nature. Every plant, every animal, every human is a living testimony to this great law, and the error of the ages is in looking for strength or power from without. The world within is the Universal Fountain of Supply, and the world without is the outlet to the stream. Our ability to receive depends upon our recognition of this Universal Fountain—this Infinite Energy—of which each individual is an outlet and is one with every other individual.

Recognition is a mental process; mental action is therefore the interaction of the individual upon Universal Mind. As Universal Mind is the intelligence which pervades all space and animates all living things, this mental action and reaction is the law of causation. But the principle of causation does not obtain in the individual but in Universal Mind. It is not an objective faculty but a subjective process, and the results are seen in an infinite variety of conditions and experiences. In order to express life there must be Mind; nothing can exist without Mind. Everything which exists is some manifestation of this one basic substance from which and by which all things have been created and are continually being re-created.

We live in a fathomless sea of plastic Mind Substance. This substance is ever alive and active, and it is sensitive to the highest degree. It takes form according to the mental demand. Thought forms the mold or matrix from which the substance expresses. Remember that it is in the application alone that the value consists, and a practical understanding of this law will substitute abundance for poverty, wisdom for ignorance, harmony for discord, and freedom for tyranny. Certainly there can be no greater blessing than these from a material and social standpoint.

Now make the application: Select a room where you can be alone and undisturbed; sit erect, comfortably, but do not lounge. Let your thoughts roam where they will but be perfectly still for fifteen minutes to half an hour. Continue this for three or four days or for a week until you secure full control of your physical being.

Many will find this extremely difficult; others will conquer it with ease. But it is absolutely essential to secure complete control of the body before you are ready to progress. In chapter two, you will receive instructions for the next step; in the meantime you must master this one.

Summary

- What is the world without in its relation to the world within?
  The world without is a reflection of the world within.
- Upon what does all possession depend?
  All possession is based on consciousness.
- How is the individual related to the objective world?
  The individual is related to the objective world by the objective mind; the brain is the organ of this mind.
- How is he related to Universal Mind?
  He is related to Universal Mind by the subconscious mind; the solar plexus is the organ of this mind.
- What is Universal Mind?
  Universal Mind is the life principle of every atom which is in existence.
- How can the individual act on the Universal?
  The ability of the individual to think is his ability to act upon the Universal and bring it into manifestation.
- What is the result of this action and interaction?
  The result of this action and interaction is cause and effect; every thought is a cause and every condition an effect.
- How are harmonious and desirable conditions secured?
  Harmonious and desirable conditions are obtained by right thinking.

- What is the cause of all discord, inharmony, lack, and limitation?
  Discord, inharmony, lack, and limitation are the result of wrong thinking.
- What is the source of all power?
  The source of all power is the world within, the Universal Fountain of Supply, the Infinite Energy of which each individual is an outlet.

TWO

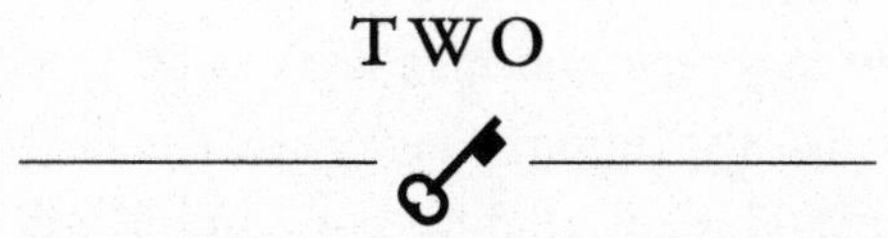

Thought Is Energy

Our difficulties are largely due to confused ideas and ignorance of our true interests. The great task is to discover the laws of Nature to which we are to adjust ourselves. Clear thinking and moral insight are, therefore, of incalculable value. All processes, even those of thought, rest on solid foundations.

The keener the sensibilities, the more acute the judgment, the more delicate the taste, the more refined the moral feelings, the more subtle the intelligence, the loftier the aspiration, the purer and more intense the gratifications existence yields. Hence it is the study of the best in thought that gives the world supreme pleasure.

The powers, uses, and possibilities of the mind under the new interpretations are incomparably more wonderful that the most extravagant accomplishment or even dreams of material progress.

Thought is energy. Active thought is active energy; concentrated thought is concentrated energy. Thought concentrated on a definite purpose becomes power. This is the power which is being used by those who do not believe in the virtue of poverty or the beauty of self-denial. They perceive that this is the talk of weaklings.

The ability to receive and manifest power depends upon the ability to recognize the Infinite Energy ever dwelling in man, constantly creating and re-creating his body and Mind, and ready at any moment to manifest through him in any needful manner. In exact proportion to the recognition of this truth will be the manifestation in the outer life of the individual.

Here we explain the method by which this is accomplished.

The operations of the mind are produced by two parallel modes of activity, one conscious and the other subconscious. Professor Davidson says: "He who thinks to illuminate the whole range of mental action by the light of his own consciousness is not unlike the one who should go about to illuminate the universe with a rushlight." The logical processes of the subconscious are carried on with a certainty and regularity which would be impossible if there existed the possibility of error. Our mind is so designed that it prepares for us the most important foundations of cognition, whilst we have not the slightest apprehension of the modus operandi.

The subconscious soul, like a benevolent stranger, works and makes provision for our benefit, pouring only the mature fruit into our lap; thus ultimate analysis of thought processes shows that the subconscious is the theater of the most important mental phenomena. It is through the subconscious that Shakespeare must have perceived, without effort, great truths which are hidden from the conscious mind of the student; that Phidias fashioned bronze; that Raphael painted Madonnas; and that Beethoven composed symphonies.

Ease and perfection depend entirely upon the degree to which we cease to depend upon the consciousness; playing the piano, skating, operating the typewriter, performing the skilled trades depend for their perfect execution on the process of the subconscious mind. The marvel of playing a brilliant piece on the piano, while at the same time conducting a vigorous conversation, shows the greatness of our subconscious powers. We are all aware of how dependent we are upon the subconscious, and the greater, the nobler, the more brilliant our thoughts are, the more it is obvious to ourselves that the origin lies beyond our ken. We find ourselves endowed with tact, instinct, and a sense of the beautiful in art, music, and so on, of whose origin or dwelling place we are wholly unconscious.

The value of the subconscious is enormous: it inspires us; it warns us; and it furnishes us with names, facts, and scenes from the storehouse of memory. It directs our thoughts and tastes, and it accomplishes tasks so intricate that no conscious mind, even if it had the power, has the capacity for.

We can walk at will; we can raise our arm whenever we choose to do so; we can give our attention through eye or ear to any subject at pleasure. On the other hand, we cannot stop our heartbeat, the circulation of the blood, the growth of stature, the formation of nerve and muscle tissue, the building of the bones, or the many other vital processes.

If we compare these two sets of action, the one decreed by the will of the moment and the other proceeding in majestic, rhythmic course, subject to no vascillation but constant at every moment, we stand in awe of the latter and ask to have the mystery explained. We see at once that these are the vital processes of our physical life, and we cannot avoid the inference that these all-important functions are designedly withdrawn from the domain of our outward will, with its variations and transitions, and placed under the direction of a permanent and dependable power within us.

Of these two powers, the outward and changeable has been termed the "conscious mind," or the "objective mind" (dealing with outward objects). The interior power is called the "subconscious mind," or the "subjective mind," and besides its work on the mental plane, it controls the regular functions which make physical life possible. It is necessary to have a clear understanding of their respective functions on the mental plane, as well as having a clear understanding of other basic principles. Perceiving and operating through the five physical senses, the conscious mind deals with the impressions and objects of the outward life. It has the faculty of discrimination, carrying with it the responsibility of choice. It has the power of reasoning—whether inductive, deductive, analytical, or syllogistic—and this power may be developed to a high degree. It is the seat of the will with all the energies that flow therefrom.

Not only can the conscious mind impress other minds, but it can direct the subconscious mind. In this way the conscious mind becomes the responsible ruler and guardian of the subconscious mind. It is this high function which can completely reverse conditions in your life. It is often true that conditions of fear, worry, poverty, disease, inharmony, and evils of all kinds dominate us by reason of false suggestions accepted by the unguarded subconscious mind. All this the trained conscious mind can entirely prevent by its vigilant, protective action. It may properly be called "the watchman at the gate" of the great subconscious domain.

One writer has expressed the chief distinction between the two phases of mind thus: "Conscious mind is reasoning will. Subconscious mind is instinctive desire, the result of past reasoning will."

The subconscious mind draws just and accurate inferences from premises furnished from outside sources. Where the premise is true, the subconscious mind reaches a faultless conclusion, but where the premise or suggestion is an error, the whole structure falls. The subconscious mind does not engage in the process of proving. It relies upon the conscious mind, "the watchman at the gate," to guard it from mistaken impressions. Receiving any suggestions as true, the subconscious mind at once proceeds to act thereon in the whole domain of its tremendous field of work. The conscious mind can suggest either truth or error. If the latter, it is at the cost of wide-reaching peril to the whole being.

The conscious mind ought to be on duty during every waking hour. When the "watchman" is "off guard," or when its calm judgment is suspended under a variety of circumstances, the subconscious mind is unguarded and left open to suggestion from all sources. During the wild excitement of panic, the height of anger, the impulses of the irresponsible mob, or at any other time of unrestrained passion the conditions are most dangerous. The subconscious mind is then open to the suggestion of fear, hatred, selfishness, greed, self-depreciation, and other negative forces derived from surrounding persons or circumstances. The result is usually unwholesome in the extreme, with effects that may endure to distress it for a long time. Hence the great importance of guarding the subconscious mind from false impressions.

The subconscious mind perceives by intuition. Hence its processes are rapid. It does not wait for the slow methods of conscious reasoning. In fact, it cannot employ them. The subconscious mind never sleeps and never rests, anymore than does your heart or your blood. It has been found that by plainly stating to the subconscious mind certain specific things to be accomplished, forces are set in operation that lead to the result desired. Here, then, is a source of power which places us in touch with omnipotence. Here is a deep principle which is well worth our most earnest study.

The operation of this law is interesting. Those who put it into operation find that when they go out to meet the person with whom they anticipate a difficult interview, something has been there before them and dissolved the supposed differences.

Everything is changed; all is harmonious. They find that when some difficult business problem presents itself they can afford to make delay and something suggests the proper solution; everything is properly arranged; in fact, those who have learned to trust the subconscious find that they have infinite resources at their command. The subconscious mind is the seat of our principles and our aspirations. It is the fount of our artistic and altruistic ideals. These instincts can only be overthrown by an elaborate and gradual process of undermining the innate principles.

The subconscious mind cannot argue controversially. Hence, if it has accepted wrong suggestions, the sure method of overcoming them is by the use of a strong counter suggestion, frequently repeated, which the mind must accept. Thus, it eventually forms new and healthy habits of thought and life, for the subconscious mind is the seat of habit. That which we do over and over becomes mechanical; it is no longer an act of judgment but has worn its deep grooves in the subconscious mind. This is favorable for us if the habit be wholesome and right. If it be harmful and wrong, the remedy is to recognize the omnipotence of the subconscious mind and suggest present actual freedom. The subconscious being creative and one with our divine source will at once create the freedom suggested.

To sum up: The normal functions of the subconscious on the physical side have to do with regular and vital processes; with the preservation of life and the restoration of health; and with the care of offspring, which includes an instinctive desire to preserve all life and improve conditions generally.

On the mental side, it is the storehouse of memory: it harbors wonderful thought messengers, who work unhampered by time or space; it is the fountain of the practical initiative and constructive forces of life; it is the seat of habit. On the spiritual side, it is the source of ideals, of aspiration, of imagination, and it is the channel through which we recognize our Divine Source. And in proportion as we recognize this divinity do we come into an understanding of the source of power.

Someone may ask, "How can the subconscious change conditions?" The reply is, because the subconscious is a part of Universal Mind, and a part must be the same in kind and quality as the whole; the only difference is one of degree. The Whole, as we know, is creative; in fact, it is the only creator there is. Consequently, we find that mind is creative, and as thought is the only activity which the mind possesses, thought must necessarily be creative also. But we shall find that there is a vast difference between simply thinking and directing our thought consciously, systematically, and constructively. When we do this we place our mind in harmony with Universal Mind, we come in tune with the Infinite, and we set in operation the mightiest force in existence—the creative power of Universal Mind. This, as everything else, is governed by Natural Law, and this law is the Law of Attraction, which is that Mind is creative and will automatically correlate with its object and bring it into manifestation.

In the last chapter, I gave you an exercise for the purpose of securing control of the physical body; if you have accomplished this you are ready to advance. This time you will begin to control your thought. Always take the same room, the same chair, and the same position if possible. In some cases it is not convenient to take the same room; in this case simply make the best use of such conditions as may be available. Now be perfectly still as before, but inhibit all thought; this will give you control over all thoughts of care, worry, and fear, and will enable you to entertain only the kind of thoughts you desire. Continue this exercise until you gain complete mastery.

You will not be able to do this for more than a few moments at a time, but the exercise is valuable because it will be a very practical demonstration of the great number of thoughts which are constantly trying to gain access to your mental world.

In the next chapter, you will receive instructions for an exercise which may be a little more interesting, but it is necessary that you master this one first.

> *Cause and effect is as absolute and undeviating in the hidden realm of thought as in the world of visible and material things. Mind is the master weaver, both of the interior garment of character and the outer garment of circumstance.*
>
> —JAMES ALLEN

Summary

- What are the two modes of mental activity?
  Conscious and subconscious.
- Upon what do ease and perfection depend?
  Ease and perfection depend entirely upon the degree to which we cease to depend upon the conscious mind.
- What is the value of the subconscious?
  It is enormous; it guides us and warns us, it controls the vital processes, and it is the seat of memory.
- What are some of the functions of the conscious mind?
  It has the faculty of discrimination; it has the power of reasoning; it is the seat of the will and may impress the subconscious.
- How has the distinction between the conscious and subconscious been expressed?
  "Conscious mind is reasoning will. Subconscious mind is instinctive desire, the result of past reasoning will."

- What method is necessary in order to impress the subconscious?
  Mentally state what is wanted.
- What will be the result?
  If the desire is in harmony with the forward movement of the Great Whole, forces will be set in motion which will bring about the result.
- What is the result of the operation of this law?
  Our environment reflects conditions corresponding to the predominant mental attitude which we entertain.
- What name has been given to this law?
  The Law of Attraction.
- How is the law stated?
  Thought is a creative energy, and it will automatically correlate with its object and bring it into manifestation.

THREE

Radiating Attraction

You have found that the individual may act on the universal and that the result of this action and interaction is cause and effect. Thought, therefore, is the cause, and the experiences with which you meet in life are the effect.

Eliminate, therefore, any possible tendency to complain of conditions as they have been, or as they are, because it rests with you to change them and make them what you would like them to be.

Direct your effort to a realization of the mental resources, always at your command, from which all real and lasting power comes.

Persist in this practice until you come to a realization of the fact that there can be no failure in the accomplishment of any proper object in life if you but understand your power and persist in your object. The mind-forces are ever ready to lend themselves to a purposeful will in the effort to crystallize thought and desire into actions, events, and conditions.

Whereas in the beginning, each function of life and each action is the result of conscious thought. The habitual actions become automatic and the thought that controls them passes into the realm of the subconscious, yet it is just as intelligent as before. It is necessary that it become automatic, or subconscious, in order that the self-conscious mind may attend to other things. The new actions will, however, in their turn, become habitual, then automatic, then subconscious in order that the mind again may be freed from this detail and advance to still other activities.

When you realize this, you will have found a source of power which will enable you to take care of any situation in life which may develop.

The necessary interaction of the conscious and subconscious mind requires a similar interaction between the corresponding systems of nerves. Judge Troward indicates the very beautiful method in which this interaction is effected. He says: "The cerebro-spinal system is the organ of the conscious mind and the sympathetic is the organ of the subconscious. The cerebro-spinal is the channel through which we receive conscious perception from the physical senses and exercise control over the movements of the body. This system of nerves has its center in the brain.

"The sympathetic system has its center in a ganglionic mass at the back of the stomach known as the solar plexus and is the channel of that mental action which unconsciously supports the vital functions of the body. The connection between the two systems is made by the vagus nerve which passes out of the cerebral region as a portion of the voluntary system to the thorax, sending out branches to the heart and lungs, and finally passing through the diaphragm, it loses its outer coating and becomes identified with the nerves of the sympathetic system, so forming a connecting link between the two and making man physically a single entity."

We have seen that every thought is received by the brain, which is the organ of the conscious; it is here subjected to our power of reasoning. When the objective mind has been satisfied that the thought is true, it is sent to the solar plexus, or the brain of the subjective mind, to be made into our flesh, to be brought forth into the world as reality. It is then no longer susceptible to any argument whatever. The subconscious mind cannot argue; it only acts. It accepts the conclusions of the objective mind as final.

The solar plexus has been likened to the sun of the body, because it is a central point of distribution for the energy which the body is constantly generating. This energy is very real energy, and this sun is a very real sun; the energy is being distributed by very real nerves to all parts of the body and is thrown off in an atmosphere which envelopes the body. If this radiation is sufficiently strong the person is called magnetic; he is said to be filled with personal magnetism. Such a person may wield an immense power for good. His presence alone will often bring comfort to the troubled minds with which he comes in contact. When the solar plexus is in active operation and is radiating life, energy, and vitality to every part of the body and to everyone whom he meets, the sensations are pleasant, the body is filled with health, and all with whom he comes in contact experience a pleasant sensation.

If there is any interruption of this radiation the sensations are unpleasant, the flow of life and energy to some part of the body is stopped; this is the cause of every ill to the human race, physical, mental, or environmental. Physical because the sun of the body is no longer generating sufficient energy to vitalize some part of the body; mental because the conscious mind is dependent upon the subconscious mind for the vitality necessary to support its thought; and environmental because the connection between the subconscious mind and Universal Mind is being interrupted.

The solar plexus is the point at which the part meets with the whole, where the finite becomes infinite, where the uncreate becomes create, the universal becomes individualized, the invisible becomes visible. It is the point at which life appears, and there is no limit to the amount of life an individual may generate from this solar center. This center of energy is omnipotent because it is the point of contact with all life and all intelligence. It can, therefore, accomplish whatever it is directed to accomplish, and herein lies the power of the conscious mind. The subconscious can and will carry out such plans and ideas as may be suggested to it by the conscious mind.

Conscious thought, then, is master of this sun center from which the life and energy of the entire body flows. The quality of the thought which we entertain determines the quality of the thought which this sun will radiate; the character of the thought which our conscious mind entertains will determine the character of the thought which this sun will radiate; and the nature of the thought which our conscious mind entertains will determine the nature of thought which this sun will radiate, and consequently will determine the nature of the experience which will result.

It is evident, therefore, that all we have to do is let our light shine; the more energy we can radiate, the more rapidly shall we be enabled to transmute undesirable conditions into sources of pleasure and profit. The important question, then, is how to let this light shine, how to generate this energy. Nonresistant thought expands the solar plexus; resistant thought contracts it. Pleasant thought expands it; unpleasant thought contracts it. Thoughts of courage, power, confidence, and hope all produce a corresponding state, but the one arch enemy of the solar plexus which must be absolutely destroyed before there is any possibility of letting any light shine is fear. This enemy must be completely destroyed; he must be eliminated; he must be expelled forever; he is the cloud which hides the sun and causes a perpetual gloom.

It is this personal devil which makes men fear the past, the present, and the future; fear themselves, their friends, and their enemies; fear everything and everybody. When fear is effectually and completely destroyed, your light will shine, the clouds will disperse, and you will have found the source of power, energy, and life. When you find that you are really one with the Infinite Power, and when you can consciously realize this power by a practical demonstration of your ability to overcome any adverse condition by the power of your thought, you will have nothing to fear; fear will have been destroyed and you will have come into possession of your birthright.

It is our attitude of mind toward life which determines the experiences with which we are to meet; if we expect nothing, we shall have nothing; if we demand much, we shall receive the greater portion. The world is harsh only as we fail to assert ourselves. The criticism of the world is bitter only to those who cannot compel room for their ideas. It is fear of this criticism that causes many ideas to fail to see the light of day.

But the man who knows that he has a solar plexus will not fear criticism or anything else; he will be too busy radiating courage, confidence, and power; he will anticipate success by his mental attitude; he will pound barriers to pieces and leap over the chasm of doubt and hesitation which fear places in his path. A knowledge of our ability to consciously radiate health, strength, and harmony will bring us into a realization that there is nothing to fear because we are in touch with Infinite Strength.

This knowledge can be gained only by making practical application of this information. We learn by doing; through practice the athlete becomes powerful. As the following statement is of considerable importance, I will put it in several ways so that you cannot fail to get the full significance of it. If you are religiously inclined, I would say, you can let your light shine. If your mind has a bias toward physical science, I would say you can wake the solar plexus. Or if you prefer the strictly scientific interpretation, I will say that you can impress your subconscious mind.

I have already told you what the result of this impression will be. It is the method in which you are now interested. You have already learned that the subconscious is intelligent and that it is creative and responsive to the will of the conscious mind. What, then, is the most natural way of making the desired impression? Mentally concentrate on the object of your desire; when you are concentrating you are impressing the subconscious. This is not the only way, but it is a simple and effective way—the most direct way—and consequently the way in which the best results are secured. It is the method which is producing such extraordinary results that many think that miracles are being accomplished. It is the method by which every great inventor, every great financier, every great statesman has been enabled to convert the subtle and invisible force of desire, faith, and confidence into actual, tangible, concrete facts in the objective world.

The subconscious mind is a part of Universal Mind. Universal Mind is the creative principle of the universe; a part must be the same in kind and quality as the whole. This means that this creative power is absolutely unlimited; it is not bound by precedent of any kind and consequently has no prior existing pattern by which to apply its constructive principle. We have found that the subconscious mind is responsive to our conscious will, which means that the unlimited creative power of Universal Mind is within control of the conscious mind of the individual.

When making a practical application of this principle, in accordance with the exercises given in the subsequent lessons, it is good to remember that it is not necessary to outline the method by which the subconscious will produce the results you desire.

The finite cannot inform the Infinite. You are simply to say what you desire, not how you are to obtain it.

You are the channel by which the undifferentiated is being differentiated, and this differentiation is being accomplished by appropriation. It only requires recognition to set causes in motion which will bring about results in accordance with your desire, and this is accomplished because the Universal can act only through the individual, and the individual can act only through the Universal; they are one.

For your exercise in this chapter, I will ask you to go one step further. I want you to not only be perfectly still and inhibit all thought as far as possible, but relax, let go, let the muscles take their normal condition; this will remove all pressure from the nerves and eliminate that tension which so frequently produces physical exhaustion. Physical relaxation is a voluntary exercise of the will, and the exercise will be found to be of great value, as it enables the blood to circulate freely to and from the brain and body.

Tension leads to mental unrest and abnormal mental activity of the mind; it produces worry, care, fear, and anxiety. Relaxation is, therefore, an absolute necessity in order to allow the mental faculties to exercise the greatest freedom. Make this exercise as thorough and complete as possible; mentally determine that you will relax every muscle and nerve, until you feel quiet and restful and at peace with yourself and the world. The solar plexus will then be ready to function, and you will be surprised at the result.

Summary

- What system of nerves is the organ of the conscious mind?
  The cerebro-spinal.
- What system of nerves is the organ of the subconscious mind?
  The sympathetic.

- What is the central point of distribution for energy which the body is constantly generating?
  The solar plexus.
- How may this distribution be interrupted?
  By resistant, critical, discordant thoughts, and especially fear.
- What is the result of such interruption?
  Every ill with which the human race is afflicted.
- How may this energy be controlled and directed?
  By conscious thought.
- How may fear be completely eliminated?
  By an understanding and recognition of the true source of all power.
- What determines the experiences with which we meet in life?
  Our predominant mental attitude.
- How may we awaken the solar plexus?
  Mentally concentrate upon the condition which we desire to see manifested in our lives.
- What is the creative principle of the universe?
  Universal Mind.

FOUR

Energy Is Power

HERE I offer to you chapter four. This chapter will show you why what you think, do, feel is an indication of what you are.

Thought is energy, and energy is power, and it is because of all the religions, sciences, and philosophies with which the world has heretofore been familiar that the manifestation of this energy—instead of the energy itself—has been limited to effects, while causes have been ignored or misunderstood.

For this reason, we have God and the Devil in religion, positive and negative in science, and good and bad in philosophy.

The Master Key reverses the process; it is interested only in cause, and letters received from students tell a marvelous story. They indicate conclusively that students are finding the cause whereby they may secure for themselves health, harmony, abundance, and whatever else may be necessary for their welfare and happiness.

Life is expressive, and it is our business to express ourselves harmoniously and constructively. Sorrow, misery, unhappiness, disease, and poverty are not necessities, and we are constantly eliminating them.

But this process of eliminating consists in rising above and beyond limitation of any kind. He who has strengthened and purified his thought need not concern himself about microbes, and he who has come into an understanding of the Law of Abundance will go at once to the source of supply.

It is thus that fate, fortune, and destiny will be controlled as readily as a captain controls his ship, or an engineer his train.

The "I" of you is not the physical body; that is simply an instrument which the "I" uses to carry out its purposes. The "I" cannot be the mind, for the mind is simply another instrument which the "I" uses with which to think, reason, and plan.

The "I" must be something which controls and directs both the body and the mind; something which determines what they shall do and how they shall act. When you come into a realization of the true nature of this "I," you will enjoy a sense of power which you have never before known.

Your personality is made up of countless individual characteristics, peculiarities, habits, and traits of character; these are the result of your former method of thinking, but they have nothing to do with the real "I." When you say "I think" the "I" tells the mind what it shall think; when you say "I go" the "I" tells the physical body where it shall go. The real nature of this "I" is spiritual, and it is the source of the real power which comes to men and women when they come into a realization of their true nature.

The greatest and most marvelous power which this "I" has been given is the power to think, but few people know how to think constructively or correctly. Consequently they achieve only indifferent results. Most people allow their thoughts to dwell on selfish purposes—the inevitable result of an infantile mind. When a mind becomes mature, it understands that the germ of defeat is in every selfish thought.

The trained mind knows that every transaction must benefit every person who is in any way connected with the transaction, and any attempt to profit by the weakness, ignorance, or necessity of another will inevitably operate to his disadvantage. This is because the individual is a part of the Universal. A part cannot antagonize any other part, but, on the contrary, the welfare of each part depends upon a recognition of the interest of the whole.

Those who recognize this principle have a great advantage in the affairs of life: they do not wear themselves out; they can eliminate vagrant thoughts with facility; they can readily concentrate to the highest possible degree on any subject; and they do not waste time or money upon objects which can be of no possible benefit to them. If you cannot do these things, it is because you have thus far not made the necessary effort. Now is the time to make the effort. The result will be exactly in proportion to the effort expended. One of the strongest affirmations for strengthening the will and realizing your power to accomplish is, "I can be what I will to be."

Every time you repeat it, realize who and what this "I" is; try to come into a thorough understanding of the true nature of the "I." If you do, you will become invincible; that is, provided that your objects and purposes are constructive and are therefore in harmony with the creative principle of the Universe. If you make use of this affirmation, use it continuously, night and morning and as often during the day as you think of it, and continue to do so until it becomes a part of you; form the habit.

Unless you do this, you had better not start at all because modern psychology tells us that when we start something and do not complete it, or make a resolution and do not keep it, we are forming the habit of failure—absolute, ignominious failure. If you do not intend to do a thing, do not start; if you do start, see it through even if the heavens fall; if you make up your mind to do something, do it; let nothing and no one interfere. Once the "I" in you has determined this, the thing is settled; the die is cast, there is no longer any argument.

If you carry out this idea, beginning with small things which you know you can control, and gradually increase the effort (but never under any circumstances allowing your "I" to be overruled), you will find that you can eventually control yourself. Many men and women have found to their sorrow that it is easier to control a kingdom than to control themselves. But when you have learned to control yourself, you will have found the world within, which controls the world without; you will have become irresistible; men and things will respond to your every wish without any apparent effort on your part. This is not so strange or impossible as it may appear when you remember that the world within is controlled by the "I" and that this "I" is a part or one with the Infinite "I," which is the Universal Energy or Spirit, usually called God.

This is not a mere statement or theory made for the purpose of confirming or establishing an idea, but it is a fact which has been accepted by the best religious thought as well as the best scientific thought.

Herbert Spender said: "Amid all the mysteries by which we are surrounded, nothing is more certain than that we are ever in the presence of an Infinite and Eternal Energy from which all things proceed." Lyman Abbott, in an address delivered before the alumni of Bangor Theological Seminary, said: "We are coming to think of God as dwelling in man rather than as operating on men from without."

Science goes a little way in its search and stops. Science finds the ever-present Eternal Energy, but religion finds the power behind this energy and locates it within man. But this is by no means a new discovery; the Bible says exactly the same thing, and the language is just as plain and convincing: "Know ye not that ye are the temple of the living God?" Here, then, is the secret of the wonderful creative power of the world within.

Here is the secret of power, of mastery. To overcome does not mean to go without things. Self-denial is not success. We cannot give unless we get; we cannot be helpful unless we are strong. The Infinite is not bankrupt, and we who are the representatives of Infinite Power should not be bankrupt either. If we wish to be of service to others, we must have power and more power, but to get it we must give it; we must be of service.

The more we give the more we shall get; we must become a channel whereby the Universal can express activity. The Universal is constantly seeking to express itself, to be of service; it seeks the channel whereby it can find the greatest activity, where it can do the most good, where it can be of greatest service to mankind. The Universal cannot express through you as long as you are busy with your plans, your own purposes; quiet the senses, seek inspiration, focus the mental activity on the within, dwell in the consciousness of your unity with Omnipotence. "Still water runs deep"; contemplate the multitudinous opportunities to which you have spiritual access by the Omnipresence of Power.

Visualize the events, circumstances, and conditions which these spiritual connections may assist in manifesting. Realize the fact that the essence and soul of all things is spiritual and that the spiritual is real because it is the life of all there is. When the spirit is gone, the life is gone; it is dead; it has ceased to exist. These mental activities pertain to the world within, to the world of cause; and the conditions and circumstances which result are the effect. It is thus that you become a creator. This is important work, and the higher, loftier, grander, and more noble ideals that you can conceive, the more important the work will become.

Overwork, over-play, or too much bodily activity of any kind produces conditions of mental apathy and stagnation. This makes it impossible to do the more important work which results in a realization of conscious power. We should, therefore, seek the Silence frequently. Power comes through repose; it is in the Silence that we can be still. When we are still, we can think; and thought is the secret of all attainment.

Thought is a mode of motion and is carried by the Law of Vibration the same as light or electricity. It is given vitality by the emotions through the Law of Love; it takes form and expression by the Law of Growth; it is a product of the spiritual "I," hence its divine, spiritual, and creative nature. From this it is evident that in order to express power, abundance, or any other constructive purpose, the emotions must be called upon to give feeling to the thought so that it will take form. How may this purpose be accomplished? This is the vital point; how may we develop the faith, the courage, the feeling which will result in accomplishment?

The reply is, by exercise; mental strength is secured in exactly the same way that physical strength is secured: by exercise. We think something, perhaps with difficulty the first time; we think the same thing again, and it becomes easier this time; we think it again and again; it then becomes a mental habit. We continue to think the same thing and finally it becomes automatic; we can no longer help thinking this thing; we are now positive of what we think; there is no longer any doubt about it. We are sure; we know.

In the last chapter, I asked you to relax, to let go physically. Now, I am going to ask you to let go mentally. If you practiced the exercise given in the last chapter fifteen or twenty minutes a day in accordance with the instructions, you can no doubt relax physically; and anyone who cannot consciously do this quickly and completely is not a master of himself. He has not obtained freedom; he is still a slave to conditions. But I shall assume that you have mastered the exercise and are ready to take the next step, which is mental freedom.

And now, after taking your usual position, remove all tension by completely relaxing, and then mentally let go of all adverse conditions, such as hatred, anger, worry, jealousy, envy, sorrow, trouble, or disappointment of any kind. You may say that you cannot "let go" of these things, but you can; you can do so by mentally determining to do so—by voluntary intention and persistence.

The reason that some cannot do this is because they allow themselves to be controlled by the emotions instead of by their intellect. But those who will be guided by the intellect will gain the victory. You will not succeed the first time you try, but practice makes perfect, in this as in everything else. You must succeed in dismissing, eliminating, and completely destroying these negative and destructive thoughts because they are the seed which is constantly germinating into discordant conditions of every conceivable kind and description.

There is nothing truer than that the quality of thought which we entertain correlates certain externals in the outside world. This is the Law from which there is no escape. And it is this Law, this correlative of the thought with its object, that from time immemorial has led the people to believe in special providence.

—Helen Wilmans

Summary

- What is thought?
  Thought is spiritual energy.
- How is it carried?
  By the Law of Vibration.
- How is it given vitality?
  By the Law of Love.
- How does it take form?
  By the Law of Growth.
- What is the secret of its creative power?
  It is a spiritual activity.
- How may we develop the faith, courage, and enthusiasm which will result in accomplishment?
  By a recognition of our spiritual nature.
- What is the secret of power?
  Service.
- Why is this so?
  Because we get what we give.
- What is the Silence?
  A physical stillness.
- Of what value is it?
  It is the first step to self-control, self-mastery.

FIVE

Thought Is Creative

And now you reach chapter five. After studying this chapter carefully, you will see that every conceivable force or object or fact is the result of mind in action.

Mind in action is thought, and thought is creative. Men are thinking now as they never thought before.

Therefore, this is a creative age, and the world is awarding its richest prizes to the thinkers. Matter is powerless, passive, inert. Mind is force, energy, power. Mind shapes and controls matter. Every form which matter takes is but the expression of some pre-existing thought.

But thought works no magic transformations; it obeys Natural Law; it sets in motion natural forces; it releases natural energies; it manifests in your conduct and actions, and these in turn react upon your friends and acquaintances, and eventually upon the whole of your environment. You can originate thought, and, since thoughts are creative, you can create for yourself the things you desire.

At least 90 percent of our mental life is subconscious, so those who fail to make use of this mental power live within very narrow limits. The subconscious can and will solve any problem for us if we know how to direct it. The subconscious processes are always at work; the only question is, are we to be simply passive recipients of this activity, or are we to consciously direct the work? Shall we have a vision of the destination to be reached and the dangers to be avoided, or shall we simply drift?

We have found that mind pervades every part of the physical body and is always capable of being directed or impressed by authority coming from the objective or the more dominant portion of the mind. The mind, which pervades the body, is largely the result of heredity, which, in turn, is simply the result of all the environments of all past generations on the responsive and ever-moving life forces. An understanding of this fact will enable us to use our authority when we find some undesirable trait of character manifesting. We can consciously use all the desirable characteristics with which we have been provided, and we can repress and refuse to allow the undesirable ones to manifest.

Again, this mind which pervades our physical body is not only the result of hereditary tendencies but the result of home, business, and social environment, where countless impressions, ideas, prejudices, and similar thoughts have been received. Much of this has been received from others, the result of opinions, suggestions, or statements; much of it is the result of our own thinking, but nearly all of it has been accepted with little or no examination or consideration.

The idea seemed plausible, then the conscious received it and passed it on to the subconscious, where it was taken up by the sympathetic system and passed on to be built into our physical body. "The word has become flesh." This, then, is the way we are consistently creating and re-creating ourselves; we are today the result of our past thinking, and we shall be what we are thinking today. The Law of Attraction is not bringing to us the things we should like, the things we wish for, or the things someone else has; but it brings us "our own," the things which we have created by our thought processes, whether consciously or unconsciously. Unfortunately, many of us are creating these things unconsciously.

If either of us were building a home for ourselves, how careful we would be in regard to the plans; how we should study every detail; how we should watch the material and select only the best of everything. And yet how careless we are when it comes to building our mental home, which is infinitely more important than any physical home, as everything which can possibly enter into our lives depends upon the character of the material which enters into the construction of our mental home.

What is the character of this material? We have seen that it is the result of the impressions which we have accumulated in the past and stored away in our subconscious mentality. If these impressions have been of fear, worry, care, anxiety, or if they have been despondent, negative, doubtful, then the texture of the material which we are weaving today will be of the same negative material. Instead of being of any value, it will be mildewed and rotten and will bring us only more toil and care and anxiety. We shall be forever busy trying to patch it up and make it appear at least genteel.

But if we have stored away nothing but courageous thought; if we have been optimistic, positive, and have immediately thrown any kind of negative thought on the scrap pile; if we have refused to have anything to do with it, have refused to associate with it or to become identified with it in any way, what then is the result? Our mental material is now of the best kind; we can weave any kind of material we want; we can use any color we wish. We know that the texture is firm, that the material is solid, that it will not fade, and that we have no fear, no anxiety concerning the future. There is nothing to cover, there are no patches to hide.

These are psychological facts; there is no theory or guesswork about these thinking processes; there is nothing secret about them. In fact, they are so plain that everyone can understand them. The thing to do is to have a mental housecleaning, to have this housecleaning every day, and to keep the house clean. Mental, moral, and physical cleanliness are absolutely indispensable if we are to make progress of any kind.

When this mental housecleaning process has been completed, the material which is left will be suitable for the making of the kind of ideals or mental images which we desire to realize. There is a fine estate awaiting a claimant. Its broad acres, with abundant crops, running water, and fine timber, stretch away as far as the eye can see. There is a mansion, spacious and cheerful, with rare pictures, a well-stocked library, rich hangings, and every comfort and luxury. All the heir has to do is to assert his heirship, take possession, and use the property. He must use it and he must not let it decay, for use is the condition on which he holds it. To neglect it is to lose possession.

In the domain of mind and spirit, in the domain of practical power, such an estate is yours. You are the heir! You can assert your heirship and possess and use this rich inheritance. Power over circumstances is one of its fruits; health, harmony, and prosperity are assets upon its balance sheet. It offers you poise and peace. It costs you only the labor of studying and harvesting its great resources. It demands no sacrifice except the loss of your limitations, your servitudes, your weakness. It clothes you with self-honor and puts a scepter in your hands.

To gain this estate, three processes are necessary: you must earnestly desire it, you must assert your claim, and you must take possession. You admit that these are not burdensome conditions.

You are familiar with the subject of heredity. Darwin, Huxley, Haeckel, and other physical scientists have piled evidence mountain high that heredity is a law attending progressive creation. It is progressive heredity which gives man his erect attitude, his power of motion, his organs of digestion, his blood circulation, his nerve force, his muscular force, his bone structure, and his host of other faculties on the physical side. There are even more impressive facts concerning heredity of mind force. All these constitute what may be called your human heredity.

But there is a heredity which the physical scientists have not compassed; it lies beneath and antecedent to all their researches. At a point where they throw up their hands in despair, saying they cannot account for what they see, this divine heredity is found in full sway. It is the benignant force which decrees primal creation. It thrills down from the Divine, direct into every created being. It originates life, which the physical scientist has not done nor ever can do. It stands out among all forces supreme, unapproachable. No human heredity can approach it. No human heredity measures up to it.

This Infinite Life flows through you, is you. Its doorways are but the faculties which comprise your consciousness. To keep open these doors is the secret of power. Is it not worthwhile to make the effort? The great fact is that the source of all life and all power is from within. Persons, circumstances, and events may suggest need and opportunities, but the insight, strength, and power to answer these needs will be found within. Avoid counterfeits. Build firm foundations for your consciousness upon forces which flow direct from the Infinite Source, the Universal Mind of which you are the image and likeness.

Those who have come into possession of this inheritance are never quite the same again. They have come into possession of a sense of power hitherto undreamed of. They can never again be timid, weak, vacillating, or fearful. They are indissolubly connected with Omnipotence. Something in them has been aroused; they have suddenly discovered that they possess a tremendous latent ability of which they were heretofore entirely unconscious.

This power is from within, but we cannot receive it unless we give it. Use is the condition upon which we hold this inheritance. We are each of us but the channel through which the Omnipotent Power is being differentiated into form; unless we give, the channel is obstructed and we can receive no more. This is true on every plane of existence and in every field of endeavor and all walks of life. The more we give, the more we get. The athlete who wishes to get strong must make use of the strength he has; the more he gives the more he will get. The financier who wishes to make money must make use of the money he has, for only by using it can he get more.

The merchant who does not keep his goods going out will soon have none coming in; the corporation which fails to give efficient service will soon lack customers; the attorney who fails to get results will soon lack clients, and so it goes everywhere. Power is contingent upon a proper use of the power already in our possession; what is true in every field of endeavor, every experience in life is true of the power from which every other power known among men is begotten—spiritual power. Take away the spirit and what is left? Nothing.

If then the spirit is all there is, upon the recognition of this fact must depend the ability to demonstrate all power, whether physical, mental, or spiritual.

All possession is the result of the accumulative attitude of mind, or the money consciousness; this is the magic wand which will enable you to receive the idea, and it will formulate plans for you to execute. You will find as much pleasure in the execution as in the satisfaction of attainment and achievement.

Now, go to your room, take the same seat, the same position as heretofore, and mentally select a place which has pleasant associations. Make a complete mental picture of it: see the buildings, grounds, trees, friends, associations, everything complete. At first, you will find yourself thinking of everything under the sun, except the ideal upon which you desire to concentrate. But do not let that discourage you. Persistence will win, but persistence requires that you practice these exercises every day without fail.

Summary

- What proportion of our mental life is subconscious?
  At least 90 percent.
- Is this vast mental storehouse generally utilized?
  No.
- Why not?
  Few understand or appreciate the fact that it is an activity which they may consciously direct.
- Where has the conscious mind received its governing tendencies?
  From heredity, which means that it is the result of all the environments of all past generations.
- What is the Law of Attraction bringing to us?
  Our "own."
- What is our "own"?
  What we inherently are, which is the result of our past thinking, both conscious and subconscious.
- Of what is the material with which we construct our mental home composed?
  The thoughts which we entertain.

- What is the secret of power?
  A recognition of the omnipresence of Omnipotence.
- Where does it originate?
  All life and all power is from within.
- Upon what is the possession of power contingent?
  Upon a proper use of the power already in our possession.

SIX

Thought, Action, and Effect

IT IS my privilege to offer chapter six. This chapter will give you an excellent understanding of the most wonderful piece of mechanism which has ever been created—a mechanism whereby you may create for yourself health, strength, success, prosperity, or any other condition which you desire.

Necessities are demands, and demands create action, and actions bring about results. The process of evolution is constantly building our tomorrows out of our todays. Individual development, like Universal development, must be gradual with an ever-increasing capacity and volume.

The knowledge that, if we infringe upon the rights of others, we become moral thorns and find ourselves entangled at every turn of the road, should be an indication that success is contingent upon the highest moral ideal, which is "The greatest good to the greatest number." Aspiration, desire, and harmonious relations constantly and persistently maintained will accomplish results. The greatest hindrance is erroneous and fixed ideas.

To be in tune with Eternal Truth we must possess poise and harmony within. In order to receive Intelligence the receiver must be in tune with the transmitter.

Thought is a product of Mind, and Mind is creative, but this does not mean that the Universal will change its modus operandi to suit us or our ideas, but it does mean that we can come into harmonious relationship with the Universal. When we have accomplished this we may ask anything to which we are entitled, and the way will be made plain.

Universal Mind is so wonderful that it is difficult to understand its utilitarian powers, its possibilities, and its unlimited producing effects. We have found that Mind is not only all intelligence but all substance. How, then, is it to be differentiated in form? How are we to secure the effect which we desire?

Ask any electrician what the effect of electricity will be and he will reply that "Electricity is a form of motion, and its effect will depend upon the mechanism to which it is attached." Upon this mechanism will depend whether we shall have heat, light, power, music, or any of the other marvelous demonstrations of power to which this vital energy has been harnessed.

What effect can be produced by thought? The reply is that thought is mind in motion (just as wind is air in motion), and its effect will depend entirely on the "mechanism to which it is attached." Here, then, is the secret of all mental power; it depends entirely on the mechanism which we attach.

What is this mechanism? You know something of the mechanism which has been invented by Edison, Bell, Marconi, and other electrical wizards, by which place and space and time have become only figures of speech, but did you ever stop to think that the mechanism which has been given to you for transforming the Universal, Omnipresent Potential Power invented by a greater inventor than Edison?

We are accustomed to examining the mechanism of the implements which we use for tilling the soil, and we try to get an understanding of the mechanism of the automobile which we drive, but most of us are content to remain in absolute ignorance of the greatest piece of mechanism which has ever come into existence: the brain of man. Let us examine the wonders of this mechanism; perhaps we shall thereby get a better understanding of the various effects of which it is the cause.

In the first place, there is the great mental world in which we live and move and have our being. This world is omnipotent, omniscient, and omnipresent; it will respond to our desire in direct ratio to our purpose and faith, so the purpose must be in accordance with the Law of Our Being. That is, it must be creative or constructive; our faith must be strong enough to generate a current of sufficient strength to bring our purpose into manifestation. "As thy faith is, so be it unto thee" bears the stamp of scientific test.

The effects which are produced in the world without are the result of the action and reaction of the individual upon the Universal; that is the process which we call thinking. The brain is the organ through which this process is accomplished—think of the wonder of it all! Do you love music, flowers, or literature, or are you inspired by the thought of ancient or modern genius? Remember, every beauty to which you respond must have its corresponding outline in your brain before you can appreciate it.

There is not a single virtue or principle in the storehouse of Nature which the brain cannot express. The brain is an embryonic world, ready to develop at any time as necessity may arise.

If you can comprehend that this is a scientific truth and one of the wonderful laws of Nature, it will be easier for you to get an understanding of the mechanism by which these extraordinary results are being accomplished.

The nervous system has been compared to an electric circuit with its battery of cells in which force is originated, and its white matter to insulated wires by which the current is conveyed. It is through these channels that every impulse or desire is carried through the mechanism. The spinal cord is the great motor and sensory pathway by which messages are conveyed to and from the brain; then there is the blood supply plunging through the veins and arteries, renewing our energy and strength; the perfectly arranged structure upon which the entire physical body rests; and finally, the delicate and beautiful skin, clothing the entire mechanism in a mantle of beauty.

This then is the "Temple of the Living God" where the individual "I" is given control. It is his understanding and control of the mechanism upon which the results depend. Every thought sets the brain cells in action; at first the substance upon which the thought is directed fails to respond, but if the thought is sufficiently refined and concentrated, the substance finally yields and expresses perfectly. This influence of the mind can be exerted upon any part of the body, causing the elimination of any undesirable effect.

A perfect conception and understanding of the laws governing in the mental world cannot fail to be of inestimable value in the transaction of business, as it develops the power of discernment and gives a clearer understanding and appreciation of facts.

The man who looks within instead of without cannot fail to make use of the mighty forces which will eventually determine his course in life and so bring him into vibration with all that is best, strongest, and most desirable.

Attention or concentration is probably the most important essential in the development of mind culture. The possibilities of attention, when properly directed, are so startling that they would hardly appear credible to the uninitiated. The cultivation of attention is the distinguishing characteristic of every successful man or woman and is the highest personal accomplishment which can be acquired.

The power of attention can be more readily understood by comparing it with a magnifying glass in which rays of sunlight are focused; they possess no particular strength as long as the glass is moved about and the rays are directed from one place to another. But let the glass be held perfectly still and let the rays be focused on one spot for any length of time, and the effect will become immediately apparent.

So it is with the power of thought: let power be dissipated by scattering the thought from one object to another, and no result is apparent; but focus this power through attention or concentration on any single purpose for any length of time, and nothing becomes impossible.

A very simple remedy for a very complex situation, some will say. All right, try it, you who have had no experience in concentrating the thought on a definite purpose or object. Choose any single object, and concentrate your attention on it for a definite purpose for even ten minutes; you cannot do it. The mind will wander a dozen times, and it will be necessary to bring it back to the original purpose. Each time the effect will have been lost, and at the end of the ten minutes, nothing will have been gained because you have not been able to hold your thought steadily to the purpose.

It is, however, through attention that you will finally be able to overcome obstacles of any kind that appear in your path onward and upward, and the only way to acquire this wonderful power is by practice. Practice makes perfect, in this as in anything else.

In order to cultivate the power of attention, bring a photograph with you to the same seat in the same room in the same position as heretofore. Examine it closely at least ten minutes; note the expression of the eyes, the form of the features, the clothing, the way the hair is arranged. In fact, note every detail shown on the photograph carefully. Now cover it, close your eyes, and try to see it mentally. If you can see every detail perfectly and can form a good mental image of the photograph, you are to be congratulated; if not, repeat the process until you can. This step is simply for the purpose of preparing the soil; in the next chapter we shall be ready to sow the seed.

It is by such exercises as these that you will finally be able to control your mental moods, your attitude, your consciousness. Great financiers are learning to withdraw from the multitude more and more, that they may have more time for planning, thinking, and generating the right mental moods. Successful businessmen are constantly demonstrating the fact that it pays to keep in touch with the thought of other successful businessmen. A single idea may be worth millions of dollars, and these ideas can only come to those who are receptive, who are prepared to receive them, who are in a successful frame of mind.

Men are learning to place themselves in harmony with Universal Mind; they are learning the unity of all things; they are learning the basic methods and principles of thinking, and this is changing conditions and multiplying results. They are finding that circumstances and environment follow the trend of mental and spiritual progress; they find that growth follows knowledge, action follows inspiration, and opportunity follows perception—always the spiritual first, then the transformation into the infinite and unlimited possibilities of achievement. As the individual is but the channel for the differentiation of the Universal, these possibilities are necessarily inexhaustible.

Thought is the process by which we may absorb the Spirit of Power and hold the result in our inner consciousness until it becomes a part of our ordinary consciousness. The method of accomplishing this result by the persistent practice of a few fundamental principles, as explained in this system, is the Master Key which unlocks the storehouse of Universal Truth.

The two great sources of human suffering at present are bodily disease and mental anxiety. These may be readily traced to the infringement of Natural Law. This is, no doubt, owing to the fact that, so far, knowledge has largely remained partial, but the clouds of darkness, which have accumulated through long ages, are beginning to roll away with many of the miseries that attend imperfect information.

That a man can change himself, improve himself, re-create himself, control his environment, and master his own destiny is the conclusion of every mind who is wide-awake to the power of right thought in constructive action.

—Christian Larsen

Summary

- What are some of the effects which can be produced by electricity?
  Heat, light, power, music.
- Upon what do these various effects depend?
  Upon the mechanism to which electricity is attached.
- What is the result of the action and interaction of the individual mind upon the Universal?
  The conditions and experiences with which we meet.

- How may these conditions be changed?
  By changing the mechanism by which the Universal is differentiated in form.
- What is this mechanism?
  The brain.
- How may it be changed?
  By the process we call thinking. Thoughts produce brain cells, and these cells respond to the corresponding thought in the Universal.
- Of what value is the power of concentration?
  It is the highest personal accomplishment which can be acquired and the distinguishing characteristic of every successful man or woman.
- How may it be acquired?
  By faithfully practicing the exercises in this system.
- Why is this so important?
  Because it will enable us to control our thoughts, and since thoughts are causes, conditions must be effects. If we can control the cause, we can also control the effect.
- What is changing conditions and multiplying results in the objective world?
  Men are learning the basic methods of constructive thinking.

SEVEN

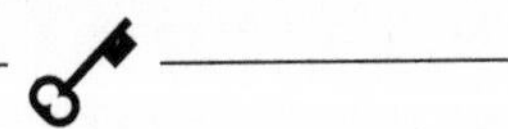

Idealization, Visualization, Realization

THROUGH ALL the ages man has believed in an invisible power, through which and by which all things have been created and are continually being re-created. We may personalize this power and call it God, or we may think of it as the Essence or Spirit which permeates all things, but in either case the effect is the same.

As far as the individual is concerned, the objective, the physical, the visible is the personal—that which can be cognized by the senses. It consists of body, brain, and nerves. The subjective is the spiritual, the invisible, the impersonal.

The personal is conscious because it is a personal entity. The impersonal, being the same in kind and quality as all other-being, is not conscious of itself and has therefore been termed the subconscious.

The personal, or conscious, has the power of will and choice and can therefore exercise discrimination in the selection of methods that bring about the solution of difficulties.

The impersonal, or spiritual, being a part or one with the source and origin of all power, can necessarily exercise no such choice, but, on the contrary, it has infinite resources at its command. It can and does bring about results by methods which the human or individual mind can have no possible conception.

You will, therefore, see that it is your privilege to depend upon the human will with all its limitations and misconceptions, or you may utilize the potentialities of Infinity by making use of the subconscious mind. Here, then, is the scientific explanation of the wonderful power which has been put within your control if you but understand, appreciate, and recognize it.

One method of consciously utilizing this Omnipotent Power is outlined in this chapter.

Visualization is the process of making mental images, and the image is the mold or model which will serve as a pattern from which your future will emerge.

Make the pattern clear and make it beautiful; do not be afraid. Make it grand, and remember that no limitation can be placed upon you by anyone but yourself. You are not limited as to cost or material; draw on the Infinite for your supply, construct it in your imagination. It will have to be there before it will ever appear anywhere else. Make the image clear and clean-cut, hold it firmly in the mind, and you will gradually and constantly bring the thing nearer to you. You can be what you *will* to be.

This is another psychological fact which is well known, but unfortunately, reading about it will not bring about any result which you may have in mind; it will not even help you to form the mental image, much less bring it into manifestation. Work is necessary—labor, hard mental labor, the kind of effort which so few are willing to put forth.

The first step is idealization. It is likewise the most important step because it is the plan on which you are going to build. It must be solid; it must be permanent. The architect, when he plans a 30-story building, has every line and detail pictured in advance. The engineer, when he spans a chasm, first ascertains the strength requirements of a million separate parts.

They see the end before a single step is taken; so you are to picture in your mind what you want. You are sowing the seed, but, before sowing any seed, you want to know what the harvest is to be. This is idealization. If you are not sure, return to your chair daily until the picture becomes plain; it will gradually unfold. First the general plan will be dim, but it will take shape. The outline will take form, then the details, and you will gradually develop the power by which you will be enabled to formulate plans which eventually materialize in the objective world. You will come to know what the future holds for you.

Then comes the process of visualization. You must see the picture more and more completely, see the detail, and, as the details begin to unfold, the ways and means for bringing it into manifestation will develop; one thing will lead to another. Thought will lead to action, action will develop methods, methods will develop friends, friends will bring about circumstances, and, finally, the third step, or materialization, will have been accomplished.

We all recognize the universe must have been thought into shape before it ever could have become a material fact. And if we are willing to follow along the lines of the Great Architect of the universe, we shall find our thoughts taking form, just as the universe took concrete form. It is the same mind operating through the individual. There is no difference in kind or quality; the only difference is one of degree.

The architect visualizes his building, he sees it as he wishes it to be. His thought becomes a plastic mold from which the building will eventually emerge—a high one or a low one, a beautiful one or a plain one. His vision takes form on paper, the necessary material is utilized, and eventually the building stands complete.

The inventor visualizes his idea in exactly the same manner. For instance, Nikola Tesla—he with the giant intellect, one of the greatest inventors of all ages, the man who has brought forth the most amazing realities—always visualizes his inventions before attempting to work them out. He did not rush to embody them in form and then spend his time in correcting defects. Having first built up the idea in his imagination, he held it there as a mental picture to be reconstructed and improved by his thought. "In this way," he writes in the *Electrical Experimenter,* "I am enabled to rapidly develop and perfect a conception without touching anything. When I have gone so far as to embody in the invention every possible improvement I can think of, and see no fault anywhere, I put into concrete the product of my brain. Invariably my devise works as I conceived it should; in twenty years there has not been a single exception."

If you can conscientiously follow these directions, you will develop faith, the kind of faith that is the "Substance of things hoped for, the evidence of things not seen"; you will develop confidence, the kind of confidence that leads to endurance and courage; you will develop the power of concentration which will enable you to exclude all thoughts except the ones which are associated with your purpose. The law is that thought will manifest in form, and only one who knows how to be the divine thinker of his own thoughts can ever take a master's place and speak with authority.

Clearness and accuracy are obtained only by repeatedly having the image in mind. Each repeated action renders the image more clear and accurate than the preceding, and, in proportion to the clearness and accuracy of the image, will the outward manifestation be. You must build it firmly and securely in your mental world—the world within—before it can take form in the world without, and you can build nothing of value, even in the mental world, unless you have the proper material. When you have the material, you can build anything you wish, but be sure of your material. You cannot make broadcloth from shoddy. This material will be brought out by millions of silent mental workers and fashioned into the form of the image which you have in mind.

Think of it! You have over five million of these mental workers, ready and in active use; brain cells they are called. Besides this, there is another reserve force of at least an equal number, ready to be called into action at the slightest need. Your power to think, then, is almost unlimited, and this means that your power to create the kind of material which is necessary to build for yourself any kind of environment which you desire is practically unlimited.

In addition to these millions of mental workers, you have billions of mental workers in the body, every one of which is endowed with sufficient intelligence to understand and act upon any message or suggestion given. These cells are all busy creating and re-creating the body, but, in addition to this, they are endowed with psychic activity whereby they can attract to themselves the substance necessary for perfect development.

They do this by the same law and in the same manner that every form of life attracts to itself the necessary material for growth. The oak, the rose, the lily all require certain material for their most perfect expression, and they secure it by silent demand, the Law of Attraction, and the most certain way for you to secure what you require for your most complete development.

Make the mental image; make it clear, distinct, perfect; hold it firmly. The ways and means will develop; supply will follow the demand; you will be led to do the right thing at the right time and in the right way. Earnest desire will bring about confident expectation, and this in turn must be reinforced by firm demand. These three cannot fail to bring about attainment, because the earnest desire is the feeling, the confident expectation is the thought, and the firm demand is the will, and, as we have seen, feeling gives vitality to thought and the will holds it steadily until the Law of Growth brings it into manifestation.

Is it not wonderful that man has such tremendous power within himself, such transcendental faculties concerning that of which he had no conception? Is it not strange that we have always been taught to look for strength and power without? We have been taught to look everywhere but within, and whenever this power manifested in our lives we were told that it was something supernatural.

There are many who have come to an understanding of this wonderful power and who make serious and conscientious efforts to realize health, power, and other conditions, and seem to fail. They do not seem able to bring the law into operation. The difficulty in nearly every case is that they are dealing with externals. They want money, power, health, and abundance, but they fail to realize that these are effects and can come only when the cause is found.

Those who will give no attention to the world without will seek only to ascertain the Truth, will look only for wisdom, will find that this wisdom will unfold and disclose the source of all power and it will manifest in thought and purpose that which will create the external conditions desired. This Truth will find expression in noble purpose and courageous action.

Create ideals only, give no thought to external conditions, make the world within beautiful and opulent, and the world without will express and manifest the condition which you have within. You will come into a realization of your power to create ideals, and these ideals will be projected into the world of effect.

For instance, a man is in debt. He will be continually thinking about the debt, concentrating on it, and, as thoughts are causes, the result is that he not only fastens the debt closer to him but actually creates more debt. He is putting the great Law of Attraction into operation with the usual and inevitable result—loss leads to greater loss.

What, then, is the correct principle? Concentrate on the things you want, not on the things you do not want. Think of abundance; idealize the methods and plans for putting the Law of Abundance into operation. Visualize the condition which the Law of Abundance creates; this will result in manifestation.

If the law operates perfectly to bring about poverty, lack, and every form of limitation for those who are continually entertaining thoughts of lack and fear, it will operate with the same certainty to bring about conditions of abundance and opulence for those who entertain thoughts of courage and power.

This is a difficult problem for many: we are too anxious; we manifest anxiety, fear, distress; we want to do something; we want to help; we are like a child who has just planted a seed and every fifteen minutes goes and stirs up the earth to see if it is growing. Of course, under such circumstances, the seed will never germinate, and yet this is exactly what many of us do in the mental world. We must plant the seed and leave it undisturbed. This does not mean that we are to sit down and do nothing; we will do more and better work than we have ever done before, new channels will constantly be provided, new doors will open—all that is necessary is to have an open mind and be ready to act when the time comes.

Thought force is the most powerful means of obtaining knowledge, and if concentrated on any subject, it will solve the problem. Nothing is beyond the power of human comprehension, but in order to harness thought force and make it do your bidding, work is required. Remember that thought is the fire that creates the steam that turns the wheel of fortune upon which your experiences depend.

Ask yourself a few questions and then reverently await the response. Do you not now and then feel the self with you? Do you assert this self or do you follow the majority? Remember that majorities are always led, they never lead. It was the majority that fought, tooth and nail, against the steam engine, the power loom, and every other advance or improvement ever suggested.

For your exercise in this chapter, visualize your friend; see him exactly as you last saw him; see the room, the furniture, recall the conversation. Now see his face—see it distinctly; then talk to him about some subject of mutual interest. See his expression change, watch him smile. Can you do this? Go on to arouse his interest, by telling him a story of adventure; see his eyes light up with the spirit of fun or excitement. Can you do all of this? If so, your imagination is good, and you are making excellent progress.

Summary

- What is visualization?
  The process of making mental pictures.
- What is the result of this method of thought?
  By holding the image or picture in mind, we can gradually but surely bring the thing nearer to us. We can be what we will *to be.*
- What is idealization?
  It is a process of visualizing the plans which will eventually materialize in our objective world.
- Why are clearness and accuracy necessary?
  Because "seeing" creates feeling, and feeling creates being. First the mental, then the emotional, then the illimitable possibilities of achievement.

- How are they obtained?
  Each repeated action renders the image more accurate than the former one.
- How is the material for the construction of your mental image secured?
  By millions of mental workers called brain cells.
- How do you secure the necessary conditions for bringing about the materialization of your ideal in the objective world?
  By the Law of Attraction—the natural law by which all conditions and experiences are brought about.
- What three steps are necessary in order to bring this law into operation?
  Earnest desire, confident expectation, firm demand.
- Why do many people fail?
  Because they concentrate on loss, disease, and disaster. The law is operating perfectly; the things they fear are coming upon them.
- What is the alternative?
  Concentrate on the ideals that you desire to see manifested in your life.

EIGHT

The Power of Imagination

IN THIS chapter you will find that you may freely choose what you think, but the result of your thought is governed by an immutable law! Is this not a wonderful thought? Is it not wonderful to know that our lives are not subject to caprice or variability of any kind? That they are governed by Natural Law. This stability is our opportunity because by complying with the law we can secure the desired effect with invariable precision.

It is the law which makes the universe one grand paean of harmony. If it were not for law, the universe would be a chaos instead of a cosmos.

Here, then, is the secret of the origin of both good and evil: this is all the good and evil there ever was or ever will be.

Let me illustrate. Thought results in action. If your thought is constructive and harmonious, the result will be good; if your thought is destructive or inharmonious, the result will be evil.

There is, therefore, but one law, one principle, one cause, one Source of Power, and good and evil are simply words which have been coined to indicate the result of our action, or our compliance or noncompliance with this law.

The importance of this is well illustrated in the lives of Emerson and Carlyle. Emerson loved the good, and his life was a symphony of peace and harmony; Carlyle hated the bad, and his life was a record of perpetual discord and inharmony.

Here we have two grand men, each intent upon achieving the same ideal, but one makes use of constructive thought and is therefore in harmony with Natural Law, the other makes use of destructive thought and therefore brings upon himself discord of every kind and character.

It is evident, therefore, that we are to hate nothing, not even the bad, because hatred is destructive, and we shall soon find that by entertaining destructive thought we are sowing the wind and in turn shall reap the whirlwind.

Thought contains a vital principle because, as the creative principle of the universe, its nature will lead it to combine with other similar thoughts. As the one purpose of life is growth, all principles underlying existence must contribute to give it effect. Thought, therefore, takes form and the Law of Growth eventually brings it into manifestation.

You may freely choose what you think, but the result of your thought is governed by Immutable Law. Any line of thought persisted in cannot fail to produce its result in the character, health, and circumstances of the individual. Methods whereby we can substitute habits of constructive thinking for those which we have found produce only undesirable effects are therefore of primary importance.

We all know that this is by no means easy. Mental habits are difficult to control, but it can be done. The way to do it is to begin at once to substitute constructive thought for destructive thought; Form the habit of analyzing every thought. If its manifestation in the objective will be a benefit, not only to yourself but to all whom it may affect in any way, keep it; treasure it. It is of value; it is in tune with the Infinite; it will grow and develop and produce fruit a hundredfold. On the other hand, it will be well for you to keep this quotation from George Matthew Adams in mind: "Learn to keep the door shut, keep out of your mind, out of your office, and out of your world every element that seeks admittance with no definite helpful end in view."

If your thought has been critical or destructive and has resulted in any condition of discord or inharmony in your environment, it may be necessary for you to cultivate a mental attitude which will be conducive to constructive thought. The imagination will be found to be a great assistance in this direction; the cultivation of the imagination leads to the development of the ideal out of which your future will emerge.

The imagination gathers up the material by which the mind weaves the fabric in which your future is to be clothed. Imagination is the light by which we can penetrate new worlds of thought and experience. Imagination is the mighty instrument by which every discoverer, every inventor opened the way from precedent to experience. Precedent said, "It cannot be done"; experience said, "It is done." Imagination is a plastic power, molding the things of sense into new forms and ideals. Imagination is the constructive form of thought which must precede every constructive form of action.

A builder cannot build a structure of any kind until he has first received the plans from the architect, and the architect must get them from his imagination.

The captain of industry cannot build a giant corporation, which may coordinate hundreds of smaller corporations and thousands of employees and utilize millions of dollars of capital, until he has first created the entire work in his imagination. Objects in the material world are as clay in the potter's hand; it is in the Master Mind that the real things are created, and it is by the use of the imagination that the work is done. In order to cultivate the imagination it must be exercised. Exercise is necessary to cultivate mental muscle as well as physical muscle; it must be supplied with nourishment or it cannot grow.

Do not confuse imagination with fancy or that form of daydreaming in which some people like to indulge. Daydreaming is a form of mental dissipation which may lead to mental disaster.

Constructive imagination means mental labor, considered by some to be the hardest kind of labor, but if so, it yields the greatest returns. All the great things in life have come to men and women who had the capacity to think, to imagine, and to make their dreams come true. When you have become thoroughly conscious of the fact that Mind is the only creative principle, that it is the Omnipotent, Omniscient, and Omnipresent, and that you can consciously come into harmony with this Omnipotence through your power of thought, you will have taken a long step in the right direction.

The next step is to place yourself in position to receive this power. As it is omnipresent, it must be within you. We know that this is so because we know that all power is from within, but it must be developed, unfolded, cultivated. In order to do this we must be receptive, and this receptivity is acquired just as physical strength is gained: by exercise.

The Law of Attraction will certainly and unerringly bring to you the conditions, environment, and experiences in life corresponding with your habitual, characteristic, predominant mental attitude. It's not what you think once in a while when you are in church or have just read a good book, but your predominant mental attitude is what counts. You cannot entertain weak, harmful, negative thoughts ten hours a day and expect to bring about beautiful, strong, and harmonious conditions by ten minutes of strong, positive, creative thought.

Real power comes from within. All power that anybody can possibly use is within man, only waiting to be brought into visibility by his first recognizing it, then affirming it as his, and working it into his consciousness until he becomes one with it.

People say that they desire abundant life, and so they do, but so many interpret this to mean that if they will exercise their muscles or breathe scientifically, eat certain foods in certain ways, drink so many glasses of water every day of just a certain temperature, and keep out of drafts, they will attain the abundant life they seek. The result of such methods is but indifferent. However, when man awakens to the Truth and affirms his oneness with all life, he finds that he takes on the clear eye, the elastic step, the vigor of youth; he finds that he has discovered the source of all power.

All mistakes are but the mistakes of ignorance. Knowledge-gaining and consequent power is what determines growth and evolution. The recognition and demonstration of knowledge is what constitutes power, and this power is Spiritual Power, and this Spiritual Power is the power which lies at the heart of all things; it is the Soul of the universe.

This knowledge is the result of man's ability to think; thought is, therefore, the germ of man's conscious evolution. When man ceases to advance in his thoughts and ideals, his forces immediately begin to disintegrate and his countenance gradually registers these changing conditions.

Successful men make it their business to hold ideals of the conditions which they wish to realize. They constantly hold in mind the next step necessary to the ideal for which they are striving.

Thoughts are the materials with which they build, and the imagination is their mental workshop. Mind is the ever-moving force with which they secure the persons and circumstance necessary to build their success structure, and imagination is the matrix in which all great things are fashioned.

If you have been faithful to your ideal, you will hear the call when circumstances are ready to materialize your plans, and the results will correspond in the exact ratio of your fidelity to your ideal. The ideal steadily held is what predetermines and attracts the necessary conditions for its fulfillment.

It is thus that you may weave a garment of spirit and power into the web of your entire existence; it is thus that you may lead a charmed life and be forever protected from all harm; it is thus that you may become a positive force whereby conditions of opulence and harmony may be attracted to you. This is the leaven which is gradually permeating the general consciousness and is largely responsible for the conditions of unrest which are everywhere evident.

In the last chapter, you created a mental image and you brought it from the invisible into the visible. This week I want you to take an object and follow it back to its origination—to see of what it really consists. If you do this, you will develop imagination, insight, perception, and sagacity. These come not by the superficial observation of the multitude but by a keen analytical observation which sees below the surface. It is few who know that the things they see are only effects, and understand the causes by which these effects were brought into existence.

Take the same position as heretofore and visualize a battleship: see the grim monster floating on the surface of the water; there appears to be no life anywhere about, all is silence. You know that by far the largest part of the vessel is underwater, out of sight; you know that the ship is as large and as heavy as a twenty-story skyscraper. You know that there are hundreds of men ready to spring to their appointed task instantly; you know that every department is in charge of able, trained, skilled officials who have proven themselves competent to take charge of this marvelous piece of mechanism. You know that, although it lies apparently oblivious to everything else, it has eyes which see everything for miles around, and nothing is permitted to escape its watchful vision. You know that while it appears quiet, submissive, and innocent, it is prepared to hurl a steel projectile weighing thousands of pounds at an enemy many miles away. This and much more you can bring to mind with comparatively no effort whatever. But how did the battleship come to be where it is; how did it come into existence in the first place? All of this you want to know if you are a careful observer.

Follow the great steel plates through the foundries, and see the thousands of men employed in their production. Go still further back and see the ore as it comes from the mine; see it loaded onto barges or train cars; see it melted and properly treated. Go back still further and see the architect and engineers who planned the vessel; let the thought carry you back to determine why they planned the vessel. You will see that you are now so far back that the vessel is something intangible; it no longer exists. It is only a thought existing in the brain of the architect.

But from where did the order come to plan the vessel? It probably came from the Secretary of Defense, but this vessel was likely planned long before the war was thought of. Congress would have had to pass a bill appropriating the money; possibly there was opposition and speeches for or against the bill. Whom do these Congressmen represent? They represent you and me; our line of thought begins with the battleship and ends with ourselves, and we find in the last analysis that our own thought is responsible for this and many other things, of which we seldom think. And a little further reflection will develop the most important fact of all:

if someone had not discovered the law by which this tremendous mass of steel and iron could be made to float upon the water, instead of immediately going to the bottom, the battleship could not have come into existence at all.

This law is that "the specific gravity of any substance is the weight of any volume of it compared with an equal volume of water." The discovery of this law revolutionized every kind of ocean travel, commerce, and warfare, and made the existence of the battleship, aircraft carriers, and cruise ships possible.

You will find exercises of this kind invaluable. When the thought has been trained to look below the surface, everything takes on a different appearance, the insignificant becomes significant, the uninteresting interesting. The things which we supposed to be of no importance are seen to be the only really vital things in existence.

Look to this day!
For it is life, the very life of life.
In its brief course lie all the verities
And realities of your existence;
The bliss of growth;
The glory of action;
The splendor of beauty;
For yesterday is but a dream,
And tomorrow is only a vision:
But today well lived
Makes every yesterday
A dream of happiness,
And every tomorrow a vision of hope.
Look well, therefore, to this day!

—Kalidasa (Sanskrit Poet)

Summary

- What is the imagination?
  A form of constructive thought. The light by which we penetrate new worlds of thought and experience. The mighty instrument by which every inventor or discoverer opened the way from precedent to experience.
- What is the result of imagination?
  The cultivation of the imagination leads to the development of the ideal out of which your future will emerge.
- How may it be cultivated?
  By exercise; it must be supplied with nourishment or it cannot live.
- How does imagination differ from daydreaming?
  Daydreaming is a form of mental dissipation, while imagination is a form of constructive thought which must precede every constructive action.
- What are mistakes?
  The result of ignorance.
- What is knowledge?
  The result of man's ability to think.
- What is the power with which successful men build?
  Mind is the very moving force with which they secure the persons and circumstances necessary to complete their plans.
- What predetermines the result?
  The ideal held steadily in mind attracts the necessary conditions for its fulfillment.
- What is the result of a keen analytical observation?
  The development of imagination, insight, perception, and sagacity.
- To what do these lead?
  Opulence and harmony.

NINE

Health, Wealth, and Love

IN THIS chapter you may learn to fashion the tools by which you may build for yourself any condition you desire. If you wish to change conditions, you must change yourself. Your whims, your wishes, your fancies, your ambitions may be thwarted at every step, but your inmost thoughts will find expression just as certainly as the plant springs from the seed.

Suppose, then, we desire to change conditions. How are we to bring this about? The reply is simple: by the Law of Growth. Cause and effect are as absolute and undeviating in the hidden realm of thought as in the world of material things.

Hold in mind the condition desired; affirm it as an already existing fact. This indicates the value of a powerful affirmation, and by constant repetition it becomes a part of ourselves. We are actually changing ourselves; we are making ourselves what we want to be.

Character is not a thing of chance, but it is the result of continued effort. If you are timid, vacillating, self-conscious, or if you are overanxious or harassed by thoughts of fear or impending danger, remember that it is axiomatic that "two things cannot exist in the same place at the same time."

Exactly the same thing is true in the mental and spiritual world, so that your remedy is plainly to substitute thoughts of courage, power, self-reliance, and confidence for those of fear, lack, and limitation.

The easiest and most natural way to do this is to select an affirmation which seems to fit your particular case.

The positive thought will destroy the negative as certainly as light destroys darkness, and the results will be just as effectual.

Act is the blossom of thought, and conditions are the result of action, so that you constantly have in your possession the tools by which you will certainly and inevitably make or unmake yourself, and joy or suffering will be the reward.

There are only three things which can possibly be desired in the world without, and each of them can be found in the world within. The secret of finding them is simply to apply the proper "mechanism" of attachment to the Omnipotent Power to which each individual has access.

The three things which all mankind desires and which are necessary for his highest expression and complete development are health, wealth, and love. All will admit that health is absolutely essential; no one can be happy if the physical body is in pain. All will not so readily admit that wealth is necessary, but all must admit that a sufficient supply at least is necessary; and what would be considered sufficient for one would be considered absolute and painful lack for another. And as Nature provides not only enough but abundantly, wastefully, lavishly, we realize that any lack or limitation is only the limitation which has been made by an artificial method of distribution.

All will probably admit that love is the third, or maybe some will say the first, essential necessary to the happiness of mankind; at any rate, those who possess all three—health, wealth, and love—find nothing else which can be added to their cup of happiness. We have found that the Universal Substance is "all health," "all wealth," and "all love" and that the mechanism of attachment whereby we can consciously connect with this Infinite Supply is in our method of thinking. To think correctly is therefore to enter into the "Secret Place of the Most High."

What shall we think? If we know this, we shall have found the proper mechanism of attachment which will relate us to "whatsoever things we desire." This mechanism may seem very simple when I give it to you, but read on; you will find that it is in reality the Master Key, the "Aladdin's lamp," if you please; you will find that it is the foundation, the imperative condition, the Absolute Law of well-doing, which means, well-being.

To think correctly, accurately, we must know the Truth. The Truth then is the underlying principle in every business or social relation. It is a condition precedent to every right action. To know the Truth, to be sure, to be confident affords a satisfaction beside which no other is at all comparable; it is the only solid ground in a world of doubt, conflict, and danger.

To know the Truth is to be in harmony with the Infinite and Omnipotent Power. To know the Truth is, therefore, to connect yourself with a power which is irresistible and which will sweep away every kind of discord, inharmony, doubt, or error of any kind; "the Truth is mighty and will prevail." The humblest intellect can readily foretell the result of any action when he knows that it is based on Truth, but the mightiest intellect, the most profound and penetrating mind loses its way hopelessly and can form no conception of the results which may ensue when his hopes are based on a premise which he knows to be false.

Every action which is not in harmony with Truth, whether through ignorance or design, will result in discord and eventual loss in proportion to its extent and character. How then are we to know the Truth in order to attach this mechanism which will relate us to the Infinite?

We can make no mistake about this if we realize that Truth is the vital principle of Universal Mind and is omnipresent. For instance, if you require health, a realization of the fact that the "I" in you is spiritual and that all spirit is one, that wherever a part is the Whole must be, will bring about a condition of health; every cell in the body must manifest the Truth as you see it. If you see sickness, the cells will manifest sickness; if you see perfection, they must manifest perfection. The affirmation "I am whole, perfect, strong, powerful, loving, harmonious, and happy" will bring about harmonious conditions. The reason for this is because the affirmation is in strict accordance with the Truth, and when Truth appears every form of error or discord must necessarily disappear.

You have found that the "I" is spiritual; it must necessarily then always be no less than perfect. The affirmation "I am whole, perfect, strong, powerful, loving, harmonious, and happy" is therefore an exact scientific statement. Thought is a spiritual activity, and spirit is creative; therefore, the result of holding this thought in mind must necessarily bring about conditions in harmony with the thought.

If you require wealth, a realization of the fact that the "I" in you is one with Universal Mind, which is all substance and is omnipotent, will assist you in bringing into operation the Law of Attraction. And this law will bring you into vibration with those forces which make for success and bring about conditions of power and affluence in direct proportion with the character and purpose of your affirmation.

Visualization is the mechanism of the attachment which you require, as it is a very different process from seeing. Seeing is physical and is therefore related to the objective world, the world without, but visualization is a product of the imagination and is therefore a product of the subjective mind, the world within. It, therefore, possesses vitality; it will grow. The thing visualized will manifest itself in form. The mechanism is perfect; it was created by the Master Architect who "doeth all things well," but unfortunately sometimes the operator is inexperienced or inefficient. Practice and determination will overcome this defect.

If you require love, try to realize that the only way to get love is by giving; the more you give the more you will get, and the only way in which you can give it is to fill yourself with it, until you become a magnet. This method was explained in another lesson.

He who has learned to bring the greatest spiritual truths into touch with the so-called lesser things of life has discovered the secret of the solution to his problem. One is always quickened, made more thoughtful by his nearness of approach to great ideas, great events, great natural objects, and great men. Lincoln is said to have begotten in all who came near him the feeling awakened when one approaches a mountain, and this sense asserts itself most keenly when one comes to realize that he has laid hold upon things that are eternal, the power of Truth.

It is sometimes an inspiration to hear from someone who has actually put these principles to the test, someone who has demonstrated them in their own life. A letter from Frederick Elias Andrews offers the following insight:

I was about thirteen years old when Dr. T. W. Marsee, since passed over, said to my mother: "There is no possible chance, Mrs. Andrews. I lost my little boy the same way, after doing everything for him that it was possible to do. I have made a special study of these cases, and I know there is no possible chance for him to get well." She turned to him and said: "Doctor, what would you do if he were your boy?" and he answered, "I would fight, fight, as long as there is a breath of life to fight for."

That was the beginning of a long drawn-out battle, with many ups and downs, the doctors all agreeing that there was no chance for a cure, though they encouraged and cheered us the best they could. But at last the victory came, and I have grown from a little, crooked, twisted, cripple, going about on my hands and knees, to a strong, straight, well-formed man.

Now, I know you want the formula, and I will give it to you as briefly and quickly as I can.

I built up an affirmation for myself, taking the qualities I most needed, and affirming for myself over and over again, "I am whole, perfect, strong, powerful, loving, harmonious, and happy." I kept up this affirmation, always the same, never varying, till I could wake up in the night and find myself repeating, "I am whole, perfect, strong, powerful, loving, harmonious, and happy." It was the last thing on my lips at night and the first thing in the morning.

Not only did I affirm it for myself, but for others that I knew needed it. I want to emphasize this point. Whatever you desire for yourself, affirm it for others, and it will help you both. We reap what we sow. If we send out thoughts of love and health, they return to us like bread cast upon the waters; but if we send out thoughts of fear, worry, jealousy, anger, hate, etc., we will reap the results in our own lives.

It used to be said that man is completely built-over every seven years, but some scientists now declare that we build ourselves over entirely every eleven months; so we are really only eleven months old. If we build the defects back into our bodies year after year, we have no one to blame but ourselves.

Man is the sum total of his own thoughts; so the question is, how are we going to entertain only the good thoughts and reject the evil ones? At first we can't keep the evil thoughts from coming, but we can keep from entertaining them. The only way to do this is to forget them—which means, get something for them. This is where the ready-made affirmation comes into play.

When a thought of anger, jealousy, fear, or worry creeps in, just start your affirmation going. The way to fight darkness is with light; the way to fight cold is with heat; the way to overcome evil is with good. For myself, I never could find any help in denials. Affirm the good, and the bad will vanish.

If there is anything you require, it will be well for you to make use of this affirmation; it cannot be improved upon. Use it just as it is; take it into the Silence with you, until it sinks into your subconsciousness and you can use it anywhere—in your car, in the office, at home. This is the advantage of spiritual methods; they are always available. Spirit is omnipresent, ever ready; all that is required is a proper recognition of its omnipotence and a willingness or desire to become the recipient of its beneficent effects.

If our predominant mental attitude is one of power, courage, kindliness, and sympathy, we shall find that our environment will reject conditions in correspondence with these thoughts; if it is weak, critical, envious, and destructive, we shall find our environment reflecting conditions corresponding to these thoughts.

Thoughts are causes, and conditions are effects. Herein is the explanation of the origin of both good and evil. Thought is creative and will automatically correlate with its object. This is Cosmological Law (Universal Law), the Law of Attraction, the Law of Cause and Effect. The recognition and application of this law will determine both beginning and end; it is the law by which in all ages and in all times the people were led to believe in the power of Prayer. "As thy faith is, so be it unto thee" is simply another, shorter, better way of stating it.

This week visualize a plant: take a flower, the one you most admire, and bring it from the unseen into the seen. Plant the tiny seed, water it, care for it, place it where it will get the direct rays of the morning sun, and see the seed burst; it is now a living thing, something which is alive and beginning to search for the means of subsistence. See the roots penetrating the earth, watch them shoot out in all directions, and remember that they are living cells dividing and subdividing, that they will soon number in the millions, that each cell is intelligent and knows what it wants and how to get it. See the stem shoot forward and upward, watch it burst through the surface of the earth, see it divide and form branches, see how perfect and symmetrical each branch is formed, see the leaves begin to form, and then see the tiny stems, each one holding aloft a bud. As you watch you, see the bud begin to unfold and your favorite flower comes to view. And now if you will concentrate intently, you will become conscious of a fragrance; it is the fragrance of the flower as the breeze gently sways the beautiful creation which you have visualized.

When you are enabled to make your vision clear and complete, you will be enabled to enter into the spirit of a thing; it will become very real to you. You will be learning to concentrate, and the process is the same, whether you are concentrating on health, a favorite flower, an ideal, a complicated business proposition, or any other problem of life.

Every success has been accomplished by persistent concentration upon the object in view.

> *Thought means life, since those who do not think do not live in any high or real sense. Thinking makes the man.*
>
> —A. B. Alcott

Summary

- What is the imperative condition of all well-being?
  Well-doing.
- What is the condition precedent to every right action?
  Right thinking.
- What is the underlying condition necessary in every business transaction or social relation?
  To know the Truth.
- What is the result of a knowledge of the Truth?
  We can readily predict the result of any action that is based upon a true premise.
- What is the result of any action based upon a false premise?
  We can form no conception of the results which may ensue.
- How may we know the Truth?
  By a realization of the fact that Truth is the Vital Principle of the

Universe and is therefore omnipresent.

- What is the nature of Truth?
  It is spiritual.
- What is the secret of the solution to every problem?
  To apply spiritual Truth.
- What is the advantage of spiritual methods?
  They are always available.
- What are the necessary requirements?
  A recognition of the omnipotence of Spiritual Power and a desire to become the recipient of its beneficent effects.

TEN

Cause and Effect

IF YOU get a thorough understanding of the thought contained in chapter ten, you will have learned that nothing happens without a definite cause. You will be enabled to formulate your plans in accordance with exact knowledge. You will know how to control any situation by bringing adequate causes into play. When you win, as you will, you will know exactly why.

The ordinary man, who has no definite knowledge of cause and effect, is governed by his feelings or emotions. He thinks chiefly to justify his action. If he fails as a businessman, he says that luck is against him. If he dislikes music, he says that music is an expensive luxury. If he is a poor office man, he says that he could succeed better at some outdoor work. If he lacks friends, he says his individuality is too fine to be appreciated.

He never thinks his problem through to the end. In short, he does not know that every effect is the result of a certain definite cause, but he seeks to console himself with explanations and excuses. He thinks only in self-defense.

On the contrary, the man who understands that there is no effect without an adequate cause thinks impersonally. He gets down to bedrock facts regardless of consequences. He is free to follow the trail of truth wherever it may lead. He sees the issue clear to the end, and he meets the requirements fully and fairly. The result is that the world gives him all that it has to give in friendship, honor, love, and approval.

Abundance is a natural law of the Universe. The evidence of this law is conclusive; we see it on every hand. Everywhere Nature is lavish, wasteful, extravagant. Nowhere is economy observed in any created thing. Profusion is manifested in everything. The millions and millions of trees and flowers and plants and animals and the vast scheme of reproduction where the process of creating and re-creating is forever going on—all indicates the lavishness with which Nature has made provision for man. That there is an abundance for everyone is evident, but that many fail to participate in this abundance is also evident. They have not yet come into a realization of the universality of all substance, and that Mind is the active principle whereby we are related to the things we desire.

All wealth is the offspring of power; possessions are of value only as they confer power. Events are significant only as they affect Power; all things represent certain forms and degrees of power.

Knowledge of cause and effect as shown by the laws governing electricity and chemical affinity, and gravitation enables man to plan courageously and execute fearlessly. These laws are called Natural Law because they govern in the physical world, but all power is not physical power; there is also mental power, and there is moral and spiritual power.

Spiritual Power is superior because it exists on a higher plane. It has enabled man to discover the law by which these wonderful forces of Nature could be harnessed and made to do the work of hundreds and thousands of men. It has enabled man to discover laws whereby time and space have been annihilated and the Law of Gravity to be overcome. The operation of this law is dependent upon spiritual contact, as Henry Drummond well says:

> In the physical world as we know it, there exists the organic and the inorganic. The inorganic of the mineral world is absolutely cut off from the plant or animal world; the passage is hermetically sealed. These barriers have never yet been crossed. No change of substance, no modification of environment, no chemistry, no electricity, no form of energy, no evolution of any kind can ever endow a single atom of the mineral world with the attribute of life.
>
> Only by the bending down into this dead world of some living form can those dead atoms be gifted with the properties of vitality; without this contact with life they remain fixed in the inorganic sphere forever. Huxley says that the doctrine of biogenesis (or life only from life) is victorious all along the line, and Tyndall is compelled to say: "I affirm that no shred of trustworthy evidence exists to prove that life in our day has ever appeared independent of antecedent life."
>
> Physical laws may explain the inorganic, biology explains and accounts for the development of the organic, but on the point of contact science is silent. A similar passage exists between the natural world and the spiritual world; this passage is hermetically sealed on the natural side. The door is closed; no man can open it, no organic change, no mental energy, no moral effort, no progress

of any kind can enable any human being to enter the spiritual world.

But as the plant reaches down into the mineral world and touches it with the mystery of life, so the Universal Mind reaches down into the human mind and endows it with new, strange, wonderful, and even marvelous qualities. All men or women who have ever accomplished anything in the world of industry, commerce, or art have accomplished because of this process.

Thought is the connecting link between the Infinite and the finite, between the Universal and the individual. We have seen that there is an impassable barrier between the organic and the inorganic and that the only way that matter can unfold is to be impregnated with life. As a seed reaches down into the mineral world and begins to unfold and reach out, the dead matter begins to live, a thousand invisible fingers begin to weave a suitable environment for the new arrival, and as the Law of Growth begins to take effect, we see the process continue until the lily finally appears. Even "Solomon in all his glory was not arrayed like one of these."

Even so, a thought is dropped into the Invisible Substance of the Universal Mind—that substance from which all things are created—and as it takes root, the Law of Growth begins to take effect. We find that conditions and environment are but the objective form of our thought.

The law is that thought is an active vital form of dynamic energy which has the power to correlate with its object and bring it out of the Invisible Substance from which all things are created into the visible or objective world. This is the law by which and through which all things come into manifestation; it is the Master Key by which you are admitted into the Secret Place of the Most High and are "given dominion over all things." With an understanding of this law, you may "decree a thing and it shall be established unto thee."

It could not be otherwise; if the Soul of the Universe as we know it is the Universal Spirit, then the Universe is simply the condition which the Universal Spirit has made for itself. We are simply individualized spirit and are creating the conditions for our growth in exactly the same way. This creative power depends upon our recognition of the potential power of the Spirit, or Mind, and must not be confused with evolution. Creation is the calling into existence of that which does not exist in the objective world. Evolution is simply the unfolding of potentialities involved in things which already exist.

In taking advantage of the wonderful possibilities opened up to us through the operation of this law, we must remember that we contribute nothing to its efficacy, just as the Great Teacher said: "It is not I that doeth the works, but the Father that dwelleth in me, He doeth the work." We must take exactly the same position; we can do nothing to assist in the manifestation, we simply comply with the law, and the all-originating Mind will bring about the result.

The great error of the present day is the idea that man has to originate the intelligence whereby the Infinite can proceed to bring about a specific purpose or result. Nothing of this kind is necessary; the Universal Mind can be depended upon to find the ways and means for bringing about any necessary manifestation. We must, however, create the ideal, and this ideal should be perfect.

We know that the laws governing electricity have been formulated in such a way that this invisible power can be controlled and used for our benefit and comfort in thousands of ways. We know that electricity carries messages around the world, that ponderous machinery does its bidding, that it now illuminates practically the whole world, but we know too that if we consciously or ignorantly violate its law by touching a live wire when it is not properly insulated, the result will be unpleasant and possibly disastrous. A lack of understanding of the laws governing in the invisible world has the same result, and many people are suffering the consequences all the time.

It has been explained that the Law of Causation depends upon polarity; a circuit must be formed. This circuit cannot be formed unless we operate in harmony with the law. How shall we operate in harmony with the law unless we know what the law is? How shall we know what the law is? We know by study, by observation.

We see the law in operation everywhere; all Nature testifies to the operation of the law by silently, constantly expressing itself in the Law of Growth. Where there is growth there must be life; where there is life there must be harmony, so that everything that has life is constantly attracting to itself the conditions and the supply which is necessary for its most complete expression.

If your thought is in harmony with the creative principle of Nature, it is in tune with the Infinite Mind and will form the circuit; it will not return to you void. But it is possible for you to think thoughts that are not in tune with the Infinite, and when there is no polarity, the circuit is not formed. What, then, is the result? What is the result when a dynamo is generating electricity, the circuit is cut off, and there is no outlet? The dynamo stops.

It will be exactly the same with you if you entertain thoughts which are not in accordance with the Infinite and cannot therefore be polarized: there is no circuit; you are isolated; the thoughts cling to you, harass you, worry you, and finally bring about disease and possibly death. The physician may not diagnose the case exactly in this way, and he may give it some fancy name which has been manufactured for the various ills which are the result of wrong thinking, but the cause is the same nevertheless.

Constructive thought must necessarily be creative, but creative thought must be harmonious. This eliminates all destructive or competitive thought.

Wisdom, strength, courage, and all harmonious conditions are the result of power, and we have seen that all power is from within. Likewise, every lack, limitation, or adverse circumstance is the result of weakness, and weakness is simply an absence of power: it comes from nowhere, it is nothing. The remedy then is simply to develop power, and this is accomplished in exactly the same manner that all power is developed—by exercise.

This exercise consists in making an application of your knowledge; knowledge will not apply itself. You must make the application because abundance will not come to you out of the sky and neither will it drop into your lap. A conscious realization of the Law of Attraction and the intention to bring it into operation for a certain, definite, and specific purpose, and the will to carry out this purpose, will bring about the materialization of your desire by the natural law of transference. If you are in business, it will increase and develop along regular channels, possibly new or unusual channels of distribution will be opened, and when the law becomes fully operative, you will find that the things you seek are seeking you.

This week select a blank space on the wall, or any other convenient spot, from where you usually sit and mentally draw a black horizontal line about six inches long; try to see the line as plainly as though it were painted on the wall. Now mentally draw two vertical lines of equal length (six inches) connecting with this horizontal line at either end; draw another horizontal line connecting with the two vertical lines to make a square. Try to see the square perfectly; when you can do so draw a circle within the square. Place a point in the center of the circle, then draw the point toward you about 10 inches. Now you have a cone on a square base. You will remember that your work was all in black; change it to white, to red, to yellow.

If you can do this, you are making excellent progress and will soon be enabled to concentrate on any problem you may have in mind.

> *When any object or purpose is clearly held in thought, its precipitation, in tangible and visible form, is merely a question of time. The vision always precedes and itself determines the realization.*
>
> —Lillian Whiting

Summary

- What is wealth?
  Wealth is the offspring of power.
- Of what value are possessions?
  Possessions are of value only as they confer power.
- Of what value is a knowledge of cause and effect?
  It enables men to plan courageously and execute fearlessly.
- How does life originate in the inorganic world?
  Only by the introduction of some living form. There is no other way.
- What is the connecting link between the finite and the Infinite?
  Thought is the connecting link.
- Why is that so?
  Because the Universal can manifest only through the individual.
- Upon what does causation depend?
  Upon polarity; a circuit must be formed. The Universal is the positive side of the battery of life, the individual is the negative, and thought forms the circuit.

- Why do many fail to secure harmonious conditions?
  They do not understand the law; there is no polarity; they have not formed the circuit.
- What is the remedy?
  A conscious recognition of the Law of Attraction with the intention to bring it into existence for a definite purpose.
- What will be the result?
  Thought will correlate with its object and bring it into manifestation because thought is a product of the spiritual man, and spirit is the creative principle of the Universe.

A vivid thought brings the power to paint it; and in proportion to the depth of its source is the force of its projection.

—Emerson

ELEVEN

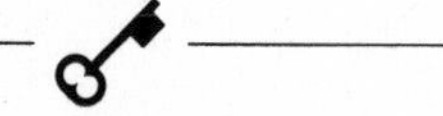

Answers from Nature

Your life is governed by law—by actual, immutable principles that never vary. Law is in operation at all times, in all places. Fixed laws underlie all human actions. For this reason, men who control giant industries are enabled to determine with absolute precision just what percentage of every hundred thousand people will respond to any given set of conditions.

It is well, however, to remember that while every effect is the result of a cause, the effect in turn becomes a cause, which creates other effects, which in turn create still other causes. When you put the Law of Attraction into operation you must remember that you are starting a train of causation for good or otherwise which may have endless possibilities.

We frequently hear it said, "A very distressing situation came into my life which could not have been the result of my thought, as I certainly never entertained any thought which could have had such a result." We fail to remember that like attracts like in the mental world and that the thought which we entertain brings to us certain friendships and companionships, and these in turn bring about conditions and environment, which in turn are responsible for the conditions of which we complain.

Inductive reasoning is the process of the objective mind by which we compare a number of separate instances with one another until we see the common factor that gives rise to them all. Induction proceeds by comparison of facts; it is this method of studying Nature which has resulted in the discovery of a reign of law which has marked an epoch in human progress. It is the dividing line between superstition and intelligence; it has eliminated the elements of uncertainty and caprice from men's lives and substituted law, reason, and certitude. It is the watchman at the gate mentioned in a former lesson.

When, by virtue of this principle, the world to which the senses were accustomed had been revolutionized; when the sun had been arrested in its course; when the apparently flat earth had been shaped into a ball and set whirling around it; when the inert matter had been resolved into active elements; when the universe presented itself wherever we directed the telescope and microscope, full of force, motion, and life; we were constrained to ask by what possible means the delicate forms of organization in the midst of it are kept in order and repair.

Like poles and like forces repel themselves or remain impenetrable to each other, and this cause seems sufficient to assign a proper place and distance to stars, men, and forces in general. As men of different virtues enter into partnership, so do opposite poles attract each other; elements that have no property in common, like acids and gases, cling to each other in preference; and a general exchange is kept up between the surplus and the demand.

As the eye seeks and receives satisfaction from colors complementary to those which are given, so does need, want, and desire, in the largest sense, induce, guide, and determine action. It is our privilege to become conscious of the principle and to act in accordance with it. Georges Cuvier sees a tooth belonging to an extinct race of animals. This tooth wants a body for the performance of its function, and it defines the peculiar body it stands in need of with such precision that Cuvier is able to reconstruct the frame of this animal.

Perturbations are observed in the motion of Uranus. Urbain Leverrier needs another star at a certain place to keep the solar system in order, and Neptune appears in the place and hour appointed. The instinctive wants of the animal and the intellectual wants of Cuvier, and the wants of Nature and of the mind of Leverrier were alike, and thus the results; here the thoughts of an existence, there an existence. A well-defined lawful want, therefore, furnishes the reason for the more complex operations of Nature.

Having recorded correctly the answers furnished by Nature, having stretched our senses with the growing science over her surface, and having joined hands with the levers that move the earth we become conscious of such a close, varied, and deep contact with the world without that our wants and purposes become no less identified with the harmonious operations of this vast organization than the life, liberty, and happiness of the citizen identified with the existence of his government.

As the interests of the individual are protected by the arms of the country, added to his own, and his needs may depend upon certain supply in the degree that they are felt more universally and steadily, in the same manner does conscious citizenship in the republic of Nature secure us from the annoyances of subordinate agents by alliance with superior powers and by appeal to the fundamental laws of resistance or inducement offered to mechanical or chemical agents. Distribute the labor to be performed between them and man to the best advantage of the inventor.

If Plato could have witnessed the pictures executed by the sun with the assistance of the photographer or a hundred similar illustrations of what man does by induction, he would perhaps have been reminded of the intellectual midwifery of his master and, in his own mind, might have arisen the vision of a land where all manual, mechanical labor and repetition is assigned to the power of Nature, where our wants are satisfied by purely mental operations set in motion by the will, and where the supply is created by the demand.

However distant that land may appear, induction has taught men to make strides toward it and has surrounded him with benefits which are, at the same time, rewards for past fidelity and incentives for more assiduous devotion. It is also an aid in concentrating and strengthening our faculties for the remaining part, giving unerring solution for individual as well as universal problems by the mere operations of mind in the purest form.

Here we find a method, the spirit of which is to believe that what is sought has been accomplished in order to accomplish it—a method bequeathed upon us by the same Plato who, outside of this sphere, could never find how the ideas became realities. This conception is also elaborated by Swedenborg in his doctrine of correspondences; and a still greater teacher has said, "What things soever ye desire, when ye pray, believe that ye receive them, and ye shall have them" (Mark 11:24). The difference of the tenses in this passage is remarkable.

We are first to believe that our desire has already been fulfilled and its accomplishment will then follow. This is a concise direction for making use of the creative power of thought by impressing on the Universal Subjective Mind the particular thing which we desire as an already existing fact.

We are thus thinking on the plane of the absolute and eliminating all consideration of conditions or limitation, planting a seed which, if left undisturbed, will finally germinate into external fruition.

To review: Inductive reasoning is the process of the objective mind, by which we compare a number of separate instances with one another until we see the common factor that gives rise to them all. We see people in every civilized country on the globe securing results by some process which they do not seem to understand and to which they usually attach more or less mystery. Our reason is given to us for the purpose of ascertaining the law by which these results are accomplished.

The operation of this thought process is seen in those fortunate natures that possess everything that others must acquire by toil—in those who never have a struggle with conscience because they always act correctly, and can never conduct themselves otherwise than with tact; in those who learn everything easily, complete everything they begin with a happy knack, live in eternal harmony with themselves without ever reflecting much what they do or ever experiencing difficulty or toil.

The fruit of this thought is, as it were, a gift of the gods, but a gift which few as yet realize, appreciate, or understand. The recognition of the marvelous power, which is possessed by the mind under proper conditions, and the fact that this power can be utilized, directed, and made available for the solution of every human problem, is of transcendental importance.

All truth is the same, whether stated in modern scientific terms or in the language of apostolic times. There are timid souls who fail to realize that the very completeness of Truth requires various statements—that no one human formula will show every side of it.

Changing emphasis, new language, novel interpretations, and unfamiliar perspectives are not, as some suppose, signs of departure from Truth, but on the contrary, they are evidence that the Truth is being apprehended in new relations to human needs and is becoming more generally understood.

The Truth must be told to each generation and to every people in new and different terms, so that when the Great Teacher said, "Believe that ye receive and ye shall receive," or when Paul said, "Faith is the substance of things hoped for, the evidence of things not seen," or when modern science says, "The Law of Attraction is the law by which thought correlates with its object," each statement, when subjected to analysis, is found to contain exactly the same Truth, the only difference being in the form of presentation.

We are standing on the threshold of a new era. The time has arrived when man has learned the secrets of mastery, and the way is being prepared for a new social order, more wonderful than anything ever heretofore dreamed of. The conflict of modern science with theology, the study of comparative religions, the tremendous power of new social movements—all of these are but clearing the way for the new order. They may have destroyed traditional forms which have become antiquated and impotent, but nothing of value has been lost.

A new faith has been born—a faith which demands a new form of expression—and this faith is taking form in a deep consciousness of power, which is being manifested in the present spiritual activity found on every hand. The spirit which sleeps in the mineral, breathes in the vegetable, moves in the animal, and reaches its highest development in man is Universal Mind, and it behooves us to span the gulf between being and doing, theory and practice, by demonstrating our understanding of the dominion which we have been given.

By far the greatest discovery of all the centuries is the power of thought. The importance of this discovery has been a little slow in reaching the general consciousness, but it has arrived. Already in every field of research, the importance of this greatest of all great discoveries is being demonstrated.

You ask in what does the creative power of thought consist? It consists in creating ideas, and these in turn objectify themselves by appropriating, inventing, observing, discerning, discovering, analyzing, ruling, governing, combining, and applying matter and force. It can do this because it is intelligent creative power.

Thought reaches its loftiest activity when plunged into its own mysterious depth, when it breaks through the narrow compass of self and passes from truth to truth to the region of eternal light where all which is, was, or ever will be melts into one grand harmony. From this process of self-contemplation comes inspiration which is Creative Intelligence and which is undeniably superior to every element, force, or law of Nature because it can understand, modify, govern, and apply them to its own ends and purposes and therefore, possess them.

Wisdom begins with the dawn of reason, and reason is but an understanding of the knowledge and principles whereby we may know the true meaning of things. Wisdom, then, is illuminated reason, and wisdom leads to humility, for humility is a large part of wisdom. We all know many who have achieved the seemingly impossible, who have realized life-long dreams, who have changed everything including themselves. We have sometimes marveled at the demonstration of an apparently irresistible power, which seemed to be ever available just when it was most needed, but it is all clear now. All that is required is an understanding of certain definite fundamental principles and their proper application.

For your exercise in this chapter, concentrate on the quotation taken from the Bible, "What things soever ye desire, when ye pray, believe that ye receive them, and ye shall have them" (Mark 11:24); notice that there is no limitation. "What things soever" is very definite and implies that the only limitation which is placed upon us is our ability to think, to be equal to the occasion, to rise to the emergency, to remember that faith is not a shadow but a substance, "the substance of things hoped for, the evidence of things not seen" (Hebrews 11:1).

Death is but the natural process whereby all material forms are thrown into the crucible for reproduction in fresh diversity.

Summary

- What is inductive reasoning?
  The process of the objective mind by which we compare a number of separate instances with each other until we see the common factor which gives rise to them all.
- What has this method of studying accomplished?
  It has resulted in the discovery of a reign of law which has marked an epoch in human progress.
- What is it that guides and determines action?
  It is need, want, and desire which in the largest sense induce, guide, and determine action.
- What is the formula for the unerring solution of every individual problem?
  We are to believe that our desire has already been fulfilled; its accomplishment will then follow.
- What great teachers advocated it?
  Jesus, Plato, Swedenborg.
- What is the result of this thought process?
  We are thinking on the plane of the absolute and planting a seed which, if left undisturbed, will germinate into fruition.
- Why is it scientifically exact?
  Because it is Natural Law.

- What is faith?
  "Faith is the substance of things hoped for, the evidence of things unseen."
- What is the Law of Attraction?
  The law by which faith is brought into manifestation.
- What importance do you attach to an understanding of this law?
  It has eliminated the elements of uncertainty and caprice from men's lives and substituted law, reason, and certitude.

TWELVE

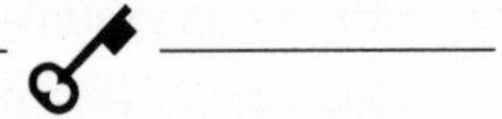

The Law of Attraction

CHAPTER TWELVE is offered herewith. In the fourth paragraph following you will find this statement: "You must first have the knowledge of your power; second, the courage to dare; third, the faith to do." If you concentrate upon the thoughts given, if you give them your entire attention, you will find a world of meaning in each sentence and will attract to yourself other thoughts in harmony with them; you will soon grasp the full significance of the vital knowledge upon which you are concentrating.

Knowledge does not apply itself; we as individuals must make the application, and the application consists in fertilizing the thought with a living purpose.

The time and thought which most persons waste in aimless effort would accomplish wonders if properly directed with some special object in view. In order to do this, it is necessary to center your mental force upon a specific thought and hold it there, to the exclusion of all other thoughts. If you have ever looked through the viewfinder of a camera, you found that when the object was not in focus, the impression was indistinct and possibly blurred; but when the proper focus was obtained the picture was clear and distinct. This illustrates the power of concentration. Unless you can concentrate upon the object which you have in view, you will have but a hazy, indifferent, vague, indistinct, and blurred outline of your ideal, and the results will be in accordance with your mental picture.

There is no purpose in life that cannot be best accomplished through a scientific understanding of the creative power of thought. This power to think is common to all. Man *is* because he thinks. Man's power to think is infinite, consequently his creative power is unlimited.

We know that thought is building for us the thing we think of and actually bringing it nearer, yet we find it difficult to banish fear, anxiety, or discouragement, all of which are powerful thought forces which continually send the things we desire further away; our thoughts are often one step forward and two steps backward. The only way to keep from going backward is to keep going forward. Eternal vigilance is the price of success. There are three steps, and each one is absolutely essential. You must first have the knowledge of your power; second, the courage to dare; third, the faith to do.

With this as a basis, you can construct an ideal business, an ideal home, ideal friends, and an ideal environment; you are not restricted as to material or cost. Thought is omnipotent and has the power to draw on the infinite bank of Primary Substance for all that it requires. infinite resources are therefore at your command.

But your ideal must be sharp, clear-cut, definite; to have one ideal today, another tomorrow, and a third next week means to scatter your forces and accomplish nothing; your result will be a meaningless and chaotic combination of wasted material. Unfortunately this is the result which many are securing, and the cause is self-evident. If a sculptor started out with a piece of marble and a chisel and changed his ideal every fifteen minutes, what result could he expect? And why should you expect any different result in molding the greatest and most plastic of all substances, the only real Substance?

The result of this indecision and negative thought is often found in the loss of material wealth. Supposed independence, which required many years of toil and effort, suddenly disappears. It is often found then that money and property are not independence at all. On the contrary, the only independence is found to be a practical working knowledge of the creative power of thought.

This practical working method cannot come to you until you learn that the only real power which you can have is the power to adjust yourself to divine and unchangeable principles. You cannot change the Infinite, but you can come into an understanding of Natural Law. The reward of this understanding is a conscious realization of your ability to adjust your thought faculties with the Universal Thought which is omnipresent. Your ability to cooperate with this Omnipotence will indicate the degree of success with which you meet.

The power of thought has many counterfeits, which are more or less fascinating, but the results are harmful instead of helpful. Of course, worry, fear, and all negative thoughts produce a crop after their kind; those who harbor thoughts of this kind must inevitably reap what they have sown.

Again, there are the phenomena seekers who gormandize on the so-called proofs and demonstrations obtained at materializing séances. They throw open their mental doors and soak themselves in the most poisonous currents which can be found in the psychic world. They do not seem to understand that it is the ability to become negative, receptive, and passive, and thus drain themselves of all their vital force, which enables them to bring about these vibratory thought forms.

There are also the Hindu worshippers who see in the materializing phenomena, which are performed by the so-called adepts, a source of power, forgetting, or never seeming to realize, that as soon as the will is withdrawn the forms wither and the vibratory forces of which they are composed vanish.

Telepathy, or thought transference, has received considerable attention, but as it requires a negative mental state on the part of the receiver, the practice is harmful. A thought may be sent with the intention of hearing or seeing, but it will bring the penalty attached to the inversion of the principle involved. In many instances, hypnotism is positively dangerous to the subject as well as the operator. No one familiar with the laws governing in the mental world would think of attempting to dominate the will of another, for by so doing, he will gradually (but surely) divest himself of his own power.

All of these perversions have their temporary satisfaction and, for some, a keen fascination, but there is an infinitely greater fascination in a true understanding of the world of power within—a power which increases with use; is permanent instead of fleeting; is potent as a remedial agency to bring about the remedy for past error or results of wrong thinking, as well as a prophylactic agency protecting us from all manner and form of danger; and is an actual creative force with which we can build new conditions and a new environment.

The law is that thought will correlate with its object and bring forth in the material world the correspondence of the thing thought or produced in the mental world. We then discern the absolute necessity of seeing that every thought has the inherent germ of Truth in order that the Law of Growth will bring into manifestation good, for good alone confers permanent power.

The principle, which gives the thought the dynamic power to correlate with its object and therefore to master every adverse human experience, is the Law of Attraction, which is another name for love. This is an eternal and fundamental principle, inherent in all things, in every system of philosophy, in every religion, and in every science; there is no getting away from the Law of Love. It is feeling that imparts vitality to thought; feeling is desire, and desire is love. Thought impregnated with love becomes invincible.

We find this truth emphasized wherever the power of thought is understood. Universal Mind is not only Intelligence but Substance, and this substance is the attractive force which brings electrons together by the Law of Attraction so that they form atoms; the atoms in turn are brought together by the same law and form molecules; molecules take objective forms. And so we find that the Law of Love is the creative force behind every manifestation, not only of atoms but of worlds, of the universe, of everything of which the imagination can form any conception.

It is the operation of this marvelous Law of Attraction which has caused men in all ages and all times to believe that there must be some personal being who responded to their petitions and desires, and manipulated events in order to comply with their requirements.

It is the combination of thought and love which forms the irresistible force called the Law of Attraction. All Natural Law are irresistible; the Law of Gravity, the Law of Electricity, or any other law operates with mathematical exactitude. There is no variation; it is only the channel of distribution which may be imperfect. If a bridge falls, we do not attribute the collapse to any variation of the Law of Gravity. If a light fails us, we do not conclude that the laws governing electricity cannot be depended upon, and if the Law of Attraction seems to be imperfectly demonstrated by an inexperienced or uninformed person, we are not to conclude that the greatest and most infallible law upon which the entire system of creation depends has been suspended. We should rather conclude that a little more understanding of the law is required, for the same reason that a correct solution of a difficult problem in mathematics is not always readily and easily obtained.

Things are created in the mental or spiritual world before they appear in the outward act or event. By the simple process of governing our thought forces today, we help create the events which will come into our lives in the future, perhaps even tomorrow. Educated desire is the most potent means of bringing into action the Law of Attraction.

Man is so constituted that he must first create the tools or implements by which he gains the power to think. The mind cannot comprehend an entirely new idea until a corresponding, vibratory brain cell has been prepared to receive it. This explains why it is so difficult for us to receive or appreciate an entirely new idea; we have no brain cell capable of receiving it and we are therefore incredulous. We do not believe it.

If, therefore, you have not been familiar with the omnipotence of the Law of Attraction and the scientific method by which it can be put into operation, or if you have not been familiar with the unlimited possibilities which it opens to those who are enabled to take advantage of the resources it offers, begin now and create the necessary brain cells which will enable you to comprehend the unlimited powers which may be yours by cooperating with Natural Law. This is done by concentration or attention.

The intention governs the attention; power comes through repose. It is by concentration that deep thoughts, wise speech, and all forces of high potentiality are accomplished. It is in the Silence that you get in touch with the omnipotent power of the subconscious mind from which all power is evolved. He who desires wisdom, power, or permanent success of any kind will find it only within; it is an unfoldment. The unthinking may conclude that the Silence is very simple and easily attained, but it should be remembered that only in Absolute Silence may one come into contact with Divinity itself, learn of unchangeable law, and open for himself the channels by which persistent practice and concentration lead to perfection.

This week, go to the same room, and take the same chair and the same position as previously. Be sure to relax, let go both mentally and physically. Always do this; never try to do any mental work under pressure. See that there are no tense muscles or nerves, that you are entirely comfortable. Now realize your unity with Omnipotence; get in touch with this power; come to a deep and vital understanding, appreciation, and realization of the fact that your ability to think is your ability to act upon the Universal Mind and bring it into manifestation. Realize that it will meet any and every requirement, that you have exactly the same potential ability which any individual ever did have or ever will have. Each is but an expression or manifestation of the One, all are parts of the Whole; there is no difference in kind or quality, the only difference being one of degree.

Thought cannot conceive of anything that may not be brought to expression. He who first uttered it may be only the suggester, but the doer will appear.

—Wilson

Summary

- How may any purpose in life be best accomplished?
  Through a scientific understanding of the spiritual nature of thought.
- What three steps are absolutely essential?
  The knowledge of our power, the courage to dare, the faith to do.
- How is this practical working knowledge secured?
  By an understanding of Natural Laws.
- What is the reward for an understanding of these laws?
  A conscious realization of our ability to adjust ourselves to divine and unchanging principle.
- What will indicate the degree of success with which we meet?
  The degree to which we realize that we cannot change the Infinite but must cooperate with it.
- What is the principle which gives thought its dynamic power?
  The Law of Attraction, which rests on vibration, which in turn rests upon the Law of Love. Thought impregnated with love becomes invincible.
- Why is this law irresistible?
  Because it is a natural law. All Natural Law is irresistible and unchangeable and acts with mathematical exactitude. There is no deviation or variation.
- Why then does it sometimes seem to be difficult to find the solution to our problems in life?
  For the same reason that it is sometimes difficult to find the correct solution to a difficult mathematical problem: the operator is uninformed or inexperienced.
- Why is it impossible for the mind to grasp an entirely new idea?
  We have no corresponding, vibratory brain cells capable of receiving the idea.
- How is wisdom secured?
  By concentration; it is an unfoldment; it comes from within.

THIRTEEN

The Process

PHYSICAL SCIENCE is responsible for the marvelous age of invention in which we are now living, but spiritual science is now setting out on a career whose possibilities no one can foretell.

Spiritual science has previously been the football of the uneducated, the superstitious, the mystical, but men are now only interested in definite methods and demonstrated facts.

We have come to know that thinking is a spiritual process, that vision and imagination preceded action and event, that the day of the dreamer has come.

The following lines by Mr. Herbert Kaufman are interesting in this connection: "They are the architects of greatness, their vision lies within their souls, they peer beyond the veils and mists of doubt and pierce the walls of unborn Time. The belted wheel, the trail of steel, the churning screw are shuttles in the loom on which they weave their magic tapestries. Makers of Empire, they have fought for bigger things than crowns and higher seats than thrones. Your homes are set upon the land a dreamer found. The pictures on its walls are visions from a dreamer's soul. They are the chosen few—the blazers of the way. Walls crumble and empires fall, the tidal wave sweeps from the sea and tears a fortress from its rocks. The rotting nations drop off from Time's bough, and only things the dreamers make live on."

Chapter thirteen tells why the dreams of the dreamer come true. It explains the Law of Causation by which dreamers, inventors, authors, and financiers bring about the realization of their desires. It explains the law by which the thing pictured upon our mind eventually becomes our own.

It has been the tendency, and, as might be proved, a necessity for science to seek the explanation of everyday facts by a generalization of those others which are less frequent and form the exception. Thus does the eruption of the volcano manifest the heat which is continually at work in the interior of the earth and to which the latter owes much of her configuration.

Thus does lightning reveal a subtle power constantly busy to produce changes in the inorganic world, and, as dead languages now seldom heard were once ruling among the nations, so does a giant tooth in Siberia or a fossil in the depth of the earth not only bear record of the evolution of past ages but thereby explains to us the origin of the hills and valleys which we inhabit today.

In this way, a generalization of facts which are rare, strange, or form the exception has been the magnetic needle guiding all the discoveries of inductive science. This method is founded upon reason and experience and thereby destroyed superstition, precedent, and conventionality.

It is several hundred years since Lord Bacon recommended this method of study, to which the civilized nations owe the greater part of their prosperity and the more valuable part of their knowledge; which purged the mind from narrow prejudices and denominated theories more effectually than by the keenest irony; which called the attention of men from Heaven to earth more successfully by surprising experiments than by the most forcible demonstration of their ignorance; and which educated the inventive faculties more powerfully by the near prospect of useful discoveries thrown open to all than by talk of bringing to light the innate laws of our mind.

The method of Bacon has seized the spirit and aim of the great philosophers of Greece and carried them into effect by the new means of observation which another age offered. It gradually revealed a wondrous field of knowledge in the infinite space of astronomy, in the microscopic egg of embryology, and in the dim age of geology, disclosing an order of the pulse which the logic of Aristotle could never have unveiled, and analyzing into formerly unknown elements the material combinations which no dialectic of the scholastics could force apart.

It has lengthened life; it has mitigated pain; it has extinguished diseases; it has increased the fertility of the soil; it has given new securities to the mariner; it has spanned great rivers with bridges of form unknown to our fathers; it has guided the thunderbolt from Heaven to earth; it has lighted up night with the splendor of day; it has extended the range of human vision; it has multiplied the power of the human muscles; it has accelerated motion; it has annihilated distance; it has facilitated intercourse, correspondence, all friendly offices, all dispatch of business; it has enabled men to descend into the depths of the sea, to soar into the air, to penetrate securely into the noxious recesses of the earth.

This then is the true nature and scope of induction. But the greater the success which men have achieved in the inductive science, the more does the whole tenor of their teachings and example impress us with the necessity of observing carefully, patiently, accurately, with all the instruments and resources at our command, and with the individual facts, before venturing upon a statement of general laws.

To ascertain the bearing of the spark drawn from the electric machine under every variety of circumstances, we may be emboldened with Benjamin Franklin to address, in the form of a kite, the question to the cloud about the nature of the lightning. To assure ourselves of the manner in which bodies fall with the exactness of Galileo and that of Newton, we may dare to ask the moon about the force that fastens it to the earth.

In short, by the value we set upon Truth, by our hope in a steady and universal progress, not to permit a tyrannical prejudice to neglect or mutilate unwelcome facts, but to rear the superstructure of science upon the broad and unchangeable basis of full attention paid to the most isolated as well as the most frequent phenomena.

An ever-increasing material may be collected by observation, but the accumulated facts are of very different value for the explanation of nature, and as we esteem most highly those useful qualities of men which are of the rarest occurrence, so does natural philosophy sift the facts and attach a preeminent importance to that striking class which cannot be accounted for by the usual and daily observation of life.

If then, we find that certain persons seem to possess unusual power, what are we to conclude? First, we may say, it is not so, which is simply an acknowledgment of our lack of information because every honest investigator admits that there are many strange and previously unaccountable phenomena constantly taking place. Those, however, who become acquainted with the creative power of thought will no longer consider them unaccountable.

Second, we may say that they are the result of supernatural interference, but a scientific understanding of Natural Law will convince us that there is nothing supernatural. Every phenomenon is the result of an accurate, definite cause, and the cause is Immutable Law or Principle, which operates with invariable precision whether the law is put into operation consciously or unconsciously.

Third, we may say that we are on "forbidden ground," that there are some things which we should not know. This objection was used against every advance in human knowledge. Every individual who ever advanced a new idea, whether Columbus, Darwin, Galileo, Fulton, or Emerson, was subjected to ridicule or persecution, so this objection should receive no serious consideration. On the contrary, we should carefully consider every fact which is brought to our attention; by doing this we will more readily ascertain the law upon which it is based.

It will be found that the creative power of thought will explain every possible condition or experience, whether physical, mental, or spiritual. Thought will bring about conditions in correspondence with the predominant mental attitude. Therefore, if we fear disaster, as fear is a powerful form of thought, disaster will be the certain result of our thinking. It is this form of thought which frequently sweeps away the result of many years of toil and effort.

If we think of some form of material wealth we may secure it. By concentrated thought and with the proper effort put forth, the required conditions will be brought about. This will result in bringing about the circumstances necessary to realize our desires; but we often find that when we secure the things we thought we wanted, they do not have the effect we expected. That is, the satisfaction is only temporary, or possibly is the reverse of what we expected.

What, then, is the proper method of procedure? What are we to think in order to secure what we really desire? What you and I desire, what we all desire, what everyone is seeking is happiness and harmony. If we can be truly happy, we shall have everything the world can give. If we are happy ourselves, we can make others happy. But we cannot be happy unless we have health, strength, congenial friends, pleasant environment, sufficient supply, not only to take care of our necessities but to provide for those comforts and luxuries to which we are entitled.

The old orthodox way of thinking was to be "a worm," to be satisfied with our portion whatever it is. But the modern idea is to know that we are entitled to the best of everything, that the "Father and I are one" and that the "Father" is the Universal Mind, the Creator, the Original Substance from which all things proceed. Now, admitting that this is all true in theory, that it has been taught for two thousand years, that it is the essence of every system of philosophy or religion, how are we to make it practical in our lives? How are we to get the actual, tangible results here and now?

In the first place, we must put our knowledge into practice. Nothing can be accomplished in any other way. The athlete may read books and lessons on physical training all his life, but unless he begins to give out strength by actual work he will never receive any strength; he will eventually get exactly what he gives, but he will have to give it first. It is exactly the same with us: we will get exactly what we give, but we shall have to give it first. It will then return to us many fold. And the giving is simply a mental process because thoughts are causes and conditions are effects; therefore, in giving thoughts of courage, inspiration, health, or help of any kind, we are setting causes in motion which will bring about their effect.

Thought is a spiritual activity and is therefore creative, but make no mistake: thought will create nothing unless it is consciously, systematically, and constructively directed. Herein is the difference between idle thinking, which is simply a dissipation of effort, and constructive thinking, which means practically unlimited achievement.

We have found that everything we get comes to us by the Law of Attraction. A happy thought cannot exist in an unhappy consciousness; therefore the consciousness must change, and, as the consciousness changes, all conditions necessary to meet the changed consciousness must gradually change in order to meet the requirements of the new situation.

In creating a mental image or an ideal, we are projecting a thought into the Universal Substance from which all things are created. This Universal Substance is omnipresent, omnipotent, and omniscient. Are we to inform the omniscient as to the proper channel to be used to materialize our demand? Can the finite advise the Infinite? This is the cause of failure, of every failure. We recognize the omnipresence of the Universal Substance, but we fail to appreciate the fact that this substance is not only omnipresent but is omnipotent and omniscient, and consequently will set causes in motion concerning which we may be entirely ignorant.

We can best conserve our interests by recognizing the Infinite Power and Infinite Wisdom of the Universal Mind, and in this way become a channel whereby the Infinite can bring about the realization of our desire. This means that recognition brings about realization; therefore, for your exercise in this chapter, make use of the principle. Recognize the fact that you are a part of the Whole and that a part must be the same in kind and quality as the Whole; the only difference there can possibly be is in degree.

When this tremendous fact begins to permeate your consciousness, when you really come into a realization of the fact that you (not your body, but the Ego), the "I," the spirit which thinks is an integral part of the Great Whole; that it is the same in substance, in quality, in kind; and that the Creator could create nothing different from Himself, you will also be able to say, "The

Father and I are one." You will come into an understanding of the beauty, the grandeur, the transcendental opportunities which have been placed at your disposal.

Increase in me that wisdom
Which discovers my truest interest,
Strengthen my resolution
To perform that which wisdom dictates.

—BENJAMIN FRANKLIN

Summary

- What is the method by which natural philosophers obtain and apply their knowledge?
  To observe individual facts carefully, patiently, accurately, with all the instruments and resources at their command, before venturing upon a statement of general laws.
- How may we be certain that this method is correct?
  By not permitting a tyrannical prejudice to neglect or mutilate unwelcome facts.
- What classes of facts are esteemed most highly?
  Those which cannot be accounted for by the usual daily observation of life.
- Upon what is this principle founded?
  Upon reason and experience.
- What does it destroy?
  Superstition, precedent, and conventionality.
- How have these laws been discovered?
  By a generalization of facts which are uncommon, rare, strange, and form the exception.

- How may we account for much of the strange and heretofore unexplainable phenomena which is constantly taking place?
  By the creative power of thought.
- Why is this so?
  Because when we learn of a fact, we can be sure that it is the result of a certain definite cause and that this cause will operate with invariable precision.
- What is the result of this knowledge?
  It will explain the cause of every possible condition, whether physical, mental, or spiritual.
- How will our best interest be conserved?
  By a recognition of the fact that a knowledge of the creative nature of thought puts us in touch with Infinite Power.

FOURTEEN

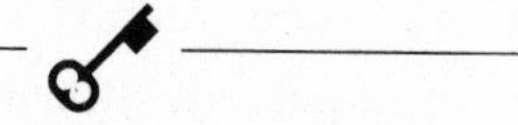

Manifestation

You have found from your study thus far that thought is a spiritual activity and is therefore endowed with creative power. This does not mean that some thought is creative but that all thought is creative. This same principle can be brought into operation in a negative way, through the process of denial.

The conscious and subconscious are but two phases of action in connection with one Mind. The relation of the subconscious to the conscious is quite analogous to that existing between a weather vane and the atmosphere.

Just as the least pressure of the atmosphere causes an action on the part of the weather vane, so does the least thought entertained by the conscious mind produce within your subconscious mind action in exact proportion to the depth of feeling characterizing the thought and the intensity with which the thought is indulged.

It follows that if you deny unsatisfactory conditions, you are withdrawing the creative power of your thought from these conditions. You are cutting them away at the root; you are sapping their vitality.

Remember that the Law of Growth necessarily governs every manifestation in the objective, so that a denial of unsatisfactory conditions will not bring about instant change. A plant will remain visible for some time after its roots have been cut, but it will gradually fade away and eventually disappear. Similarly, the withdrawal of your thought from the contemplation of unsatisfactory conditions will gradually, but surely, terminate these conditions.

You will see that this is an exactly opposite course from the one which we would naturally be inclined to adopt. It will therefore have an exactly opposite effect to the one usually secured. Most persons concentrate intently upon unsatisfactory conditions, thereby giving the condition that measure of energy and vitality which is necessary in order to supply a vigorous growth.

The Universal Energy in which all motion, light, heat, and color have their origin does not partake of the limitation of the many effects of which it is the cause; it is supreme over them all. This Universal Substance is the source of all power, wisdom, and intelligence. To recognize this Intelligence is to acquaint yourself with the knowing quality of Mind and, through it, to move upon the Universal Substance, bringing it into harmonious relations in your affairs.

This is something that the most learned physical science teacher has not attempted—a field of discovery upon which he has not yet launched. In fact, but few of the materialistic schools have ever caught the first ray of this light. It does not seem to have dawned upon them that wisdom is just as much present everywhere as are force and substance.

Some will say, if these principles are true, why are we not demonstrating them? As the fundamental principle is obviously correct, why do we not get proper results? We do. We get results in exact accordance with our understanding of the law and our ability to make the proper application. We secured no results from the laws governing electricity until someone formulated the law and showed us how to apply it.

This puts us in an entirely new relation to our environment, opening up possibilities previously undreamed of, and this by an orderly sequence of law which is naturally involved in our new mental attitude. Mind is creative, and the principle upon which this law is based is sound, legitimate, and inherent in the nature of things. But this creative power does not originate in the individual but in the Universal, which is the source and fountain of all energy and substance. The individual is simply the channel for the distribution of this energy; the individual is the means by which the Universal produces the various combinations which result in the formation of phenomena.

We know that scientists have resolved matter into an immense number of molecules; these molecules have been resolved into atoms, and the atoms into electrons. The discovery of electrons in high vacuum glass tubes containing fused terminals of hard metal indicates conclusively that these electrons fill all space, that they exist everywhere, that they are omnipresent. They fill all material bodies and occupy the whole of what we call empty space. This, then, is the Universal Substance from which all things proceed.

Electrons would forever remain electrons unless directed where to go to be assembled into atoms and molecules, and this director is Mind. A number of electrons revolving around a center of force constitutes an atom; atoms unite in absolutely regular mathematical ratios and form molecules; and these unite with each other to form a multitude of united compounds to build the Universe.

The lightest known atom is hydrogen, and this is 1,700 times heavier than an electron. An atom of mercury is 300,000 times heavier than an electron. Electrons are pure negative electricity, and as they have the same potential velocity as all other cosmic energy, such as heat, light, electricity, and thought, neither time nor space require consideration. The manner in which the velocity of light was ascertained is interesting.

The velocity of light was obtained by the Danish astronomer Roemer in 1676 by observing the eclipses of Jupiter's moons. When the earth was nearest to Jupiter, the eclipse appeared about eight and one-half minutes too soon for the calculations; when the earth was most remote from Jupiter, they were about eight and one-half minutes too late. Roemer concluded the reason to be that it required seventeen minutes for light from the planet to traverse the diameter of the earth's orbit, which measured the difference of the distances of the earth from Jupiter. This calculation has since been verified, and it proves that light travels about 186,000 miles a second.

Electrons manifest in the body as cells, and they possess Mind and Intelligence sufficient for them to perform their functions in the human physical anatomy. Every part of the body is composed of cells, some of which operate independently, others in communities. Some are busy building tissue, while others are engaged in forming the various toxin secretions necessary for the body. Some act as carriers of material; others are the surgeons whose work it is to repair damage; others are scavengers, carrying off waste; others are constantly ready to repel invaders or other undesirable intruders of the germ family.

All these cells are moving for a common purpose, and each one is not only a living organism but has sufficient Intelligence to enable it to perform its necessary duties. It is also endowed with sufficient intelligence to conserve the energies and perpetuate its own life. It must, therefore, secure sufficient nourishment, and it exercises choice in the selection of such nourishment.

Each cell is born, reproduces itself, dies, and is absorbed. The maintenance of health and life itself depends upon the constant regeneration of these cells. It is, therefore, apparent that there is mind in every atom of the body; this mind is negative mind, and the power of the individual to think makes him positive so that he can control this negative mind. This is the scientific explanation for metaphysical healing, and will enable anyone to understand the principle upon which this remarkable phenomenon rests.

This negative mind, which is contained in every cell of the body, has been called the subconscious mind because it acts without our conscious knowledge. We have found that this subconscious mind is responsive to the will of the conscious mind.

All things have their origin in Mind, and appearances are the result of thought; we see that things in themselves have no origin, permanency, or reality. Since they are produced by thought, they can be erased by thought.

In mental as in natural science, experiments are being made, and each discovery lifts man one step higher toward his possible goal. We find that every man is the reflection of the thought he has entertained during his lifetime. This is stamped on his face, his form, his character, his environment.

Behind every effect there is a cause, and if we follow the trail to its starting point, we shall find the Creative Principle out of which it grew. Proofs of this are now so complete that this Truth is generally accepted.

The objective world is controlled by an unseen and, heretofore, unexplainable power. We have, heretofore, personalized this power and called it God. We have now, however, learned to look upon it as the permeating Essence or Principle of all that exists—the Infinite or Universal Mind.

The Universal Mind, being infinite and omnipotent, has unlimited resources at its command, and when we remember that it is also omnipresent, we cannot escape the conclusion that we must be an expression or manifestation of that Mind.

A recognition and understanding of the resources of the subconscious mind will indicate that the only difference between the subconscious and the Universal is one of degree. They differ only as a drop of water differs from the ocean. They are the same in kind and quality; the difference is one of degree only.

Do you—can you—appreciate the value of this all-important fact; do you realize that a recognition of this tremendous fact places you in touch with Omnipotence? The subconscious mind being the connecting link between the Universal Mind and the conscious mind, is it not evident that the conscious mind can consciously suggest thoughts which the subconscious mind will put into action. As the subconscious is one with the Universal, is it not evident that no limit can be placed upon its activities?

A scientific understanding of this principle will explain the wonderful results which are secured through the power of Prayer. The results which are secured in this way are not brought about by any special dispensations of providence; on the contrary, they are the result of the operation of a perfectly natural law. There is, therefore, nothing either religious or mysterious about it. Yet there are many who are not ready to enter into the discipline necessary to think correctly, even though it is evident that wrong thinking has brought failure.

Thought is the only reality; conditions are but the outward manifestations; as the thought changes, all outward or material conditions must change in order to be in harmony with their creator, which is thought. But the thought must be clear-cut, steady, fixed, definite, unchangeable; you cannot take one step forward and two steps backward; neither can you spend twenty or thirty years of your life building up negative conditions as the result of negative thoughts and then expect to see them all melt away as the result of fifteen or twenty minutes of right thinking.

If you enter into the discipline necessary to bring about a radical change in your life, you must do so deliberately, after giving the matter careful thought and full consideration, and then you must allow nothing to interfere with your decision.

This discipline, this change of thought, this mental attitude will not only bring you the material things which are necessary for your highest and best welfare, but it will bring health and harmonious conditions generally. If you wish harmonious conditions in your life, you must develop a harmonious mental attitude.

Your world without will be a reflection of your world within.

For your exercise in this chapter, concentrate on Harmony, and when I say concentrate, I mean all that the word implies. Concentrate so deeply, so earnestly, that you will be conscious of nothing but harmony. Remember, we learn by doing. Reading these lessons will get you nowhere. It is in the practical application that the value consists.

Learn to keep the door shut, keep out of your mind and out of your world every element that seeks admittance with no definite helpful end in view.

—George Matthew Adams

Summary

- What is the source of all wisdom, power, and intelligence?
  Universal Mind.
- Where do all motion, light, heat, and color have their origin?
  In the Universal Energy, which is one manifestation of Universal Mind.
- Where does the creative power of thought originate?
  In Universal Mind.
- What is thought?
  Mind in motion.
- How is the Universal differentiated in form?
  The individual is the means by which the Universal produces the various combinations which result in formation of phenomena.
- How is this accomplished?
  The power of the individual to think is his ability to act upon the Universal and bring it into manifestation.
- What is the first form which the Universal takes so far as we know?
  Electrons, which fill all space.
- Where do all things have their origin?
  In Mind.
- What is the result of a change of thought?
  A change in conditions.
- What is the result of a harmonious mental attitude?
  Harmonious conditions in life.

FIFTEEN

Metamorphosis

THOUGHT, IMMATERIAL though it may be, is the matrix that shapes the issues of life. The Mind has been active in all fields during this fruitful century, but it is to science that we must look for the thoughts that have shaped all thinking.

Experiments with plant parasites indicate that even the lowest order of life is enabled to take advantage of Natural Law. This experiment was made by Jacques Loch, MD, PhD, a member of the Rockefeller Institute: "In order to obtain the material, potted rose bushes are brought into a room and placed in front of a closed window. If the plants are allowed to dry out, the aphids (parasites), previously wingless, change to winged insects. After the metamorphosis, the animals leave the plants, fly to the window, and then creep upward on the glass."

It is evident that these tiny insects found that the plants on which they had been thriving were dead and that they could therefore secure nothing more to eat and drink from this source. The only method by which they could save themselves from starvation was to grow temporary wings and fly, which they did.

Experiments such as these indicate that Omniscience as well as Omnipotence is omnipresent and that the tiniest living thing can take advantage of it in an emergency.

Chapter fifteen will tell you more about the law under which we live. It will explain that these laws operate to our advantage; that all conditions and experiences that come to us are for our benefit; that we gain strength in proportion to the effort expended; and that our happiness is best attained through a conscious cooperation with Natural Law.

The laws under which we live are designed solely for our advantage. These laws are immutable, and we cannot escape from their operation. All the great Eternal Forces act in solemn Silence, but it is in our power to place ourselves in harmony with them and thus express a life of comparative peace and happiness. Difficulties, inharmonies, and obstacles indicate that we are either refusing to give out what we no longer need or refusing to accept what we require.

Growth is attained through an exchange of the old for the new, of the good for the better; it is a conditional or reciprocal action for each of us is a complete thought entity, and this completeness makes it possible for us to receive only as we give.

We cannot obtain what we lack if we tenaciously cling to what we have. We are able to consciously control our conditions as we come to sense the purpose of what we attract, and we are able to extract from each experience only what we require for our further growth. Our ability to do this determines the degree of harmony or happiness we attain.

The ability to appropriate what we require for our growth continually increases as we reach higher planes and broader visions; the greater our abilities to know what we require, the more certain we shall be to discern its presence, to attract it, and to absorb it. Nothing may reach us except what is necessary for our growth.

All conditions and experiences that come to us do so for our benefit. Difficulties and obstacles will continue to come until we absorb their wisdom and gather from them the essentials of further growth. That we reap what we sow is mathematically exact. We gain permanent strength exactly to the extent of the effort required to overcome difficulties.

The inexorable requirements of growth demand that we exert the greatest degree of attraction for what is perfectly in accord with us. Our highest happiness will be best attained through our understanding of and conscious cooperation with Natural Law. In order to possess vitality, thought must be impregnated with love. Love is a product of the emotions. It is, therefore, essential that the emotions be controlled and guided by the intellect and reason.

It is love which imparts vitality to thought and thus enables it to germinate. The Law of Attraction, or the Law of Love, for they are one and the same, will bring to it the necessary material for its growth and maturity.

The first form which thought will find is language, or words; this determines the importance of words, as they are the first manifestation of thought—the vessels in which thought is carried. They take hold of the ether and, by setting it in motion, reproduce the thought to others in the form of sound. Thought may lead to action of any kind, but whatever the action, it is simply the thought attempting to express itself in visible form. It is evident, therefore, that if we wish desirable conditions, we can afford to entertain only desirable thoughts.

This leads to the inevitable conclusion that if we wish to express abundance in our lives, we can afford to think abundance only.

As words are only thoughts taking form, we must be especially careful to use nothing but constructive and harmonious language, which, when finally crystallized into objective forms, will prove to our advantage.

We cannot escape from the pictures we incessantly photograph in the mind, and this photography of erroneous conceptions is exactly what is being done by the use of words when we use any form of language which is not identified with our welfare. We manifest more and more life as our thought becomes clarified and takes higher planes. This is obtained with greater facility as we use word pictures that are clearly defined and relieved of the conceptions attached to them on lower planes of thought.

It is with words that we must express our thoughts, and if we are to make use of higher forms of truth, we may use only such material as has been carefully and intelligently selected with this purpose in view. This wonderful power of clothing thoughts in the form of words is what differentiates man from the rest of the animal kingdom; by the use of the written word, he has been enabled to look back over the centuries and see the stirring scenes by which he has come into his present inheritance.

He has been enabled to come into communion with the greatest writers and thinkers of all time, and the combined record which we possess today is therefore the expression of Universal Thought as it has been seeking to take form in the mind of man.

We know that Universal Thought has for its goal the creation of form, and we know that the individual thought is likewise forever attempting to express itself in form. We also know that the word is a thought form, and a sentence is a combination of thought forms. Therefore, if we wish our ideal to be beautiful or strong, we must see that the words out of which this temple will eventually be created are exact—that they are put together carefully—because accuracy in building words and sentences is the highest form of architecture in civilization and is a passport to success.

Words are thoughts and are, therefore, an invisible and invincible power; they will finally objectify themselves in the form they are given. Words may become mental places that will live forever, or they may become shacks which the first breeze will carry away. They may delight the eye as well as the ear; they may contain all knowledge. In them we find the history of the past as well as the hope of the future; they are living messengers from which every human and superhuman activity is born.

The beauty of the word consists in the beauty of the thought; the power of the word consists in the power of the thought; and the power of the thought consists in its vitality. How shall we identify a vital thought? What are its distinguishing characteristics? It must have principle. How shall we identify principle?

There is a principle of mathematics, but none of error; there is a principle of health, but none of disease; there is a principle of truth, but none of dishonesty; there is a principle of light, but none of darkness; and there is a principle of abundance, but none of poverty.

How shall we know that this is true? If we apply the principle of mathematics correctly we shall be certain of our results; where there is health there will be no disease. If we know the Truth, we cannot be deceived by error. If we let in light there can be no darkness, and where there is abundance there can be no poverty. These are self-evident facts, but the all-important Truth is that a thought containing principle is vital and therefore contains life; it consequently takes root and eventually—but surely and certainly—displaces the negative thoughts, which by their very nature can contain no vitality. This truth is one which seems to have been overlooked.

But this is a fact which will enable you to destroy every manner of discord, lack, and limitation. There can be no question but that he who "is wise enough to understand" will readily recognize that the creative power of thought places an invincible weapon in his hands and makes him a master of destiny.

In the physical world there is a law of compensation which is that "the appearance of a given amount of energy anywhere means the disappearance of the same amount somewhere else," and so we find that we can get only what we give. If we pledge ourselves to a certain action, we must be prepared to assume the responsibility for the development of that action. The subconscious cannot reason. It takes us at our word; we have asked for something and we are now to receive it; we have made our bed, we are now to lie in it; the die has been cast; the threads will carry out the pattern we have made.

For this reason, insight must be exercised so that the thought which we entertain contains no mental, moral, or physical germ which we do not wish objectified in our lives. Insight is a faculty of the mind whereby we are enabled to examine facts and conditions at long range—a kind of human telescope; it enables us to understand the difficulties, as well as the possibilities, in any undertaking.

Insight enables us to be prepared for the obstacles which we shall meet; we can therefore overcome them before they have any opportunity of causing difficulty. Insight enables us to plan to our advantage and turn our thought and attention in the right direction, instead of into channels which can yield no possible return. Insight is, therefore, absolutely essential for the development of any great achievement, but with it we may enter, explore, and possess any mental field. Insight is a product of the world within and is developed in the Silence by concentration.

For your exercise in this chapter, concentrate on insight; take your accustomed position and focus the thought on the fact that to have a knowledge of the creative power of thought does not mean to possess the art of thinking. Let the thought dwell on the fact that knowledge does not apply itself; that our actions are not governed by knowledge but by custom, precedent, and habit; that the only way we can get ourselves to apply knowledge is by a determined conscious effort. Call to mind the fact that knowledge unused passes from the mind and that the value of the information is in the application of the principle. Continue this line of thought until you gain sufficient insight to formulate a definite program for applying this principle to your own particular problem.

Think truly, and thy thoughts
Shall the world's famine feed;
Speak truly, and each word of thine
Shall be a fruitful seed;
Live truly, and thy life shall be
A great and noble creed.

—Horatio Bonar

Summary

- What determines the degree of harmony which we attain?
  Our ability to appropriate what we require for our growth from each experience.
- What do difficulties and obstacles indicate?
  That they are necessary for our wisdom and spiritual growth.
- How may these difficulties be avoided?
  By a conscious understanding of and cooperation with Natural Law.

- What is the principle by which thought manifests itself in form?
  The Law of Attraction.
- How is the necessary material secured by which the growth, development, and maturity of an idea take form?
  The Law of Love, which is the Creative Principle of the Universe, imparts vitality to the thought, and the Law of Attraction brings the necessary substance by the Law of Growth.
- How are desirable conditions secured?
  By entertaining desirable thoughts only.
- How are undesirable conditions brought about?
  By thinking, discussing, and visualizing conditions of lack, limitation, disease, inharmony, and discord of every kind. This mental photography of erroneous conceptions is taken up by the subconscious, and the Law of Attraction will inevitably crystallize it into objective form. That we reap what we sow is scientifically exact.
- How can we overcome every kind of fear, lack, limitation, poverty, and discord?
  By substituting principle for error.
- How may we recognize principle?
  By a conscious realization of the fact that Truth invariably destroys error. We do not have to laboriously shovel the darkness out; all that is necessary is to turn on the light. The same principle applies to every form of negative thought.
- What is the value of insight?
  It enables us to understand the value of making application of the knowledge which we gain. Many seem to think that knowledge will automatically apply itself, which is by no means true.

SIXTEEN

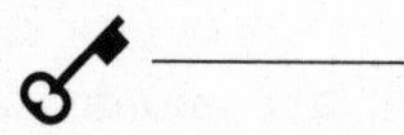

The Cycle of Seven

To every man there openeth a way,
And the high soul climbs the high way,
And the low soul gropes the low;
And in between on the misty flats,
The rest drift to and fro.
But to every man there openeth
A high way and a low
And every man decideth
The way his soul shall go.

—John Oxenham

The vibratory activities of the planetary universe are governed by a law of periodicity. Everything that lives has periods of birth, growth, fruitage, and decline. These periods are governed by the Septimal Law.

The Law of Sevens governs the days of the week, the phases of the moon, the harmonies of sound, light, heat, electricity, magnetism, atomic structure. It governs the lives of individuals and of nations, and it dominates the activities of the commercial world.

Life is growth, and growth is change, and each seven-year period takes us into a new cycle. The first seven years is the period of infancy. The next seven the period of childhood, representing the beginning of individual responsibility. The next seven represents the period of adolescence. The fourth period marks the attainment of full growth. The fifth period is the constructive period, when men begin to acquire property, possessions, a home and family. The next, from thirty-five to forty-two, is a period of reactions and changes, and this in turn is followed by a period of reconstruction, adjustment, and recuperation, so as to be ready for a new cycle of sevens, beginning with the fiftieth year.

There are many who think that the world is just about to pass out of the sixth period; that it will soon enter into the seventh period, the period of readjustment, reconstruction, and harmony; the period which is frequently referred to as the Millennium.

Those familiar with these cycles will not be disturbed when things seem to go wrong, but they can apply the principle outlined in these lessons with the full assurance that a higher law will invariably control all other laws and that through an understanding and conscious operation of spiritual laws, we can convert every seeming difficulty into a blessing.

Wealth is a product of labor. Capital is an effect, not a cause; a servant, not a master; a means, not an end. The most commonly accepted definition of wealth is that it consists of all useful and agreeable things which possess exchange value. It is this exchange value which is the predominant characteristic of wealth. When we consider the small addition made by wealth to the happiness of the possessor, we find that the true value consists not in its utility but in its exchange. This exchange value makes it a medium for securing the things of real value whereby our ideals may be realized.

Wealth should then never be desired as an end but simply as a means of accomplishing an end. Success is contingent upon a higher ideal than the mere accumulation of riches, and he who aspires to such success must formulate an ideal for which he is willing to strive. With such an ideal in mind, the ways and means can and will be provided, but the mistake must not be made of substituting the means for the end. There must be a definite fixed purpose, an ideal.

Prentice Mulford said: "The man of success is the man possessed of the greatest spiritual understanding, and every great fortune comes of superior and truly spiritual power." Unfortunately, there are those who fail to recognize this power; they forget that Andrew Carnegie's mother had to help support the family when they came to America, that W. Averell Harriman's father was a poor clergyman with a salary of only $200 a year, that Sir Thomas Lipton started with only 25 cents. These men had no other power to depend upon, but it did not fail them.

The power to create depends entirely upon spiritual power; there are three steps: idealization, visualization, and materialization. Every captain of industry depends upon this power exclusively. In an article in *Everybody's Magazine*, Henry M. Flagler, the Standard Oil multi-millionaire, admitted that the secret of his success was his power to see a thing in its completeness. The following conversation with the reporter shows his power of idealization, concentration, and visualization, all spiritual powers: "Did you actually envision to yourself the whole thing? I mean, did you, or could you, really close your eyes and see the tracks? And the trains running? And hear the whistles blowing? Did you go as far as that?" "Yes." "How clearly?" "Very clearly."

Here we have a vision of the law, we see cause and effect, we see that thought necessarily precedes and determines action. If we are wise, we shall come into a realization of the tremendous fact that no arbitrary condition can exist for a moment, and that human experience is the result of an orderly and harmonious sequence. The successful businessman is more often than not an idealist and is ever striving for higher and higher standards. The subtle forces of thought as they crystallize in our daily moods is what constitutes life.

Thought is the plastic material with which we build images of our growing conception of life. Use determines its existence. As in all other things our ability to recognize it and use it properly is the necessary condition for attainment. Premature wealth is but the forerunner of humiliation and disaster because we cannot permanently retain anything which we do not merit or which we have not earned.

The conditions with which we meet in the world without correspond to the conditions which we find in the world within. This is brought about by the Law of Attraction. How, then, shall we determine what is to enter into the world within?

Whatever enters the mind through the senses or the objective mind will impress the mind and result in a mental image which will become a pattern for the creative energies. These experiences are largely the result of environment, chance, past thinking, and other forms of negative thought and must be subjected to careful analysis before being entertained. On the other hand, we can form our own mental images through our own interior processes of thought regardless of the thoughts of others, regardless of exterior conditions, regardless of environment of every kind, and it is by the exercise of this power that we can control our own destiny, body, mind, and soul.

It is by the exercise of this power that we take our fate out of the hands of chance and consciously make for ourselves the experiences which we desire, because when we consciously realize a condition, that condition will eventually manifest in our lives; it is, therefore, evident that in the last analysis, thinking is the one great cause in life. Therefore, to control thought is to control circumstances, conditions, environment, and destiny.

How then are we to control thought; what is the process? To think is to create a thought, but the result of the thought will depend upon its form, its quality, and its vitality. The form will depend upon the mental images from which it emanates; this will depend upon the depth of the impression, the predominance of the idea, the clarity of the vision, the boldness of the image. The quality depends upon its substance, and this depends upon the material of which the mind is composed; if this material has been woven from thoughts of vigor, strength, courage, determination, the thought will possess these qualities.

And finally, the vitality depends upon the feeling with which the thought is impregnated. If the thought is constructive, it will possess vitality; it will have life, it will grow, develop, expand, it will be creative; it will attract to itself everything necessary for its complete development. If the thought is destructive, it will have within itself the germ of its own dissolution; it will die, but in the process of dying, it will bring sickness, disease, and every other form of discord.

This we call evil, and when we bring it upon ourselves some of us are disposed to attribute our difficulties to a supreme being, but this Supreme Being is simply Mind in equilibrium. It is neither good nor bad, it simply is. Our ability to differentiate it into form is our ability to manifest good or evil. Good and evil therefore are not entities, they are simply words which we use to indicate the result of our actions, and these actions are in turn predetermined by the character of our thought.

If our thought is constructive and harmonious, we manifest good; if it is destructive and discordant, we manifest evil. If you desire to visualize a different environment, the process is simply to hold the ideal in mind until your vision has been made real; give no thought to persons, places, or things; these have no place in the absolute; the environment you desire will contain everything necessary; the right persons and the right things will come at the right time and in the right place.

It is sometimes not plain how character, ability, attainment, achievement, environment, and destiny can be controlled through the power of visualization, but this is an exact scientific fact.

You will readily see that what we think determines the quality of mind and that the quality of mind in turn determines our ability and mental capacity, and you can readily understand that the improvement in our ability will naturally be followed by increase in attainment and a greater control of circumstances.

It will thus be seen that Natural Law works in a perfectly natural and harmonious manner; everything seems to "just happen." If you want any evidence of this fact simply compare results of your efforts in your own life when your actions were prompted by high ideals and when you had selfish or ulterior motives in mind. You will need no further evidence.

If you wish to bring about the realization of any desire, form a mental picture of success in your mind by consciously visualizing your desire; in this way you will be compelling success, you will be externalizing it in your life by scientific methods.

We can only see what already exists in the objective world, but what we visualize already exists in the spiritual world, and this visualization is a substantial token of what will one day appear in the objective world if we are faithful to our ideal. The reason for this is not difficult; visualization is a form of imagination; this process of thinking forms impressions on the mind, and these impressions in turn form concepts and ideals, and they in turn are the plans from which the Master Architect will weave the future.

The psychologists have come to the conclusion that there is but one sense, the sense of feeling, and that all other senses are but modifications of this one sense; this being true, we know why feeling is the very fountainhead of power, why the emotions so easily overcome the intellect, and why we must put feeling into our thought if we wish results. Thought and feeling is the irresistible combination.

Visualization must, of course, be directed by the will; we are to visualize exactly what we want; we must be careful not to let the imagination run wild. Imagination is a good servant but a poor master, and unless it is controlled it may easily lead us into all kinds of speculations and conclusions which have no basis or foundation of fact whatever. Every kind of plausible opinion is liable to be accepted without any analytical examination, and the inevitable result is mental chaos.

We must, therefore, construct only such mental images as are known to be scientifically true. Subject every idea to a searching analysis and accept nothing which is not scientifically exact. When you do this you will attempt nothing but what you know you can carry out, and success will crown your efforts; this is what businessmen call farsightedness; it is much the same as insight, and it is one of the great secrets of success in all important undertakings.

For your exercise in this chapter, try to bring yourself to a realization of the important fact that harmony and happiness are states of consciousness and do not depend upon the possession of things, that things are effects and come as a consequence of correct mental states. So if we desire material possession of any kind, our chief concern should be to acquire the mental attitude which will bring about the result desired. This mental attitude is brought about by a realization of our spiritual nature and our unity with Universal Mind which is the substance of all things. This realization will bring about everything which is necessary for our complete enjoyment. This is correct, scientific thinking. When we succeed in bringing about this mental attitude it is comparatively easy to realize our desire as an already accomplished fact; when we can do this we shall have found the Truth which makes us free from every lack or limitation of any kind.

A man might frame and let loose a star, to roll in its orbit, and yet not have done so memorable a thing before God as he who lets a golden-orbed thought to roll through the generations of time.

—Henry Ward Beecher

Summary

- Upon what does wealth depend?
  Upon an understanding of the creative nature of thought.
- Upon what does its true value consist?
  Upon its exchange value.
- Upon what does success depend?
  Upon spiritual power.
- Upon what does this power depend?
  Upon use; use determines its existence.
- How may we take our fate out of the hands of chance?
  By consciously realizing the conditions which we desire to see manifested in our lives.

- What then is the great business of life?
  Thinking.
- Why is this so?
  Because thought is spiritual and therefore creative. To consciously control thought is therefore to control circumstances, conditions, environment, and destiny.
- What is the source of all evil?
  Destructive thinking.
- What is the source of all good?
  Correct, scientific thinking.
- What is scientific thinking?
  A recognition of the creative nature of spiritual energy and our ability to control it.

The greatest events of an age are its best thoughts.
It is the nature of thought to find its way into action.

—John Bovee Dods

SEVENTEEN

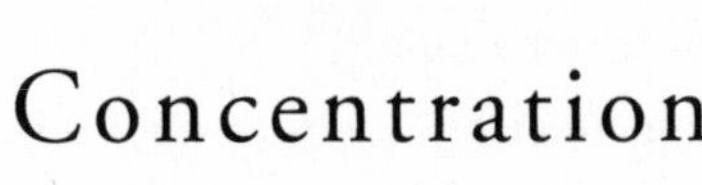

Concentration and Desire

THE KIND of deity which a man, consciously or unconsciously, worships indicates the intellectual status of the worshipper.

Ask the Indian of God, and he will describe to you a powerful chieftain of a glorious tribe. Ask the pagan of God, and he will tell you of a god of fire, a god of water, a god of this, that, and the other.

Ask the Israelite of God, and he will tell you of the God of Moses, who conceived it expedient to rule by coercive measures, hence the Ten Commandments; or ask of Joshua, who led the Israelites into battle, confiscated property, murdered the prisoners, and laid waste to cities.

The so-called heathen made "graven images" of their gods, whom they were accustomed to worship, but among the most intelligent, at least, these images were but the visible fulcrums with which they were enabled to mentally concentrate on the qualities which they desired to externalize in their lives.

We of the twentieth century worship a God of Love in theory, but in practice we make for ourselves "graven images" of wealth, power, fashion, custom, and conventionality. We "fall down" before them and worship them. We concentrate on them, and they are thereby externalized in our lives.

The student who masters the contents of chapter seventeen will not mistake the symbols for the reality; he will be interested in causes rather than effects. He will concentrate on the realities of life and will then not be disappointed in the results.

We are told that man has "dominion over all things"; this dominion is established through Mind. Thought is the activity which controls every principle beneath it. The Highest Principle, by reason of its superior essence and qualities, necessarily determines the circumstances, aspects, and relation of everything with which it comes in contact. The vibrations of mental forces are the finest and consequently the most powerful in existence. To those who perceive the nature and transcendency of mental force, all physical power sinks into insignificance.

We are accustomed to look upon the universe with a lens of five senses, and from these experiences our anthropomorphic conceptions originate, but true conceptions are only secured by spiritual insight. This insight requires a quickening of the vibrations of Mind and is only secured when the mind is continuously concentrated in a given direction. Continuous concentration means an even, unbroken flow of thought and is the result of patient, persistent, persevering, and well-regulated system.

Great discoveries are the result of long-continued investigation. The science of mathematics requires years of concentrated effort to master it, and the greatest science—that of Mind—is revealed only through concentrated effort.

Concentration is much misunderstood; there seems to be an idea of effort or activity associated with it, when just the contrary is necessary. The greatness of an actor lies in the fact that he forgets himself in the portrayal of his character, becoming so identified with it that the audience is swayed by the realism of the performance. This will give you a good idea of true concentration; you should be so interested in your thought, so engrossed in your subject, as to be conscious of nothing else. Such concentration leads to intuitive perception and immediate insight into the nature of the object concentrated upon.

All knowledge is the result of concentration of this kind; it is thus that the secrets of Heaven and earth have been wrested; it is thus that the mind becomes a magnet and the desire to know draws the knowledge, irresistibly attracts it, and makes it your own.

Desire is largely subconscious; conscious desire rarely realizes its object when the latter is out of immediate reach. Subconscious desire arouses the latent faculties of the mind, and difficult problems seem to solve themselves.

The subconscious mind may be aroused and brought into action in any direction and made to serve us, for any purpose, by concentration. The practice of concentration requires the control of the physical, mental, and physical being; all modes of consciousness, whether physical, mental, or physical, must be under control.

Spiritual Truth is therefore the controlling factor; it is this which will enable you to grow out of limited attainment and reach a point where you will be able to translate modes of thought into character and consciousness.

Concentration does not mean mere thinking of thoughts but the transmutation of these thoughts into practical values; the average person has no conception of the meaning of concentration. There is always the cry "to have" but never the cry "to be"; they fail to understand that they cannot have one without the other, that they must first find the "kingdom" before they can have the "things added." Momentary enthusiasm is of no value; it is only with unbounded self-confidence that the goal is reached.

The mind may place the ideal a little too high and fall short of the mark; it may attempt to soar on untrained wings and, instead of flying, fall to earth; but that is no reason for not making another attempt. Weakness is the only barrier to mental attainment; attribute your weakness to physical limitations or mental uncertainties and try again; ease and perfection are gained by repetition.

The astronomer centers his mind on the stars and they give forth their secrets; the geologist centers his mind on the construction of the earth and we have geology; so with all things. Men center their minds on the problems of life, and the result is apparent in the vast and complex social order of the day. All mental discovery and attainment are the result of desire plus concentration; desire is the strongest mode of action; the more persistent the desire, the more authoritative the revelation. Desire added to concentration will wrench any secret from nature. In realizing great thoughts, in experiencing great emotions that correspond with great thoughts, the mind is in a state where it appreciates the value of higher things.

The intensity of one moment's earnest concentration and the intense longing to become and to attain may take you further than years of slow, normal and forced effort; it will unfasten the prison bars of unbelief, weakness, impotence, and self-belittlement, and you will come into a realization of the joy of overcoming.

The spirit of initiative and originality is developed through persistence and continuity of mental effort. Business teaches the value of concentration and encourages decision of character; it develops practical insight and quickness of conclusion. The mental element in every commercial pursuit is dominant as the controlling factor, and desire is the predominating force; all commercial relations are the externalization of desire.

Many of the sturdy and substantial virtues are developed in commercial employment; the mind is steadied and directed; it becomes efficient. The principal necessity is the strengthening of the mind so that it rises superior to the distractions and wayward impulses of instinctive life and thus successfully overcomes in the conflict between the higher and lower self.

All of us are dynamos, but the dynamo of itself is nothing; the mind must work the dynamo; then it is useful and its energy can be definitely concentrated. The mind is an engine whose power is undreamed; thought is an omni-working power. It is the ruler and creator of all form and all events occurring in form. Physical energy is nothing in comparison with the omnipotence of thought because thought enables man to harness all other natural power.

Vibration is the action of thought; it is vibration which reaches out and attracts the material necessary to construct and build. There is nothing mysterious concerning the power of thought; concentration simply implies that consciousness can be focalized to the point where it becomes identified with the object of its attention. As food absorbed is the essence of the body, so the mind absorbs the object of its attention and gives it life and being.

If you concentrate on some matter of importance, the intuitive power will be set in operation, and help will come in the nature of information which will lead to success.

Intuition arrives at conclusions without the aid of experience or memory. Intuition often solves problems that are beyond the grasp of the reasoning power. Intuition often comes with a suddenness that is startling; it reveals the Truth for which we are searching so directly that it seems to come from a higher power. Intuition can be cultivated and developed; in order to do this it must be recognized and appreciated; if the intuitive visitor is given a royal welcome when he comes, he will come again; the more cordial the welcome the more frequent his visits will become, but if he is ignored or neglected he will make his visits few and far apart.

Intuition usually comes in the Silence; great minds seek solitude frequently; it is here that all the larger problems of life are worked out. For this reason every businessman who can afford it has a private office where he will not be disturbed; if you cannot afford a private office you can at least find somewhere where you can be alone a few minutes each day to train the thought along lines which will enable you to develop that invincible power which is necessary to achieve.

Remember that fundamentally the subconscious is omnipotent; there is no limit to the things that can be done when it is given the power to act. Your degree of success is determined by the nature of your desire. If the nature of your desire is in harmony with Natural Law or Universal Mind, it will gradually emancipate the mind and give you invincible courage.

Every obstacle conquered, every victory gained will give you more faith in your power, and you will have greater ability to win. Your strength is determined by your mental attitude; if this attitude is one of success and is permanently held with an unswerving purpose, you will attract to you from the invisible domain the things you silently demand.

By keeping the thought in mind, it will gradually take tangible form. A definite purpose sets causes in motion which go out in the invisible world and find the material necessary to serve your purpose. You may be pursuing the symbols of power instead of power itself. You may be pursuing fame instead of honor, riches instead of wealth, position instead of servitude; in either event, you will find that they turn to ashes just as you overtake them.

Premature wealth or position cannot be retained because it has not been earned; we get only what we give, and those who try to get without giving always find that the law of compensation is relentlessly bringing about an exact equilibrium. The race has usually been for money and other mere symbols of power, but with an understanding of the true source of power, we can afford to ignore the symbols. The man with a large bank account finds it unnecessary to load his pockets down with gold; so with the man who has found the true source of power; he is no longer interested in its shams or pretensions.

Thought ordinarily leads outwardly in evolutionary directions, but it can be turned within where it will take hold of the basic principles of things, the heart of things, the spirit of things. When you get to the heart of things it is comparatively easy to understand and command them. This is because the spirit of a thing is the thing itself, the vital part of it, the real substance. The form is simply the outward manifestation of the spiritual activity within.

For your exercise in this chapter, concentrate as nearly as possible in accordance with the method outlined in this lesson; let there be no conscious effort or activity associated with your purpose. Relax completely; avoid any thought of anxiety as to results. Remember that power comes through repose. Let the thought dwell upon your object, until it is completely identified with it, until you are conscious of nothing else. If you wish to eliminate fear, concentrate on courage.

If you wish to eliminate lack, concentrate on abundance. If you wish to eliminate disease, concentrate on health. Always concentrate on the ideal as an already existing fact; this is the germ cell, the life principle which goes forth and sets in motion those causes which guide, direct, and bring about the necessary relation, which eventually manifest in form.

Thought is the property of those only who can entertain it.

—Ralph Waldo Emerson

Summary

- What is the true method of concentration?
  To become so identified with the object of your thought that you are conscious of nothing else.
- What is the result of this method of concentration?
  Invisible forces are set in motion which irresistibly bring about conditions in correspondence with your thought.
- What is the controlling factor in this method of thought?
  Spiritual Truth.
- Why is this so?
  Because the nature of our desire must be in harmony with Natural Law.
- What is the practical value of this method of concentration?
  Thought is transmuted into character, and character is the magnet which creates the environment of the individual.
- What is the controlling factor in every commercial pursuit?
  The mental element.
- Why is this so?
  Because Mind is the ruler and creator of all form and all events occurring in form.
- How does concentration operate?
  By the development of the powers of perception, wisdom, intuition, and sagacity.
- Why is intuition superior to reason?
  Because it does not depend upon experience or memory and frequently brings about the solution to our problems by methods concerning which we are in entire ignorance.
- What is the result of pursuing the symbols of reality?
  Symbols frequently turn to ashes just as we overtake them because the symbol is only the outward form of the spiritual activity within; therefore, unless we can possess the spiritual reality, the form disappears.

EIGHTEEN

The Value of Belief

IN ORDER to grow we must obtain what is necessary for our growth. This is brought about through the Law of Attraction. This principle is the sole means by which the individual is differentiated from the Universal.

Think, for a moment, what a man would be if he were not a husband, father, or brother, if he were not interested in the social, economical, political, or religious world. He would be nothing but an abstract, theoretical ego. He exists, therefore, only in his relation to the Whole, in his relation to other men, in his relation to society. This relation constitutes his environment and in no other way.

It is evident, therefore, that the individual is simply the differentiation of the one Universal Mind "which lighteth every man that cometh into the world," and his so-called individuality or personality consists of nothing but the manner in which he relates with the Whole.

This we call his environment, and it is brought about by the Law of Attraction. Chapter eighteen, which follows, has something more to say concerning this important law.

There is a change in the thought of the world. This change is silently transpiring in our midst and is more important than any which the world has undergone since the downfall of paganism. This present revolution, in the opinions of all classes of men, the highest and most cultured of men as well as those of the laboring class, stands unparalleled in the history of the world. Science has of late made such vast discoveries, has revealed such an infinity of resources, has unveiled such enormous possibilities and such unsuspected forces that scientific men more and more hesitate to affirm certain theories as established and beyond doubt, or to deny other theories as absurd or impossible.

A new civilization is being born; customs, creeds, and precedent are passing; vision, faith, and service are taking their place. The fetters of tradition are being melted off from humanity, and as the impurities of materialism are being consumed, thought is being liberated and Truth is rising full-robed before an astonished multitude.

The whole world is on the eve of a new consciousness, a new power, and a new realization within the self. Physical science has resolved matter into molecules, molecules into atoms, atoms into energy, and it has remained for Mr. J. A. Fleming, in an address before the Royal Institution, to resolve this energy into mind. He says, "In its ultimate essence, energy may be incomprehensible by us except as an exhibition of the direct operation of that which we call Mind or Will."

And this Mind is the indwelling and ultimate. It is imminent in matter as in spirit. It is the sustaining, energizing, all pervading spirit of the Universe. Every living thing must be sustained by this Omnipotent Intelligence, and we find the difference in individual lives to be largely measured by the degree of this Intelligence which they manifest. It is greater intelligence that places the animal in a higher scale of being than the plant, the man higher than the animal, and we find that this increased intelligence is again indicated by the power of the individual to control modes of action and thus to consciously adjust himself to his environment. It is this adjustment that occupies the attention of the greatest minds, and this adjustment consists in nothing else than the recognition of an existing order in Universal Mind, for it is well known that Mind will obey us precisely in proportion as we first obey it.

It is the recognition of Natural Law that has enabled us to annihilate time and space, to soar in the air, and to make iron float, and the greater the degree of intelligence the greater will be our recognition of Natural Law and the greater will be the power we can possess.

It is the recognition of the self as an individualization of this Universal Intelligence that enables the individual to control those forms of intelligence which have not yet reached this level of self-recognition; they do not know that this Universal Intelligence permeates all things ready to be called into action; they do not know that it is responsive to every demand, and they are therefore in bondage to the law of their own being.

Thought is creative, and the principle on which the law is based is sound and legitimate and is inherent in the nature of things; but this creative power does not originate in the individual but in the Universal, which is the source and foundation of all energy and substance; the individual is simply the channel for the distribution of this energy.

The individual is simply the means by which the Universal produces the various combinations which result in the formation of phenomena, which depends upon the Law of Vibration, whereby various rates of rapidity of motion, in the primary substance, form new substances only in certain exact numerical ratios. Thought is the invisible link by which the individual comes into communication with the Universal, the finite with the Infinite, the seen with the Unseen. Thought is the magic by which the human is transformed into a being who thinks and knows and feels and acts.

As the proper apparatus has enabled the eye to discover worlds without number millions of miles away, so, with the proper understanding, man has been enabled to communicate with Universal Mind, the source of all power.

The understanding which is usually developed is nothing more than a "belief," which means nothing at all. The savages of the Cannibal Islands believe something; but that proves nothing. The only belief which is of any value to anyone is a belief that has been put to a test and demonstrated to be a fact; it is then no longer a belief but has become a living faith or Truth. And this Truth has been put to the test by hundreds of thousands of people and has been found to be the Truth exactly in proportion to the usefulness of the apparatus which they used.

A man would not expect to locate stars hundreds of millions of miles away without a sufficiently strong telescope, and for this reason science is continually engaged in building larger and more powerful telescopes, and is continually rewarded by additional knowledge of the heavenly bodies.

So with understanding; men are continually making progress in the methods which they use to come into communication with Universal Mind and its infinite possibilities. Universal Mind manifests itself in the objective, through the principle of attraction that each atom has for every other atom, in Infinite degrees of intensity.

It is by this principle of combining and attracting that things are brought together. This principle is of universal application and is the sole means whereby the purpose of existence is carried into effect. The expression of growth is met in a most beautiful manner through the instrumentality of this Universal Principle. In order to grow we must obtain what is essential for our growth, but as we are at all times a complete thought entity, this completeness makes it possible for us to receive only as we give; growth is, therefore, conditioned on reciprocal action, and we find that on the mental plane like attracts like, that mental vibrations respond only to the extent of their vibratory harmony.

It is clear, therefore, that thoughts of abundance will respond only to similar thoughts; the wealth of the individual is seen to be what he inherently is. Affluence within is found to be the secret of attraction for affluence without. The ability to produce is found to be the real source of wealth of the individual. It is for this reason that he who has his heart in his work is certain to meet with unbounded success. He will give and continually give; and the more he gives, the more he will receive.

The great financiers of Wall Street, the captains of industry, the statesmen, the great corporation attorneys, the inventors, the physicians, the authors—what do each of these contribute to the sum of human happiness but the power of their thought?

Thought is the energy which the Law of Attraction brings into operation, which eventually manifests in abundance. Universal Mind is static mind or substance in equilibrium. It is differentiated into form by our power to think. Thought is the dynamic phase of Mind. Power depends upon consciousness of power; unless we use it, we shall lose it, and unless we are conscious of it, we cannot use it. The use of this power depends upon attention; the degree of attention determines our capacity for the acquirement of knowledge, which is another name for power.

Attention has been held to be the distinguishing mark of genius. The cultivation of attention depends upon practice. The incentive of attention is interest; the greater the interest, the greater the attention; the greater the attention, the greater the interest, action, and reaction. Begin by paying attention; before long you will have aroused interest; this interest will attract more attention, and this attention will produce more interest, and so on. This practice will enable you to cultivate the power of attention.

For your exercise in this chapter, concentrate upon your power to create; seek insight and perception; try to find a logical basis for the faith which is in you. Let the thought dwell on the fact that the physical man lives and moves and has his being in the sustainer of all organic life—air—that he must breathe to live. Then let the thought rest on the fact that the spiritual man also lives and moves and has his being in a similar but subtler energy upon which he must depend for life, and that as in the physical world no life assumes form until after a seed is sown, and no higher fruit than that of the parent stock can be produced; so in the spiritual world no effect can be produced until the seed is sown, and the fruit will depend upon the nature of the seed, so that the results which you secure depend upon your perception of law in the Mighty Domain of Causation, the highest evolution of human consciousness.

There is no thought in my mind but it quickly tends to convert itself into a power and organizes a huge instrumentality of means.

—Ralph Waldo Emerson

Summary

- How is the difference in individual lives measured?
  By the degree of Intelligence which they manifest.

- What is the law by which the individual may control other forms of intelligence?
  A recognition of the self as an individualization of the Universal Intelligence.
- Where does the creative power originate?
  In the Universal.
- How does the Universal create form?
  By means of the individual.
- What is the connecting link between the individual and the Universal?
  Thought.
- What is the principle by which the means of existence is carried into effect?
  The Law of Love.
- How is this principle brought into expression?
  By the Law of Growth.
- Upon what condition does the Law of Growth depend?
  Upon reciprocal action. The individual is complete at all times, and this makes it possible to receive only as we give.
- What is it that we give?
  Thought.
- What do we receive?
  Thought, which is substance in equilibrium and which is constantly being differentiated in form by what we think.

NINETEEN

Matter Is Changing

FEAR IS a powerful form of thought. It paralyzes the nerve centers, thus affecting the circulation of the blood.

This, in turn, paralyzes the muscular system, so that fear affects the entire being—body, brain, and nerve; physical, mental, and muscular.

Of course the way to overcome fear is to become conscious of power. What is this mysterious Vital Force which we call power? We do not know, but then, neither do we know what electricity is.

But we do know that by conforming to the requirements of the law by which electricity is governed, it will be our obedient servant; it will light our homes and our cities, run our machinery, and serve us in many useful capacities.

And so it is with Vital Force. Although we do not know what it is, and possibly may never know, we do know that it is a primary force which manifests through living bodies, and that by complying with the laws and principles by which it is governed, we can open ourselves to a more abundant inflow of this vital energy and thus express the highest possible degree of mental, moral, and spiritual efficiency.

This chapter tells of a very simple way of developing this Vital Force. If you put into practice the information outlined in this lesson, you will soon develop the sense of power which has ever been the distinguishing mark of genius.

The search for Truth is no longer a haphazard adventure, but it is a systematic process and is logical in its operation. Every kind of experience is given a voice in shaping its decision.

In seeking the Truth, we are seeking ultimate cause; we know that every human experience is an effect; then if we may ascertain the cause, and if we shall find that this cause is one which we can consciously control, the effect or the experience will be within our control also.

Human experience will then no longer be the football of fate; a man will not be the child of fortune but destiny. Fate and fortune will be controlled as readily as a captain controls his ship or an engineer his train. All things are finally resolvable into the same element, and as they are thus translatable, one into the other, they must ever be in relation and may never be in opposition to one another.

In the physical world there are innumerable contrasts, and these may, for convenience sake, be designated by distinctive names. There are sizes, colors, shades, or ends to all things. There is a North Pole and a South Pole, an inside and an outside, a seen and an unseen, but these expressions merely serve to place extremes in contrast.

They are names given to two different parts of one quantity. The two extremes are relative; they are not separate entities but are two parts or aspects of the Whole. In the mental world, we find the same law; we speak of knowledge and ignorance, but ignorance is but a lack of knowledge and is, therefore, found to be simply a word to express the absence of knowledge; it has no principle in itself.

In the moral world we again find the same law; we speak of good and evil, but good is a reality, something tangible, while evil is found to be simply a negative condition, the absence of good. Evil is sometimes thought to be a very real condition, but it has no principle, no vitality, no life; we know this because it can always be destroyed by good; just as Truth destroys error and light destroys darkness, so evil vanishes when good appears; there is therefore but one principle in the moral world.

We find exactly the same law obtaining in the spiritual world; we speak of Mind and matter as two separate entities, but clearer insight makes it evident that there is but one operative principle, and that is Mind.

Mind is the real and the eternal. Matter is forever changing; we know that in the aeons of time a hundred years is but as a day. If we stand in any large city and let the eye rest on the innumerable large and magnificent buildings, the vast array of conveniences of modern civilization, we may remember that not one of them was there just over a century ago, and if we could stand on the same spot in a hundred years, in all probability we should find that but few of them remain.

In the animal kingdom we find the same Law of Change. The millions and millions of animals come and go, a few years constituting their span of life. In the plant world the change is still more rapid. Many plants and nearly all grasses come and go in a single year. When we pass to the inorganic, we expect to find something more substantial, but as we gaze on the apparently solid continent, we are told that it arose from the ocean; we see the giant mountain and are told that the place where it now stands was once a lake; and as we stand in awe before the great cliffs in the Yosemite Valley, we can easily trace the path of the glaciers which carried all before them.

We are in the presence of continual change, and we know that this change is but the evolution of Universal Mind, the Grand Process whereby all things are continually being created anew, and we come to know that matter is but a form which Mind takes and is therefore simply a condition. Matter has no principle; Mind is the only principle.

We have then come to know that Mind is the only principle which is operative in the physical, mental, moral, and spiritual world. We also know that this mind is static, mind at rest, we also know that the ability of the individual to think is his ability to act upon Universal Mind and convert it into dynamic mind, or mind in motion. In order to do this, fuel must be applied in the form of food, for man cannot think without eating, and so we find that even a spiritual activity such as thinking cannot be converted into sources of pleasure and profit except by making use of material means.

It requires energy of some kind to collect electricity and convert it into a dynamic power; it requires the rays of the sun to give the necessary energy to sustain plant life; so it also requires energy in the form of food to enable the individual to think and thereby act upon Universal Mind.

You may know that thought is constantly and eternally taking form, is forever seeking expression (or you may not), but the fact remains that if your thought is powerful, constructive, and positive, this will be plainly evident in the state of your health, your business, and your environment; if your thought is weak, critical, destructive, and negative generally, it will manifest in your body as fear, worry, and nervousness, in your finance as lack and limitation, and in discordant conditions in your environment.

All wealth is the offspring of power; possessions are of value only as they confer power. Events are significant only as they affect power; all things represent certain forms and degrees of power. A knowledge of cause and effect as shown by the laws governing steam, electricity, chemical affinity, and gravitation enables men to plan courageously and to execute fearlessly. These laws are called natural laws because they govern the physical world, but all power is not physical power; there is also mental power, and there is moral and spiritual power.

What are our schools, our universities, but mental powerhouses, places where mental power is being developed? As there are many mighty powerhouses for the application of power to ponderous machinery, whereby raw material is collected and converted into the necessities and comforts of life, so the mental powerhouses collect the raw material and cultivate and develop it into a power which is infinitely superior to all the forces of Nature, marvelous though they may be.

What is this raw material which is being collected in these thousands of mental powerhouses all over the world and developed into a power which is evidently controlling every other power? In its static form it is Mind—in its dynamic form, it is Thought.

This power is superior because it exists on a higher plane, because it has enabled man to discover the law by which these wonderful forces of Nature could be harnessed and made to do the work of hundreds and thousands of men. It has enabled man to discover laws whereby time and space have been annihilated and the law of gravitation overcome.

Thought is the Vital Force or Energy which is being developed and which has produced such startling results in the last half century as to bring about a world which would be absolutely inconceivable to a man existing only fifty or twenty-five years ago. If such results have been secured by organizing these mental powerhouses in fifty years, what may not be expected in another fifty years?

The substance from which all things are created is infinite in quantity; we know that light travels at the rate of 186,000 miles per second, and we know that there are stars so remote that it takes light 2,000 years to reach us, and we know that such stars exist in all parts of the heavens; we know, too, that this light comes in waves, so that if the ether on which these waves travel was not continuous the light would fail to reach us; we can then only come to the conclusion that this substance, or ether, or raw material, is universally present.

How, then, does it manifest in form? In electrical science a battery is formed by connecting the opposite poles of zinc and copper, which causes a current to flow from one to the other and so provides energy. This same process is repeated in respect to every polarity, and as all form simply depends upon the rate of vibration and consequent relations of atoms to each other, if we wish to change the form of manifestation we must change the polarity. This is the principle of causation.

For your exercise in this chapter, concentrate—and when I use the word *concentrate*, I mean all that the word implies; become so absorbed in the object of your thought that you are conscious of nothing else, and do this a few minutes every day. You take the necessary time to eat in order that the body may be nourished; why not take the time to assimilate your mental food?

Let the thought rest on the fact that appearances are deceptive. The earth is not flat, neither is it stationary; the sky is not a dome, the sun does not move, the stars are not small specks of light, and matter which was once supposed to be fixed has been found to be in a state of perpetual flux. Try to realize that the day is fast approaching—its dawn is now at hand—when modes of thought and action must be adjusted to rapidly increasing knowledge of the operation of eternal principles.

Silent thought is, after all, the mightiest agent in human affairs.

—William Ellery Channing

Summary

- How are extremes placed in contrast?
  They are designated by distinctive names, such as inside and outside, top and bottom, light and dark, good and bad.
- Are these separate entities?
  No, they are parts or aspects of one Whole.
- What is the one creative principle in the physical, mental, and spiritual world?
  Universal Mind, or the Eternal Energy from which all things proceed.
- How are we related to this creative principle?
  By our ability to think.
- How does this creative principle become operative?
  Thought is the seed, which results in action, and action results in form.
- Upon what does form depend?
  Upon the rate of vibration.
- How may the rate of vibration be changed?
  By mental action.
- Upon what does mental action depend?
  Upon polarity, action, and reaction between the individual and the Universal.

- Does the creative energy originate in the individual or the Universal?

  In the Universal, but the Universal can manifest only through the individual.

- Why is the individual necessary?

  Because the Universal is static and requires energy to start it in motion. This is furnished by food, which is converted into energy, which in turn enables the individual to think. When the individual stops eating he stops thinking; then he no longer acts upon the Universal; there is consequently no longer any action or reaction. The Universal is then only pure Mind in static form—Mind at rest.

TWENTY

Balance in the Universe

For many years there has been an endless discussion as to the origin of evil. Theologians have told us that God is Love and that God is Omnipresent. If this be true, there is no place where God is not. Where, then, is evil, Satan, and Hell?

Let us see:

- God is Spirit.
- Spirit is the creative principle of the universe.
- Man is made in the image and likeness of God.
- Man is therefore a spiritual being.
- The only activity which spirit possesses is the power to think.
- Thinking is therefore a creative process.

- All form is therefore the result of the thinking process.
- The destruction of form must also be a result of the thinking process.
- Fictitious representations of form are the result of the creative power of thought, as in hypnotism.
- Apparent representations of form are the result of the creative power of thought, as in spiritualism.
- Invention, organization, and constructive work of all kinds are the result of the creative power of thought, as in concentration.
- When the creative power of thought is manifested for the benefit of humanity, we call the result good.
- When the creative power of thought is manifested in a destructive or evil manner, we call the result evil.

This indicates the origin of both good and evil; they are simply words which have been coined in order to indicate the nature of the result of the thinking or creative process. Thought necessarily precedes and predetermines action; action precedes and predetermines condition.

Chapter twenty will throw more light upon this important subject.

The spirit of a thing is that thing; it is necessarily fixed, changeless, and eternal. The spirit of you is—you; without the spirit you would be nothing. It becomes active through your recognition of it and its possibilities.

You may have all the wealth in Christendom, but unless you recognize it and make use of it, it will have no value; so with your spiritual wealth: unless you recognize it and use it, it will have no value. The one and only condition of spiritual power is use or recognition. All great things come through recognition; the scepter of power is consciousness, and thought is its messenger, and this messenger is constantly molding the realities of the invisible world into the conditions and environments of your objective world.

Thinking is the true business of life; power is the result. You are at all times dealing with the magical power of thought and consciousness. What results can you expect so long as you remain oblivious to the power which has been placed within your control? So long as you do this you limit yourself to superficial conditions and make yourself a beast of burden for those who think, those who recognize their power, those who know that unless we are willing to think we shall have to work, and the less we think the more we shall have to work, and the less we shall get for our work.

The secret of power is a perfect understanding of the principles, forces, methods, and combinations of Mind, and a perfect understanding of our relationship to Universal Mind. It is well to remember that this principle is unchangeable; if this were not so, it would not be reliable; all principles are changeless.

This stability is your opportunity; you are its active attribute, the channel for its activity; the Universal can act only through the individual. When you begin to perceive that the essence of the Universal is within yourself—is you—you begin to do things; you begin to feel your power; it is the fuel which fires the imagination, which lights the torch of inspiration, which gives vitality to thought, which enables you to connect with all the invisible forces of the Universe. It is this power which will enable you to plan fearlessly, to execute masterfully.

But perception will come only in the Silence; this seems to be the condition required for all great purposes. You are a visualizing entity. Imagination is your workshop. It is here that your ideal is to be visualized. As a perfect understanding of the nature of this power is a primary condition for its manifestation, visualize the entire method over and over again so that you may use it whenever occasion requires. The infinity of wisdom is to follow the method whereby we may have the inspiration of the omnipotent Universal Mind on demand at any time.

We can fail to recognize this world within, and so exclude it from our consciousness, but it will still be the basic fact of all existence; and when we learn to recognize it, not only in ourselves but in all persons, events, things, and circumstances, we shall have found the "Kingdom of Heaven" which we are told is within us.

Our failures are a result of the operation of exactly the same principle; the principle is unchangeable; its operation is exact, there is no deviation; if we think lack, limitation, or discord, we shall find their fruits on every hand; if we think poverty, unhappiness, or disease, the thought messengers will carry the summons as readily as any other kind of thought, and the result will be just as certain. If we fear a coming calamity, we shall be able to say with Job, "the thing I feared has come upon me"; if we think unkindly or ignorantly, we shall thus attract to ourselves the results of our ignorance.

This power of thought, if understood and correctly used, is the greatest labor-saving device ever dreamed of, but if not understood or improperly used, the result will in all probability be disastrous, as we have already seen; by the help of this power you can confidently undertake things that are seemingly impossible because this power is the secret of all inspiration, all genius.

To become inspired means to get out of the beaten path, out of the rut because extraordinary results require extraordinary means. When we come into a recognition of the unity of all things and that the source of all power is within, we tap the source of inspiration. Inspiration is the art of imbibing; the art of self-realization; the art of adjusting the individual mind to that of the Universal Mind; the art of attaching the proper mechanism to the source of all power; the art of differentiating the formless into form; the art of becoming a channel for the flow of Infinite

Wisdom; the art of visualizing perfection; the art of realizing the omnipresence of Omnipotence.

An understanding and appreciation of the fact that the Infinite Power is omnipresent and is therefore in the infinitely small as well as the infinitely large will enable us to absorb its Essence; a further understanding of the fact that this Power is Spirit and therefore indivisible will enable us to appreciate its present at all points at the same time.

An understanding of these facts, first intellectually and then emotionally, will enable us to drink deeply from this ocean of Infinite Power. An intellectual understanding will be of no assistance; the emotions must be brought into action; thought without feeling is cold. The required combination is thought and feeling.

Inspiration is from within. The Silence is necessary, the senses must be stilled, the muscles relaxed, repose cultivated. When you have thus come into possession of a sense of poise and power you will be ready to receive the information or inspiration or wisdom which may be necessary for the development of your purpose.

Do not confuse these methods with those of the clairvoyant; they have nothing in common. Inspiration is the art of receiving and makes for all that is best in life; your business in life is to understand and command these invisible forces instead of letting them command and rule you. Power implies service; inspiration implies power; to understand and apply the method of inspiration is to become a superman.

We can live more abundantly every time we breathe if we consciously breathe with that intention. The *if* is a very important condition in this case, as the intention governs the attention, and without the attention you can secure only the results which everyone else secures—that is, a supply equal to the demand.

In order to secure the larger supply your demand must be increased, and as you consciously increase the demand the supply will follow; you will find yourself coming into a larger and larger supply of life, energy, and vitality. The reason for this is not difficult to understand, but it is another of the vital mysteries of life which does not seem to be generally appreciated. If you make it your own, you will find it one of the great realities of life.

We are told that "In Him we live and move and have our being," and we are told that "He" is a spirit, and again that "He" is love, so that every time we breathe, we breathe this Life, Love, and Spirit. This is Pranic Energy, or Pranic Ether, and we could not exist a moment without it. It is the Cosmic Energy; it is the life of the solar plexus.

Every time we breathe we fill our lungs with air and at the same time vitalize our body with this Pranic Ether which is Life itself, so that we have the opportunity of making a conscious connection with all life, all intelligence, and all substance.

A knowledge of your relation and oneness with this principle that governs the universe and the simple method whereby you can consciously identify yourself with it gives you a scientific understanding of a law whereby you may free yourself from disease, from lack or limitation of any kind; in fact, it enables you to breathe the "breath of life" into your own nostrils.

This breath of life is a superconscious reality. It is the essence of the "I am." It is pure Being, or Universal Substance, and our conscious unity with it enables us to localize it and thus exercise the powers of this creative energy.

Thought is creative vibration, and the quality of the conditions created will depend upon the quality of our thought because we cannot express powers which we do not possess. We must "be" before we can "do," and we can "do" only to the extent to which we "are," and so what we do will necessarily coincide with what we "are," and what we are depends upon what we "think."

Every time you think you start a train of causation which will create a condition in strict accordance with the quality of the thought which originated it. Thought which is in harmony with Universal Mind will result in corresponding conditions. Thought which is destructive or discordant will produce corresponding results. You may use thought constructively or destructively, but the Immutable Law will not allow you to plant a thought of one kind and reap the fruit of another. You are free to use this marvelous creative power as you will, but you must take the consequences.

This is the danger from what is called "will power." There are those who seem to think that by force of will they can coerce this Law; that they can sow seed of one kind and by will power make it bear fruit of another, but the fundamental principle of creative power is in the Universal, and therefore the idea of forcing a compliance with our wishes by the power of the individual will is an inverted conception which may appear to succeed for a while but is eventually doomed to failure—because it antagonizes the very power which it is seeking to use.

It is the individual attempting to coerce the Universal, the finite in conflict with the Infinite. Our permanent well-being will be best conserved by a conscious cooperation with the continuous forward movement of the Great Whole.

For your exercise in this chapter, go into the Silence and concentrate on the fact that "In Him we live and move and have our being" is literally and scientifically exact! That you *are* because He *is*, that if He is Omnipresent, He must be in you. That if He is all in all you must be in Him! That He is Spirit and you are made in "His image and likeness" and that the only difference between His Spirit and your spirit is one of degree, that a part must be the same in kind and quality as the Whole. When you can realize this clearly you will have found the secret of the creative power of thought; you will have found the origin of both good and evil;

you will have found the secret of the wonderful power of concentration; you will have found the key to the solution of every problem whether physical, financial, or environmental.

> *The power to think, consecutively and deeply and clearly, is an avowed and deadly enemy to mistakes and blunders, superstitions, unscientific theories, irrational beliefs, unbridled enthusiasm, fanaticism.*
>
> —Frank Channing Haddock

Summary

- Upon what condition does power depend?
  Upon recognition and use.
- What is recognition?
  Consciousness.
- How do we become conscious of power?
  By thinking.
- What then is the true business of life?
  Correct, scientific thinking.
- What is correct, scientific thinking?
  The ability to adjust our thought processes to the will of the Universal. In other words, to cooperate with Natural Law.
- How is this accomplished?
  By securing a perfect understanding of the principles, forces, methods, and combinations of Mind.
- What is Universal Mind?
  The basic fact of all existence.
- What is the cause of all lack, limitation, disease, and discord?
  It is due to the operation of exactly the same Immunent Law;

the Law operates relentlessly and is continually bringing about conditions in correspondence with the thought which originated or created them.

- What is inspiration?
  The art of realizing the omnipresence of Omniscience.
- Upon what do the conditions with which we meet depend?
  Upon the quality of our thought because what we do depends upon what we are, and what we are depends upon what we think.

TWENTY-ONE

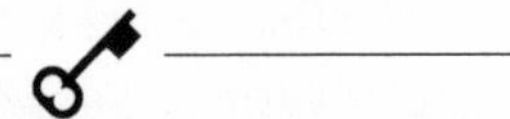

Prepare for Success

IT IS my privilege to offer chapter twenty-one. In this chapter you will find that one of the secrets of success, one of the methods of organizing victory, one of the accomplishments of the Master Mind is to think big thoughts.

And you will find that everything which we hold in our consciousness for any length of time becomes impressed upon our subconsciousness and so becomes a pattern which the Creative Energy will wave into our life and environment. This is the secret of the wonderful power of Prayer.

We know that the universe is governed by Law; that for every effect there must be a cause; and that the same cause, under the same conditions, will invariably produce the same effect.

Consequently, if Prayer has ever been answered, it will always be answered if the proper conditions are complied with. This must necessarily be true; otherwise the universe would be a chaos instead of a cosmos. The answer to Prayer is, therefore, subject to Law, and this Law is definite, exact, and scientific, just as are the laws governing gravitation and electricity. An understanding of this Law takes the foundation of Christianity out of the realm of superstition and credulity and places it upon the firm rock of scientific understanding.

But, unfortunately, there are comparatively few persons who know how to pray. They understand that there are laws governing electricity, mathematics, and chemistry, but, for some inexplicable reason, it never seems to occur to them that there are also spiritual laws and that these laws are also definite, scientific, exact, and operate with immutable precision.

The real secret of power is consciousness of power. Universal Mind is unconditional; therefore, the more conscious we become of our unity with this Mind, the less conscious we shall become of conditions and limitations, and as we become emancipated or freed from conditions we come into a realization of the unconditional. We have become free!

As soon as we become conscious of the inexhaustible power in the world within, we begin to draw on this power and apply and develop the greater possibilities which this discernment has realized, because whatever we become conscious of is invariably manifested in the objective world and is brought forth into tangible expression.

This is because the Infinite Mind, which is the source from which all things proceed, is one and indivisible, and each individual is a channel whereby this Eternal Energy is being manifested. Our ability to think is our ability to act upon this Universal Substance, and what we think is what is created or produced in the objective world.

The result of this discovery is nothing less than marvelous, and it means that Mind is extraordinary in quality, limitless in quantity, and contains possibilities without number. To become conscious of this power is to become a "live wire"; it has the same effect as placing an ordinary wire in contact with a wire that is charged. The Universal is the live wire. It carries power sufficient to meet every situation which may arise in the life of every individual. When the individual mind touches the Universal Mind it receives all the power it requires. This is the world within. All science recognizes the reality of this world, and all power is contingent upon our recognition of this world.

The ability to eliminate imperfect conditions depends upon mental action, and mental action depends upon consciousness of power; therefore, the more conscious we become of our unity with the source of all power, the greater will be our power to control and master every condition.

Large ideas have a tendency to eliminate all smaller ideas so that it is well to hold ideas large enough to counteract and destroy all small or undesirable tendencies. This will remove innumerable petty and annoying obstacles from your path. You also become conscious of a larger world of thought, thereby increasing your mental capacity as well as placing yourself in position to accomplish something of value.

This is one of the secrets of success, one of the methods of organizing victory, one of the accomplishments of the Master Mind. He thinks big thoughts. The creative energies of Mind find no more difficulty in handling large situations than small ones. Mind is just as much present in the infinitely large as in the infinitely small.

When we realize these facts concerning Mind we understand how we may bring ourselves any condition by creating the corresponding conditions in our consciousness, because everything which is held for any length of time in the consciousness eventually becomes impressed upon the subconscious and thus becomes a pattern which the Creative Energy will wave into the life and environment of the individual.

In this way conditions are produced and we find that our lives are simply the reflection of our predominant thoughts, our mental attitude; we see then that the science of correct thinking is the One Science, that it includes all other sciences.

From this science we learn that every thought creates an impression on the brain; that these impressions create mental tendencies; that these tendencies create character, ability, and purpose; and that the combined action of character, ability, and purpose determines the experiences with which we shall meet in life. These experiences come to us through the Law of Attraction; through the action of this law we meet in the world without the experiences which correspond to our world within. The predominant thought or the mental attitude is the magnet, and the law is that "like attracts like"; consequently, the mental attitude will invariably attract such conditions as correspond to its nature.

This mental attitude is our personality and is composed of the thoughts which we have been creating in our own mind. Therefore, if we wish a change in conditions all that is necessary is to change our thought; this will in turn change our mental attitude, which will in turn change our personality, which will in turn change the persons, things, and conditions, or the experiences with which we meet in life.

It is, however, no easy matter to change the mental attitude, but by persistent effort it may be accomplished; the mental attitude is patterned after the mental pictures which have been photographed in the brain; if you do not like the pictures, destroy the negatives and create new pictures; this is the art of visualization.

As soon as you have done this you will begin to attract new things, and the new things will correspond to the new pictures. To do this: impress on the mind a perfect picture of the desire which you wish to have objectified and continue to hold the picture in mind until results are obtained.

If the desire is one which requires determination, ability, talent, courage, power, or any other spiritual power, these are necessary essentials for your picture; build them in; they are the vital part of the picture; they are the feeling which combines with thought and creates the irresistible magnetic power which draws the things you require to you. They give your picture life, and life means growth, and as soon as it beings to grow, the result is practically assured.

Do not hesitate to aspire to the highest possible attainments in anything you may undertake, for the mind forces are ever ready to lend themselves to a purposeful will in the effort to crystallize its highest aspirations into acts, accomplishments, and events.

An illustration of how these mind forces operate is suggested by the method in which all our habits are formed. We do a thing, then do it again and again and again until it becomes easy and perhaps almost automatic; and the same rule applies in breaking any and all bad habits; we stop doing a thing, and then avoid it again and again until we are entirely free from it. And if we do fail now and then, we should by no means lose hope, for the Law is absolute and invincible, and gives us credit for every effort and every success, even though our efforts and successes are perhaps intermittent.

There is no limit to what this Law can do for you; dare to believe in your own idea; remember that Nature is plastic to the ideal; think of the ideal as an already accomplished fact. The real battle of life is one of ideas; it is being fought out by the few against the many; on the one side is the constructive and creative thought, on the other side the destructive and negative thought; the creative thought is dominated by an ideal, the passive thought is dominated by appearances. On both sides are men of science, men of letters, and men of affairs.

On the creative side are men who spend their time in laboratories or over microscopes and telescopes, side by side with the men who dominate the commercial, political, and scientific world; on the negative side are men who spend their time investigating law and precedent, men who mistake theology for religion, statesmen who mistake might for right, and all the millions who seem to prefer precedent to progress, who are eternally looking backward instead of forward, who see only the world without but know nothing of the world within.

In the last analysis there are but these two classes; all men will have to take their place on one side or the other; they will have to go forward or go back; there is no standing still in a world where all is motion; it is this attempt to stand still that gives sanction and force to arbitrary and unequal codes of law.

That we are in a period of transition is evidenced by the unrest which is everywhere apparent. The complaint of humanity is as a roll of Heaven's artillery, commencing with low and threatening notes and increasing until the sound is sent from cloud to cloud and the lightning splits the air and earth.

The sentries who patrol the most advanced outposts of the industrial, political, and religious world are calling anxiously to each other. What of the night? The danger and insecurity of the position they occupy and attempt to hold is becoming more apparent every hour. The dawn of a new era necessarily declares that the existing order of things cannot much longer be.

The issue between the old regime and the new, the crux of the social problem, is entirely a question of conviction in the minds of the people as to the nature of the universe. When they realize that the transcendent force of Spirit or Mind—of the cosmos—is within each individual, it will be possible to frame laws that shall consider the liberties and rights of the many instead of the privileges of the few.

As long as the people regard the Cosmic Power as a power nonhuman and alien to humanity, so long will it be comparatively easy for a supposed privileged class to rule by divine right in spite of every protest of social sentiment. The real interest of democracy is therefore to exalt, emancipate, and recognize the divinity of the human spirit—to recognize that all power is from within and that no human being has any more power than any other human being, except such as may willingly be delegated to him. The old regime would have us believe that the law was superior to the law-makers; herein is the gist of the social crime of every form of privilege and personal inequality, the institutionalizing of the fatalistic doctrine of divine election.

The Divine Mind is Universal Mind; it makes no exceptions, it plays no favorites; it does not act through sheer caprice or from anger, jealousy, or wrath; neither can it be flattered, cajoled, or moved by sympathy or petition to supply man with some need which he thinks necessary for his happiness or even his existence. The Divine Mind makes no exceptions to favor any individual; but when the individual understands and realizes his unity with the Universal Principle, he will appear to be favored because he will have found the Source of all health, all wealth, and all power.

For your exercise in this chapter, concentrate on the Truth. Try to realize that the Truth shall make you free; that is, nothing can permanently stand in the way of your perfect success when you learn to apply the scientifically correct thought methods and principles. Realize that you are externalizing in your environment your inherent soul potencies. Realize that the Silence offers an ever-available and almost unlimited opportunity for awakening the highest conception of Truth. Try to comprehend that Omnipotence itself is Absolute Silence; all else is change, activity, limitation. Silent thought concentration is therefore the true method of reaching, awakening, and then expressing the wonderful potential Power of the world within.

> *The possibilities of thought training are infinite, its consequence eternal, and yet few take the pains to direct their thinking into channels that will do them good, but instead leave all to chance.*
>
> —Orison Swett Marden

Summary

- What is the real secret of power?
  The consciousness of power because whatever we become conscious of is invariably manifested in the objective world and is brought forth into tangible expression.
- What is the source of this power?
  Universal Mind, from which all things proceed and which is One and indivisible.
- How is this power being manifested?
  Through the individual; each individual is a channel whereby this energy is being differentiated in form.
- How may we connect with this Omnipotence?
  Our ability to think is our ability to act on this Universal Energy, and what we think is what is produced or created in the objective world.
- What is the result of this discovery?
  The result is nothing less than marvelous; it opens unprecedented and limitless opportunity.
- How, then, may we eliminate imperfect conditions?
  By becoming conscious of our unity with the Source.

- What is one of the distinctive characteristics of the Master Mind?
  He thinks big thoughts; He holds ideas large enough to counteract and destroy all petty and annoying obstacles.
- How do experiences come to us?
  Through the Law of Attraction.
- How is this law brought into operation?
  By our predominant mental attitude.
- What is the issue between the old regime and the new?
  A question of conviction as to the nature of the universe. The old regime is trying to cling to the fatalistic doctrine of divine election. The new regime recognizes the divinity of the individual, the democracy of humanity.

TWENTY-TWO

Planting the Seeds

In chapter twenty-two you will find that thoughts are spiritual seeds, which, when planted in the subconscious mind, have a tendency to sprout and grow, but unfortunately the fruit is frequently not to our liking.

The various forms of inflammation, paralysis, nervousness, and diseased conditions generally are the manifestation of fear, worry, care, anxiety, jealousy, hatred, and similar thought.

The life processes are carried on by two distinct methods; first, the taking up and making use of nutritive material necessary for constructing cells; second, breaking down and excreting the waste material.

All life is based upon these constructive and destructive activities, and as food, water, and air are the only requisites necessary for the construction of cells, it would seem that the problem of prolonging life indefinitely would not be a very difficult one.

However strange it may seem, it is the second, or destructive, activity that is, with rare exception, the cause of all disease. The waste material accumulates and saturates the tissues, which causes autointoxication. This may be partial or general. In the first case the disturbance will be local; in the second place it will affect the whole system.

The problem before us in the healing of disease is to increase the inflow and distribution of vital energy throughout the system, and this can only be done by eliminating thoughts of fear, worry, care, anxiety, jealousy, hatred, and every other destructive thought, which tend to tear down and destroy the nerves and glands which control the excretion and elimination of poisonous and waste matter.

"Nourishing foods and strengthening tonics" cannot bestow life because these are but secondary manifestations to life. The primary manifestation of life and how you may get in touch with it is explained in this chapter, which I have the privilege of offering to you now.

Knowledge is of priceless value because by applying knowledge we can make our future what we wish it to be. When we realize that our present character, our present environment, our present ability, our present physical condition are all the result of past methods of thinking, we shall begin to have some conception of the value of knowledge.

If the state of our health is not all that could be desired, let us examine our method of thinking. Let us remember that every thought produces an impression on the mind; every impression is a seed which will sink into the subconscious and form a tendency; the tendency will be to attract other similar thoughts; and before we know it, we shall have a crop which must be harvested.

If these thoughts contain disease germs, the harvest will be sickness, decay, weakness, and failure; the question is, what are we thinking? What are we creating? What is the harvest to be? If there is any physical condition which it is necessary to change, the law governing visualization will be found effective. Make a mental image of physical perfection and hold it in the mind until it is absorbed by the consciousness. Many have eliminated chronic ailments in a few weeks by this method, and thousands have overcome and destroyed all manner of ordinary physical disturbances by this method in a few days, sometimes in a few minutes.

It is through the Law of Vibration that the mind exercises this control over the body. We know that every mental action is a vibration, and we know that all form is simply a mode of motion, a rate of vibration. Therefore, any given vibration immediately modifies every atom in the body, every life cell is affected, and an entire chemical change is made in every group of life cells.

Everything in the universe is what it is by virtue of its rate of vibration. Change the rate of vibration and you change the nature, quality, and form. The vast panorama of Nature, both visible and invisible, is being constantly changed by simply changing the rate of vibration; as thought is a vibration, we can also exercise this power. We can change the vibration and thus produce any condition which we desire to manifest in our bodies.

We are all using this power every minute. The trouble is that most of us are using it unconsciously and thus producing undesirable results. The problem is to use it intelligently and produce only desirable results. This should not be difficult because we all have had sufficient experience to know what produces pleasant vibration in the body; we also know the causes which produce the unpleasant and disagreeable sensations.

All that is necessary is to consult our own experience. When our thought has been uplifted, progressive, constructive, courageous, noble, kind, or in any other way desirable, we have set in motion vibrations which brought about certain results. When our thought has been filled with envy, hatred, jealousy, criticism, or any of the other thousand and one forms of discord, certain vibrations were set in motion which brought about certain other results of a different nature, and each of these rates of vibration, if kept up, crystallized in form. In the first case the result was mental, moral, and physical health, and in the second case discord, inharmony, and disease.

We can understand, then, something of the power which the mind possesses over the body. The objective mind has certain effects on the body which are readily recognized. Someone says something to you which strikes you as ludicrous and you laugh, possibly until your whole body shakes, which shows that thought has control over the muscles of your body; or someone says something which excites your sympathy and your eyes fill with tears, which shows that thought controls the glands of your body; or someone says something which makes you angry and the blood mounts to your cheek, which shows that thought controls the circulation of your blood. But as these experiences are all the results of the action of your objective mind over the body, the results are of a temporary nature; they soon pass away and leave the situation as it was before.

Let us see how the action of the subconscious mind over the body differs. You receive a wound; thousands of cells begin the work of healing at once; in a few days or a few weeks the work is complete. You may even break a bone. No surgeon on earth can weld the parts together. (I am not referring to the insertion of rods or other devices to strengthen or replace bones.) He may set the bone for you, and the subjective mind will immediately begin the process of welding the parts together, and in a short time the bone is as solid as it ever was. You may swallow poison; the subjective mind will immediately discover the danger and make violent efforts to eliminate it. You may become infected with a dangerous germ; the subjective will at once commence to build a wall around the infected area and destroy the infection by absorbing it in the white blood corpuscles which it supplies for the purpose.

These processes of the subconscious mind usually proceed without our personal knowledge or direction, and so long as we do not interfere the result, is perfect. But, as these millions of repair cells are all intelligent and respond to our thought, they are often paralyzed and rendered impotent by our thoughts of fear, doubt, and anxiety. They are like an army of workmen, ready to start an important piece of work, but every time they get started on the undertaking a strike is called, or plans changed, until they finally get discouraged and give up.

The way to health is founded on the Law of Vibration, which is the basis of all science, and this law is brought into operation by the mind, the world within. It is a matter of individual effort and practice. Our world of power is within; if we are wise we shall not waste time and effort in trying to deal with effects as we find them in the world without, which is only an external, a reflection.

We shall always find the cause in the world within; by changing the cause, we change the effect. Every cell in your body is intelligent and will respond to your direction. The cells are all creators and will create the exact pattern which you give them. Therefore, when perfect images are placed before the subjective, the creative energies will build a perfect body.

Brain cells are constructed in the same way. The quality of the brain is governed by the state of mind, or mental attitude, so that if undesirable mental attitudes are conveyed to the subjective, they will in turn be transferred to the body; we can therefore readily see that if we wish the body to manifest health, strength, and vitality, this must be the predominant thought.

We know then that every element of the human body is the result of a rate of vibration. We know that mental action is a rate of vibration. We know that a higher rate of vibration governs, modifies, controls, changes, or destroys a lower rate of vibration. We know that the rate of vibration is governed by the character of brain cells, and finally, we know how to create these brain cells; therefore, we know how to make any physical change in the body we desire, and having secured a working knowledge of the power of mind to this extent, we have come to know that there is practically no limitation which can be placed upon our ability to place ourselves in harmony with Natural Law, which is omnipotent.

This influence or control over the body by mind is coming to be more and more generally understood, and many physicians are now giving the matter their earnest attention. Dr. Albert T. Shofield, who has written several important books on the subject, says, "The subject of mental therapeutics is still ignored in medical works generally. In our physiologies no references are made to the central controlling power that rules the body for its good, and the power of the mind over the body is seldom spoken of."

No doubt many physicians treat nervous diseases of functional origin wisely and well, but what we contend is that the knowledge they display was taught at no school, was learned from no book, but it is intuitive and empirical.

This is not as it should be. The power of mental therapeutics should be the subject of careful, special, and scientific teaching in every medical school. We might pursue the subject of maltreatment, or want of treatment, in further detail and describe the disastrous results of neglected cases; but the task is an invidious one.

There can be no doubt that few patients are aware how much they can do for themselves. What the patient can do for himself, the forces he can set in motion are as yet unknown. We are inclined to believe that they are far greater than most imagine and will undoubtedly be used more and more. Mental therapeutics may be directed by the patient himself to calming the mind in excitement; by arousing feelings of joy, hope, faith, and love;

by suggesting motives for exertion; by regular mental work; by diverting the thoughts from the malady.

For your exercise in this chapter concentrate on Tennyson's beautiful lines "Speak to Him, thou, for He hears, and spirit with spirit can meet, Closer is He than breathing, and nearer than hands and feet." Then try to realize that when you do "Speak to Him" you are in touch with Omnipotence.

This realization and recognition of this Omnipresent Power will quickly destroy any and every form of sickness or suffering and substitute harmony and perfection. Then remember there are those who seem to think that sickness and suffering are sent by God; if so, every physician, every surgeon, and every Red Cross nurse is defying the will of God, and hospitals and sanitariums are places of rebellion instead of houses of mercy. Of course, this quickly reasons itself into an absurdity, but there are many who still cherish the idea.

Then let the thought rest on the fact that until recently theology has been trying to teach an impossible Creator, one who created beings capable of sinning and then allowed them to be eternally punished for such sins. Of course the necessary outcome of such extraordinary ignorance was to create fear instead of love, and so, after two thousand years of this kind of propaganda, theology is now busily engaged in apologizing for Christendom.

You will then more readily appreciate the ideal man, the man made in the image and likeness of God, and you will more readily appreciate the all-originating Mind that forms, upholds, sustains, originates, and creates all there is.

All are but parts of one stupendous Whole, whose body Nature is and God the soul.

Opportunity follows perception, action follows inspiration, growth follows knowledge, eminence follows progress. Always the spiritual first, then the transformation into the infinite and unlimited possibilities of achievement.

Summary

- How may sickness be eliminated?

  By placing ourselves in harmony with Natural Law which is Omnipotent.
- What is the process?

  A realization that man is a spiritual being and that this spirit must necessarily be perfect.
- What is the result?

  A conscious recognition of this perfection—first intellectually, then emotionally—brings about a manifestation of this perfection.
- Why is this so?

  Because thought is spiritual and therefore creative and correlates with its object and brings it into manifestation.
- Which natural law is brought into operation?

  The Law of Vibration.
- Why does this govern?

  Because a higher rate of vibration governs, modifies, controls, changes, or destroys a lower rate of vibration.
- Is this system of mental therapeutics generally recognized?

  Yes, there are literally millions of people in the United States who make use of it in one form or another (and obviously many more worldwide).
- What is the result of this system of thought?

  For the first time in the world's history every man's highest reasoning faculty can be satisfied by a demonstrable Truth which is now fast flooding the world.
- Is this system applicable to other forms of supply?

  It will meet every human requirement or necessity.
- Is this system scientific or religious?

  Both. True science and true religion are twin sisters; where one goes, the other necessarily follows.

TWENTY-THREE

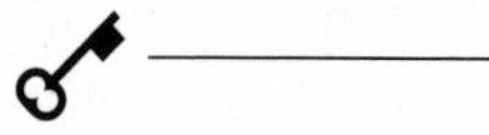

Success in Service

IN THIS chapter, which I have the honor to offer, you will find that money weaves itself into the entire fabric of our very existence; that the Law of Success is service; that we get what we give, and for this reason we should consider it a great privilege to be able to give.

We have found that thought is the creative activity behind every constructive enterprise. We can, therefore, give nothing of more practical value than our thought.

Creative thought requires attention, and the power of attention is, as we have found, the weapon of the superman. Attention develops concentration, and concentration develops Spiritual Power, and Spiritual Power is the mightiest force in existence.

This is the science which embraces all sciences. It is the art which, above all arts, is relevant to human life. In the mastery of this science and this art there is opportunity for unending progression. Perfection in this is not acquired in six days, nor in six weeks, nor in six months. It is the labor of life. Not to go forward is to go backward.

It is inevitable that the entertainment of positive, constructive, and unselfish thoughts should have a far-reaching effect for good. Compensation is the keynote of the universe. Nature is constantly seeking to strike an equilibrium. Where something is sent out something must be received, or else there would be a vacuum formed.

By observance of this rule you cannot fail to profit in such measure as to amply justify your effort along this line. The money consciousness is an attitude of mind; it is the open door to the arteries of commerce. It is the receptive attitude. Desire is the attractive force which sets the current in motion, and fear is the great obstacle by which the current is stopped or completely reversed, turned away from us.

Fear is just the opposite from money consciousness; it is poverty consciousness, and as the law is unchangeable we get exactly what we give; if we fear we get what we feared. Money weaves itself into the entire fabric of our very existence; it engages the best thought of the best minds.

We make money by making friends, and we enlarge our circle of friends by making money for them, by helping them, by being of service to them. The Law of Success then is service, and this in turn is built on integrity and justice. The man who at least is not fair in his intention is simply ignorant; he has missed the fundamental law of all exchange; he is impossible; he will lose surely and certainly; he may not know it; he may think he is winning, but he is doomed to certain defeat. He cannot cheat the Infinite. The Law of Compensation will demand of him an eye for an eye and a tooth for a tooth.

The forces of life are volatile; they are composed of our thoughts and ideals, and these in turn are molded into form; our problem is to keep an open mind, to constantly reach out for the new, to recognize opportunity, to be interested in the race rather than the goal, for the pleasure is in the pursuit rather than the possession. You can make a money magnet of yourself, but to do so you must first consider how you can make money for other people. If you have the necessary insight to perceive and utilize opportunities and favorable conditions and recognize values, you can put yourself in position to take advantage of them, but your greatest success will come as you are enabled to assist others. What benefits one must benefit all.

A generous thought is filled with strength and vitality, a selfish thought contains the germs of dissolution; it will disintegrate and pass away. Great financiers are simply channels for the distribution of wealth; enormous amounts come and go, but it would be as dangerous to stop the outgo as the income; both ends must remain open; and so our greatest success will come as we recognize that it is just as essential to give as to get.

If we recognize the Omnipotent Power that is the source of all supply, we will adjust our consciousness to this supply in such a way that it will constantly attract all that is necessary to itself, and we shall find that the more we give the more we get. Giving in this sense implies service. The banker gives his money, the merchant gives his goods, the author gives his thought, the workman gives his skill; all have something to give, but the more they can give the more they get, and the more they get the more they are enabled to give.

The financier gets much because he gives much; he thinks; he is seldom a man that lets anyone else do his thinking for him; he wants to know how results are to be secured; you must show him; when you can do this he will furnish the means by which hundreds or thousands may profit, and in proportion as they are successful will he be successful. Morgan, Rockefeller, Carnegie, and others did not get rich because they lost money for other people; on the contrary, it is because they made money for other people that they became the wealthiest men in the wealthiest country on the globe.

The average person is entirely innocent of any deep thinking; he accepts the ideas of others and repeats them, in very much the same way as a parrot; this is readily seen when we understand the method which is used to form public opinion, and this docile attitude on the part of a large majority who seem perfectly willing to let a few persons do all their thinking for them is what enables a few men in a great many countries to usurp all the avenues of power and hold the millions in subjection. Creative thinking requires attention.

The power of attention is called concentration; this power is directed by the will; for this reason we must refuse to concentrate or think of anything except the things we desire. Many are constantly concentrating upon sorrow, loss, and discord of every kind; as thought is creative it necessarily follows that this concentration inevitable leads to more loss, more sorrow, and more discord. How could it be otherwise? On the other hand, when we meet with success, gain, or any other desirable condition, we naturally concentrate upon the effects of these things and thereby create more, and so it follows that much leads to more.

How an understanding of this principle can be utilized in the business world is well told by an associate of mine: "Spirit, whatever else it may or may not be, must be considered as the Essence of Consciousness, the Substance of Mind, the reality underlying Thought. And as all ideas are phases of the activity of Consciousness, Mind, or Thought, it follows that in Spirit, and in it alone, is to be found the Ultimate Fact, the Real Thing, or Idea."

This being admitted, does it not seem reasonable to hold that a true understanding of Spirit, and its laws of manifestation, would be about the most practical thing that a practical person can hope to find? Does it not seem certain that if the practical men of the world could but realize this fact, they would "fall all over themselves" in getting to the place in which they might obtain such knowledge of spiritual things and laws? These men are not fools; they need only to grasp this fundamental fact in order to move in the direction of that which is the essence of all achievement.

Let me give you a concrete example. I know a man in Chicago whom I had always considered to be quite materialistic. He had made several successes in life, and also several failures. The last time I had a talk with him he was practically "down and out," as compared with his former business condition. It looked as if he had indeed reached "the end of his rope," for he was well advanced into the stage of middle-age, and new ideas came more slowly and less frequently to him than in former years.

He said to me, in substance: "I know that all things that 'work out' in business are the result of Thought; any fool knows that. Just now, I seem to be short on thoughts and good ideas. But if this 'All-Mind' teaching is correct, it should be possible for the individual to attain a 'direct connection' with Infinite Mind; and in Infinite Mind there must be the possibility of all kinds of good ideas which a man of my courage and experience could put to practical use in the business world and make a big success thereof. It looks good to me; and I am going to look into it."

This was several years ago. The other day I heard of this man again. Talking to a friend, I said: "What has come of our old friend X? Has he ever gotten on his feet again?" The friend looked at me in amazement. "Why," said he, "don't you know about X's great success? He is the Big Man in the '_________ Company' (naming a concern which has made a phenomenal success during the last eighteen months and is now well known, by reason of its advertisements from one end of the country to another and also abroad). He is the man who supplied the *big idea* for that concern. Why, he is about a half-million to the good and is moving rapidly toward the million mark; all in the space of eighteen months." I had not connected this man with the enterprise mentioned, although I knew of the wonderful success of the company in question. Investigation has shown that the story is true and that the above stated facts are not exaggerated in the slightest.

Now, what do you think of that? To me, it means that this man actually made the "direct connection" with Infinite Mind—Spirit—and, having found it, he set it to work for him. He "used it in his business."

Does this sound sacrilegious or blasphemous? I hope not; I do not mean it to be so. Take away the implication of personality, or magnified human nature, from the conception of the The Infinite, and you have left the conception of an Infinite Presence-Power, the Quintessence of which is Consciousness—in fact, at the last, Spirit. As this man, also, at the last, must be considered as a manifestation of Spirit; there is nothing sacrilegious in the idea that he, being spirit, should so harmonize himself with his Origin and Source that he would be able to manifest at least a minor degree of its power. All of us do this, more or less, when we use our minds in the direction of Creative Thought. This man did more; he went about it in an intensely "practical" manner.

I have not consulted him about his method of procedure, though I intend doing so at the first opportunity, but he, not only drew upon the Infinite Supply for the ideas which he needed (and which formed the seed of his success), but he also used the Creative Power of Thought in building up for himself an idealistic pattern of that which he hoped to manifest in material form, adding thereto, changing, improving its detail, from time to time—proceeding from the general outline to the finished detail. I judge this to be the facts of the case, not alone from my recollection of the conversation a few years ago, but also because I have found the same thing to be true in the cases of other prominent men who have made similar manifestation of Creative Thought.

Those who may shrink from this idea of employing the Infinite Power to aid one in his work in the material world should remember that if the Infinite objected in the least to such a procedure the thing could never happen. The Infinite is quite able to take care of itself.

Spirituality is quite practical, very practical, intensely practical. It teaches that spirit is the Real Thing, the Whole Thing, and that Matter is but plastic stuff, which Spirit is able to create, mold, manipulate, and fashion to its will. Spirituality is the most practical thing in the world—the only really and absolutely practical thing that there is!

This week concentrate on the fact that man is not a body with a spirit but a spirit with a body, and that it is for this reason that his desires are incapable of any permanent satisfaction in anything not spiritual. Money is, therefore, of no value except to bring about the conditions which we desire, and these conditions are necessarily harmonious. Harmonious conditions necessitate sufficient supply, so that if there appears to be any lack, we should realize that the idea or soul of money is service, and as this thought takes form, channels of supply will be opened, and you will have the satisfaction of knowing that spiritual methods are entirely practical.

> *We have discovered that premeditated, orderly thinking for a purpose matures that purpose into fixed form, so that we may be absolutely sure of the result of our dynamic experiment.*
>
> —FRANCIS LARIMER WARNER

Summary

- What is the Law of Success?
  Service.
- How may we be of the most service?
  Have an open mind; be interested in the race rather than the goal, in the pursuit rather than possession.
- What is the result of a selfish thought?
  It contains the germs of dissolution.
- How will our greatest success be achieved?
  By a recognition of the fact that it is just as essential to give as to receive.
- Why do financiers frequently meet with great success?
  Because they do their own thinking.
- Why do the great majority in every country remain the docile and apparently willing tools of the few?
  Because they let the few do all their thinking for them.
- What is the effect of concentrating upon sorrow and loss?
  More sorrow and more loss.
- What is the effect of concentrating upon gain?
  More gain.
- Is this principle used in the business world?
  It is the only principle which is ever used or ever can be used; there is no other principle. The fact that it may be used unconsciously does not alter the situation.

- What is the practical application of this principle?
The fact that success is an effect, not a cause, and if we wish to secure the effect we must ascertain the cause, or idea, or thought by which the effect is created.

Nurture your mind with great thoughts; to believe in the heroic makes heroes.

—Benjamin Disraeli

TWENTY-FOUR

The Master Key

Following you will find chapter twenty-four, your final lesson of this course.

If you have practiced each of the exercises a few minutes every day, as suggested, you will have found that you can get out of life exactly what you wish by first putting into life that which you wish, and you will probably agree with the student who said: "The thought is almost overwhelming, so vast, so available, so definite, so reasonable, and so usable."

The fruit of this knowledge is, as it were, a gift of the Gods; it is the Truth that makes men free, not only free from every lack and limitation, but free from sorrow, worry, and care; and is it not wonderful to realize that this law is no respecter of persons, that it makes no difference what your habit of thought may be, the way has been prepared?

If you are inclined to be religious, the greatest religious teacher the world has ever known made the way so plain that all may follow. If your mental bias is toward physical science, the law will operate with mathematical certainty. If you are inclined to be philosophical, Plato or Emerson may be your teacher, but in either case, you may reach degrees of power to which it is impossible to assign any limit.

An understanding of this principle, I believe, is the secret for which the ancient alchemists vainly sought because it explains how gold in the mind may be transmuted into gold in the heart and in the hand.

When the scientists first put the sun in the center of the solar system and sent the earth spinning around it, there was immense surprise and consternation. The whole idea was self-evidently false; nothing was more certain than the movement of the sun across the sky, and anyone could see it descend behind the western hills and sink into the sea; scholars raged and scientists rejected the idea as absurd, yet the evidence has finally carried conviction in the minds of all.

We speak of a bell as a "sounding body," yet we know that all the bell can do is to produce vibrations in the air. When these vibrations come at the rate of sixteen per second, they cause a sound to be heard in the mind. It is also possible for the mind to hear vibrations up to the rate of 38,000 vibrations per second. When the number increases beyond this, all is silence again; so we know that the sound is not in the bell, it is in our own mind.

We speak and even think of the sun as "giving light." Yet we know it is simply giving forth energy which produces vibrations in the ether at the rate of four hundred trillion a second, causing what are termed light waves, so that we know that what we call light is simply a form of energy and that the only light existing is the sensation caused in the mind by the motion of the waves.

When the number increases, the light changes in color, each change in color being caused by shorter and more rapid vibrations; so although we speak of the rose as being red, the grass as being green, or the sky as being blue, we know that the colors exist only in our minds and are the sensations experienced by us as the result of the vibrations of light waves. When the vibrations are reduced below four hundred trillion a second, they no longer affect us as light, but we experience the sensation of heat. It is evident, therefore, that we cannot depend upon the evidence of the senses for our information concerning the realities of things; if we did we should believe that the sun moved, that the world was flat instead of round, that the stars were bits of light instead of vast suns.

The whole range then of the theory and practice of any system of metaphysics consists in knowing the Truth concerning yourself and the world in which you live; in knowing that in order to express harmony, you must think harmony; in order to express health you must think health; and in order to express abundance you must think abundance; to do this you must reverse the evidence of the senses.

When you come to know that every form of disease, sickness, lack, and limitation is simply the result of wrong thinking, you will have come to know "the Truth which shall make you free." You will see how mountains may be removed. If these mountains consist only of doubt, fear, distrust, or other forms of discouragement, they are nonetheless real, and they need not only to be removed but to be "cast into the sea."

Your real work consists in convincing yourself of the Truth of these statements. When you have succeeded in doing this you will have no difficulty in thinking the Truth, and as has been shown, the Truth contains a vital principle and will manifest itself.

Those who heal diseases by mental methods have come to know this Truth; they demonstrate it in their lives and the lives of others daily. They know that life, health, and abundance are omnipresent, filling all space, and they know that those who allow disease or lack of any kind to manifest have as yet not come into an understanding of this great law.

As all conditions are thought creations and therefore entirely mental, disease and lack are simply mental conditions in which the person fails to perceive the Truth; as soon as the error is removed, the condition is removed.

The method for removing this error is to go into the Silence and know the Truth; as all mind is one mind, you can do this for yourself or anyone else. If you have learned to form mental images of the conditions desired, this will be the easiest and quickest way to secure results; if not, results can be accomplished by argument, by the process of convincing yourself absolutely of the Truth of your statement.

Remember, and this is one of the most difficult as well as most wonderful statements to grasp—remember that no matter what the difficulty is, no matter where it is, no matter who is affected, you have no patient but yourself; you have nothing to do but to convince yourself of the truth which you desire to see manifested. This is an exact scientific statement in accordance with every system of metaphysics in existence, and no permanent results are ever secured in any other way. Every form of concentration, forming mental images, argument, and autosuggestion, are all simply methods by which you are enabled to realize the Truth.

If you desire to help someone, to destroy some form of lack, limitation, or error, the correct method is not to think of the person whom you wish to help; the intention to help them is entirely sufficient, as this puts you in mental touch with the person. Then drive out of your own mind any belief of lack, limitation, disease, danger, difficulty, or whatever the trouble might be. As soon as you have succeeded in doing this, the result will have been accomplished, and the person will be free.

But remember that thought is creative, and consequently every time you allow your thought to rest on any inharmonious condition, you must realize that such conditions are apparent only, that they have no reality, that Spirit is the only reality, and it can never be less than perfect.

All thought is a form of energy, a rate of vibration, but a thought of the Truth is the highest rate of vibration known and consequently destroys every form of error in exactly the same way that light destroys darkness; no form of error can exist when the Truth appears, so that your entire mental work consists in coming into an understanding of the Truth. This will enable you to overcome every form of lack, limitation, or disease of any kind.

We can get no understanding of the Truth from the world without; the world without is relative only; Truth is Absolute. We must, therefore, find it in the world within. To train the mind to see Truth only is to express true conditions only; our ability to do this will be an indication as to the progress we are making.

The Absolute Truth is that the "I" is perfect and complete; the real "I" is spiritual and can therefore never be less than perfect; it can never have any lack, limitation, or disease. The flash of genius does not have origin in the molecular motion of the brain; it is inspired by the ego, the spiritual "I" which is one with Universal Mind, and it is our ability to recognize this unity which is the cause of all inspiration, all genius. These results are far-reaching and have effects upon generations yet to come; they are the pillars of fire which mark the path that millions follow.

Truth is not the result of logical training or of experimentation or even of observation; it is the product of a developed consciousness. Truth within a Caesar manifests in a Caesar's deportment, in his life and his action, in his influence upon social forms and progress. Your life and your actions and your influence in the world will depend upon the degree of truth which you are enabled to perceive, for truth will not manifest in creeds but in conduct.

Truth manifests in character, and the character of a man should be the interpretation of his religion, or what to him is truth, and this will in turn be evidenced in the character of his possession. If a man complains of the drift of his fortune he is just as unjust to himself as if he should deny rational truth, though it stand patent and irrefutable.

Our environment and the innumerable circumstances and accidents of our lives already exist in the subconscious personality which attracts to itself the mental and physical material which is congenial to its nature. Thus our future is being determined from our present, and if there should be apparent injustice in any feature or phase of our personal life, we must look within for the cause and try to discover the mental fact which is responsible for the outward manifestation.

It is this Truth which makes you free, and it is the conscious knowledge of this Truth which will enable you to overcome every difficulty. The conditions with which you meet in the world without are invariably the result of the conditions obtaining in the world within; therefore, it follows with scientific accuracy that by holding the perfect ideal in mind you can bring about ideal conditions in your environment.

If you see only the incomplete, the imperfect, the relative, the limited, these conditions will manifest in your life; but if you train your mind to see and realize the spiritual ego, the "I" which is forever perfect and complete, then only harmonious, wholesome, and healthful conditions will be manifested. As thought is creative, and the Truth is the highest and most perfect thought which anyone can think, it is self-evident that to think the Truth is to create that which is true, and it is again evident that when Truth comes into being that which is false must cease to be.

Universal Mind is the totality of all mind which is in existence. Spirit is Mind because Spirit is Intelligent. The words are, therefore, synonymous. The difficulty with which you have to contend is to realize that mind is not individual. It is omnipresent. It exists everywhere. In other words, there is no place where it is not. It is, therefore, Universal.

Men have, heretofore, generally used the word "God" to indicate this Universal, creative principle; but the word "God" does not convey the right meaning. Most people understand this word to mean something outside of themselves; exactly the contrary is the fact. It is our very life. Without it we would be dead. We would cease to exist. The minute the spirit leaves the body, we are as nothing. Therefore, spirit is really all there is of us.

Now, the only activity which the spirit possesses is the Power to think. Therefore, thought must be creative because spirit is creative. This Creative Power is impersonal, and your ability to think is your ability to control it and make use of it for the benefit of yourself and others. When the Truth of this statement is realized, understood, and appreciated, you will have come into possession of the Master Key, but remember that only those who are wise enough to understand, broad enough to weigh the evidence, firm enough to follow their own judgment, and strong enough to make the sacrifice exacted may enter and partake.

From now on, try to realize that this is truly a wonderful world in which we live, that you are a wonderful being, that many are awakening to a knowledge of the Truth, and as fast as they awake and come into a knowledge of the "things which have been prepared for them," they, too, realize that "Eye hath not seen, nor ear heard, neither hath it entered into the heart of man" the splendors which exist for those who find themselves in the Promised Land. They have crossed the river of judgment and have arrived at the point of discrimination between the true and the false, and they have found that all they ever willed or dreamed was but a faint concept of the dazzling reality.

Though an inheritance of acres may be bequeathed, an inheritance of knowledge and wisdom cannot. The wealthy man may pay others for doing his work for him, but it is impossible to get his thinking done for him by another or to purchase any kind of self-culture.

—S. Smiles

Summary

- Upon what principle does the theory and practice of every system of metaphysics in existence depend?
  Upon a knowledge of the Truth concerning yourself and the world in which you live.
- What is the Truth concerning yourself?
  The real "I" or ego is spiritual and can therefore never be less than perfect.
- What is the method of destroying any form of error?
  To absolutely convince yourself of the Truth concerning the condition which you wish to see manifested.
- Can we do this for others?
  The Universal Mind in which "we live and move and have our being" is one and indivisible; it is therefore just as possible to help others as to help ourselves.

- What is the Universal Mind?
  The totality of all Mind in existence.
- Where is Universal Mind?
  Universal Mind is omnipresent; it exists everywhere. There is no place where it is not. It is, therefore, within us. It is the world within. It is our spirit, our life.
- What is the nature of Universal Mind?
  It is spiritual and consequently creative. It seeks to express itself in form.
- How may we act on Universal Mind?
  Our ability to think is our ability to act on Universal Mind and bring it into manifestation for the benefit of ourselves or others.
- What is meant by thinking?
  Clear, decisive, calm, deliberate, sustained thought with a definite end in view.
- What will be the result?
  You will also be able to say, "It is not I that doeth the works, but the 'Father' that dwelleth within me, He doeth the works." You will come to know that the "Father" is Universal Mind and that He does really and truly dwell within you; in other words, you will come to know that the wonderful promises made in the Bible are fact, not fiction, and can be demonstrated by anyone having sufficient understanding.

Temples have their sacred images, and we see what influence they have always had over a great part of mankind; but, in truth, the ideas and images in men's minds are the invisible powers that constantly govern them; and to these they all pay universally a ready submission.

—Jonathan Edwards

CONTRIBUTOR BIOGRAPHIES

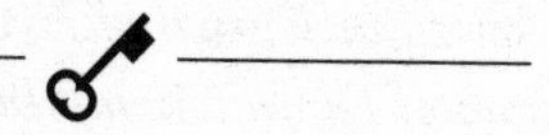

Lyman Abbott (1835–1922)

Dr. Lyman Abbott began a career in law in 1853, but soon after he changed his profession and followed his passion in the study of theology. For the next sixty years he dedicated his life to the church, working as a pastor for multiple congregations and as secretary of the American Union Freedman Commission. He devoted much time to literary work, supplying sermons for the pulpit and acting as editor for the "Literary Record" of *Harper's Magazine* and editor of the *Illinois Christian Weekly*. Dr. Abbott was the author of a number of religious books, including *Dictionary of Religious Knowledge*, *A Study in Human Nature*, and *The Theology of an Evolutionist*.

George Matthew Adams (ca. 1870s–unknown)

With the influence of a strong Baptist upbringing, Adams became a Michigan newspaper columnist, writing motivational and self-reliance stories. His column, "Today's Talk," appeared in newspapers across the country, and its inspirational tone appealed to the average American.

A. B. Alcott (1799–1888)

Amos Bronson Alcott, best known as the father of author Louisa May Alcott, was also known as a reformer, philosopher, writer, visionary, and teacher. Completely self-educated, he began his literary career by publishing articles and books describing his teaching methods and pedagogical philosophy. He published articles in both the *American Journal of Education* and its successor, the *American Annals of Education and Instruction.* Alcott was a modern man of his time, strongly advocating for a woman's right to vote and supporting the abolition of slavery.

James Allen (1864–1912)

With over nineteen books to his name, James Allen's words influenced a generation of thinkers. His work practically and eloquently blended together Buddhist teachings with a joyful exploration of the then-revolutionary Protestant philosophy that humankind is inherently good rather than sinful.

Horatio (Horatius) Bonar (1808–1889)

Horatio Bonar, a Scottish writer of popular devotional poetry, was also the author of many hymns, publishing over a dozen in the *Trinity Hymnal*; "Go, Labor On" and "Blessing and Honor and Glory and Power" became well-known all over the English-speaking world. As a reformed Presbyterian divine and churchman, he entered the ministry of the Church of Scotland and later joined the Free Church at the time of the Disruption of 1843.

F. H. Burgess (unknown)

All that is known of Frederick H. Burgess is that he was either the publisher or the editor of the Master Key Publishing Company.

William Ellery Channing (1780–1842)

William Channing, a Unitarian minister in Boston, published many sermons that were widely influential abroad as well as throughout the United States, and he acted as a spokesman during the Unitarian controversy. His work inspired both religious and literary features of the Transcendentalist movement, and he was known as a champion of human rights, effectively promoting social reform in areas of free speech, education, peace, relief for the poor, women's rights, and the abolition of slavery.

Georges Cuvier (1769–1832)

French naturalist and zoologist Georges Cuvier was instrumental in establishing the fields of comparative anatomy and paleontology, and he inspired generations of archaeologists and biologists. His work in classification of vertebrates as an exploration of the epochs of the world was at the forefront of his contemporaries. He saw clearly that each part of an organism is integrated into the whole and that development reflects the outer world that surrounds it.

John Bovee Dods (1795–1872)

When the revolutionary thinker, psychologist, and author John Dods gave a lecture to the United States Congress on "electrical psychology," he had no idea that his ideas would be forever immortalized in the Walt Whitman poem "I Sing the Body Electric." Believing that there was a connecting field between the mind and the body, Dods guessed that it was some form of electricity, though he suspected that it was more than just the newest technological phenomenon. He knew that what one generation considers magic, the next will know as science and fact.

Henry Drummond (1851–1897)

This Scotsman was a man of varied talents. In addition to working as an ordained minister and a professor of theology, he also wrote several books, including *Natural Law in the Spiritual World*, which sold seventy thousand copies in five years. Drummond's most successful book, however, was *The Greatest Thing in the World*—a meditation he wrote in 1874 that explains the importance of I Corinthians 13—which went on to sell over twelve million copies.

J. A. Fleming (1849–1945)

Sir John Ambrose Fleming was an English electrical engineer and physicist. He was knighted in 1929 for his contributions in the fields of photometry, electronics, wireless telegraphy (radio), and electrical measurements. His work eventually played a vital role in the victory of World War II. He was a devout Christian, and in the 1930s he helped to start the Evolution Protest Movement.

Elbert Henry Gary (1846–1927)

Judge Gary was one of the most outstanding corporate lawyers in the history of Illinois. From offices both in Wheaton and Chicago he handled a highly successful legal business and was active in public service. He served as county judge of DuPage County, and in 1890 he was elected as the first mayor of Wheaton. Judge Gary was a key founder of the United States Steel Corporation, bringing together partners J. P. Morgan, Andrew Carnegie, and Charles M. Schwab.

Frank Channing Haddock (unknown)

Dr. Haddock's books brought new vision to countless readers. He believed that through Sense Culture, the improvement of attention through the strengthening of the senses, will power could be learned, enhanced, and focused on any desired result. Never one for half-measures, he advised his readers that "you can no more acquire powers of mind, will, and success by merely passively reading about them." Practice with focused intent was the key to ultimate achievement.

Kalidasa (unknown)

As poet and dramatist, Kalidasa held the title Kavikulaguru (Preceptor of All Poets), bearing testimony to his stature during his life. He was an ardent worshipper of Shiva and wrote his plays and poetry largely based around Hindu mythology and philosophy. When Kalidasa lived is largely disputed, but it is believed that it was sometime between the first century BC and the fifth century AD.

Herbert Kaufman (1878–1947)

Herbert Kaufman was an American writer and newspaperman whose editorials and war poetry were widely syndicated in both the United States and Canada in such papers as *Evening Standard* and *The Times.* He also wrote numerous books, including *The Stolen Throne, Do Something!, Be Something!*, and perhaps his most popular work, *The Winning Fight.*

Christian Larsen (unknown)

Christian Larsen believed deeply that success was all in your head—proper attitude and application of powerful thoughts could lead to amazing success. In his 1912 book, *The Hidden Secret,* he taught that "the true faith is a spiritual state of mind; a state of mind that is very deep, very high, and beautiful beyond description. It is a State of mind that knows; and it knows because to be in faith is to be upon the mountaintop of intelligence, wisdom, and illumination."

Urbain Jean Joseph Leverrier (1811–1877)

French astronomer and mathematician Leverrier discovered the precise location of Neptune—within one degree—using only calculus. The ultimate example of "seek and ye shall find," Leverrier was a strict scientist who strove for precision in all of his work. He is best remembered for his unflagging pursuit of pure mathematics, science, and accurate observations as the key to knowledge.

Orison Swett Marden (1850–1924)

The founder of *Success Magazine*, Orison Swett Marden knew that he was onto something great when it first began in 1897. Having already brought his books to millions of readers through the aid of such powerful titles as *Cheerfulness as a Life Power*, *The Conquest of Worry*, and *He Can Who Thinks He Can*, Marden knew how important positive thought was for everyday people. He believed that "if you want to enlarge your life, you must first enlarge your thought of it and of yourself."

Prentice Mulford (1834–1891)

Prentice Mulford was one of the earliest pioneers of the New Thought teaching. Though eccentric, he envisioned the airplane and the radio, and he prophesized mental telepathy and practiced it. He was a figure in San Francisco's literary circles of the 1860s and wrote dozens of humorous short stories for *Overland Monthly*, *Golden Era*, and *Californian*. Living as a hermit in his later years, he became interested in mental and spiritual phenomena and wrote some of his finest works on mental/spiritual laws, including *Thoughts Are Things* and his collection of essays, *The White Cross Library*, dealing in the topic "Thought Currents and How to Use Them."

John Oxenham (unknown)

John Oxenham was just one identity for William Arthur Dunkerly, a man of many names and many talents. Using this name for his poetry and hymn writing, he explored the connection between spirituality, science, and the power of the mind.

Thomas Troward (1847–1916)

Born to British parents who were stationed in India, Thomas Troward later studied law in London, becoming a judge. Though he was a student of the Bible, he also read many of the world's religious texts, including the Koran, Hebrew texts, and Hindu scriptures, searching for the "truth" which connected all things. His lectures were widely hailed as being concise, clear, and straightforward explanations of theological concepts, and he was an inspiration to many thinkers of his day.

Francis Larimer Warner (unknown)

Warner, a New Thought pioneer and author of *Our Invisible Supply*, believed that "you cannot pour water from a pitcher until you take the pitcher in hand and begin to pour." What Warner called the Law of Supply was just one more way of explaining the Law of Attraction. He advised that we should dig deeper than our fears and refuse to let our presumptions about the world slow us down.

Lillian Whiting (unknown)

Lillian Whiting was one of the pioneer authors in the field of the attainment of success and wrote the highly acclaimed book *The World Beautiful*, which was first published in 1894.

Helen Wilmans (1831–1907)

Author, journalist, and inspiring founder of *The Woman's World*, a newspaper, as well as a weekly journal called *Freedom*, Helen Wilmans was one of the first models for successful, independent women thinkers in the United States. A strong believer in Mind over Matter, she rose up from the hardship of farm life to become a celebrated writer, teaching that "the basis of success rests in a person's power to stand alone . . . free from fear, independent of public opinion, and daring to be himself."

John Cook Wilson (1849–1915)

It is believed that the Wilson quoted in this book is in fact John Cook Wilson, the British philosopher. He was Wykeham Professor of Logic at New College, Oxford, from 1889 until his death. Of the generation brought up in the atmosphere of British idealism, he espoused the cause of philosophical realism.

GLOSSARY OF TERMS

abundance—the experience of having more than enough of whatever is needed to fully experience and express our true nature.

Aladdin's lamp—A reference to the ancient story of a boy who found an oil lamp out of which, when he wiped the dust off of it, emerged a powerful spiritual being called a "genie." The genie gave him everything he asked for, saying "your wish is my command."

Consciousness—awareness, observation; the underlying intelligence of the universe.

harmony—the effortless, orderly, beautiful coming together of all the elements and characteristics in a given experience.

idealization—Discovering and imagining a desired situation or accomplishment in its perfection.

Infinite Energy—the energy present in the quantum field.

Infinite "I"—the essence, the creative source and sustainer, of all that is.

Law of Abundance—The universal truth stating that there is more than enough of whatever is needed on the earth and in our universe to fully experience and express our true nature.

Law of Attraction—When implemented properly, this rule of Nature expresses that the mind is creative and automatically resonates with its object to bring it into manifestation.

Law of Causation (see Law of Cause and Effect)

Law of Cause and Effect (aka Law of Causation)—The unchanging, always working natural law by which every thought, word, or action may be traced back to a cause and will lead to an effect.

Law of Compensation—This universal truth states that with the appearance of a given amount of energy anywhere there must also be the disappearance of that same amount somewhere else.

Law of Creation—The unchanging, always working spiritual law by which whatever we idealize and visualize materializes.

Law of Growth—Thought takes form and expression through this natural law when it is properly planted and tended with such tools as patience, focus, and other natural laws.

Law of Love—The creative force behind every manifestation; that universal truth that provides vitality to thought through its emotional nature.

Law of Our Being—This rule of Nature states that our desire is in direct ration to our purpose and faith; this ratio must be creative or constructive to generate enough strength to bring our purpose into manifestation.

Law of Sevens (aka Septimal Law)—In accordance to the natural phases of the moon and the harmonies of sound, light, heat, electricity, magnetism, and atomic structure, this natural law follows seven-year cycles of change and governs the life of individuals, nations, and activities of the commercial world.

Law of Success—As with money and every other element of supply that's woven into the fabric of our lives, this universal truth formulates very simply that we get what we give. For this reason, we should consider it a great privilege to be able to give.

Law of Vibration—This law is ruled by the magic that transforms a human into a being who thinks and knows and feels and acts—and participates in the creation of the universe. Thought, being vibratory action similar to electricity, is the invisible link by which the individual comes into communication with the Universal.

Master Key—The fundamental insight and understanding that empowers the individual to manifest.

materialization—The physical, material experience of what has been thought about, focused on, and imagined.

Mind—The one Intelligence out of which all that is has been created and is sustained.

Mind power—the creative capacity of the individual's thoughts and feelings, combined, when in alignment with Universal Intelligence, or Truth.

Natural Law—The set of unchanging, always working laws that apply both to the world of Spirit and of Nature.

Nature—The processes, objects, and beings that make up the physical environment of the earth, our galaxy, and the rest of the universe.

Omnipotent—all-power; the only power (not simply "more powerful than . . .")

Omnipresent—everywhere present, in all things, across all time (not simply "able to show up wherever we are").

Omniscient—all-knowing; aware of every aspect of and means of accomplishing all possibilities across all time, now (not simply "able to see us wherever we are").

power—The capacity to achieve intended results.

principle—That aspect of the underlying Intelligence of the universe that we experience as unchanging processes and patterns in our inner and outer worlds.

quantum field—the apparent vacuum of space, which is filled with constantly interacting subatomic units that are called "wavicles," sometimes showing up as waves and sometimes as particles, which may best be described as tendencies toward binding ("bosons") or separating ("fermions").

Septimal Law (see Law of Sevens)

solar plexus—a spot on the torso of the human body, at the base of the sternum, several inches above the navel; also called the chi or ki spot.

Spirit—the core, or essence, of everything, including human beings.

Substance—the quantum "stuff" of the universe: the constantly interacting subatomic "wavicles," sometimes showing up as waves and sometimes as particles, which may best be described as tendencies toward binding ("bosons") or separating ("fermions"), and which form the basis for all things and all energy, everywhere

supply—The resources, including money, needed to live.

thought—This vehicle is as powerful as the fuel that's put in it, offering all or nothing to humanity depending upon the efforts expelled. It is the beginning of all that is; if you can think it, you have the power to create it.

Truth (aka the Truth)—The ideal; an infinite, eternal, power-filled understanding; the word that is the basis for all creation; the Intelligence that underlies the space-time continuum.

Universal Fountain—the process by which all needs are met.

visualization—Imagining, with as many senses as possible, a desired or intended final outcome.

wisdom—the capacity to discern what is Real, not being confused by appearances or faulty logic.

world within—Our inner processes, thoughts, and feelings; the unconscious mind.

world without—Our bodies and the environment around us; the conscious mind.